Vest Pocket
MODERN
GREEK

TITLES IN THIS SERIES

Vest Pocket
MODERN
GREEK

Formerly published as: MODERN GREEK IN A NUTSHELL

By
GEORGE C. PAPPAGEOTES, Ph.D.
and
PHILIP D. EMMANUEL
Lecturers in Modern Greek
Columbia University

PUBLISHED BY
INSTITUTE FOR LANGUAGE STUDY
Montclair, New Jersey 07042

DISTRIBUTED TO THE BOOK TRADE BY
BARNES & NOBLE BOOKS
A DIVISION OF HARPER & ROW, *PUBLISHERS*

Library of Congress Catalog Card Number: 60-53247
First paperbound edition published 1967 by Funk & Wagnalls,

Published by arrangement with Institute for Language Study

First Edition

Printed in the United States of America

9 8 7 6 5 4 3 2 1

GETTING THE MOST OUT OF YOUR COURSE

T HE WORLD is growing smaller every day. Far-sighted people who recognize the value of speaking a second language will reap the benefits of greater business success, more traveling enjoyment, easier study and finer social relationships.

VEST POCKET MODERN GREEK will unlock for you the treasure house of learning a language the easy way, with a fresh, new approach—without monotonous drills. Before you know it, you'll be speaking your new language easily and without embarrassment. You will be able to converse with fascinating people from other lands and read their books and magazines in the original language.

Much research and painstaking study has gone into the "Vest Pocket" method of learning a new language as easily as possible. This Course is the result of that research, and for the reader's convenience it is divided into several basic, closely related sections:

The KEY TO PRONUNCIATION explains the sounds of the language. Each sentence is accompanied by the phonetic spelling to help you learn the pronunciation. This method has been tested extensively and is found to be the best to enable the student to associate sounds with written forms.

The BASIC SENTENCE PATTERNS are the unique new approach to sentence construction. Here you will find sentence patterns needed in general conversation. On these basic patterns you can build sentences to suit your own particular needs.

The EVERYDAY CONVERSATIONS form the main section of this book. Here you will find a large number of situations useful for general language learning and traveling purposes. You will learn hundreds upon hundreds of conversational sentences you may need to make yourself understood. Even more important, the material is organized to provide you with a wide basis for varying the vocabulary and sentences as much as your interest and ingenuity might desire.

The OUTLINE OF GRAMMAR provides a rapid understanding of the grammatical structure of your new language. The "Basic Sentence Patterns" are closely correlated with this section to give you a quick knowledge of the language.

The two-way DICTIONARY of over 6500 entries includes all the words used in the Everyday Conversations and contains another 3000 frequently used words and expressions. It thus forms a compact and invaluable tool for the student.

Here are the tools. Use them systematically, and before you know it you will have a "feeling" for the new language. The transcriptions furnish authentic reproduction of the language to train your ear and tongue to the foreign sounds; thus you can SEE the phrase, SAY the phrase, HEAR the phrase, and LEARN the phrase.

Remember that repetition and practice are the foundation stones of language learning. Repeat and practice what you have learned as often as you can. You will be amazed (and your friends will, too) how quickly you have acquired a really practical knowledge of Modern Greek.

THE EDITORS

TABLE OF CONTENTS

KEY TO GREEK PRONUNCIATION

The pronunciation of modern Greek is not difficult for the English-speaking student as nearly all the sounds of Greek occur in English.

Moreover, modern Greek is highly "phonetic" in its spelling. Letters and combinations of letters almost always represent the same sounds. When the student has become familiar with the basic sounds which the spellings stand for, he can pronounce any Greek word correctly.

Our scheme for indicating the pronunciation of Greek letters and letter combinations is not based on a special system of phonetic symbols but on common English sounds as normally represented in English spelling.

Syllable divisions are indicated by a hyphen (-) and accented syllables are printed in capitals; thus, in the word ἄνθρωπος meaning "man", the stress would fall on the first syllable, as indicated in AHN-throh-pohs.

THE VOWELS

Modern Greek has only five vowel sounds (similar to those of Spanish):

i (as in *machine*)   *u* (as in *rule*)
e (as in *met*)   *o* (as in *port*)
          a (as in *father*)

Each of these sounds is represented by one or more letters or letter combinations because Greek adheres to its historical orthography.

The sound *i* (as in *machine* or *ee* as in *see*) is represented by the letters ι, η, υ, (and ῃ) and the letter combinations ει, οι and υι.

The sound *e* (as in *met*) is represented either by the letter ε or the letter combination αι.

The sound *a* (as in *father*) is represented by α (and ᾳ).

The sound *o* (as in *port*) is represented by ο or ω (ῳ).

The sound *u* (as in *rule* or as *oo* in *fool* or *moon*) is always represented by the letter combination ου.

In our phonetic transcription these vowels are transcribed as follows: *i* by *ee*, *e* by *eh*, *a* by *ah*, *o* by *oh*, and *u* by *oo*.

The ι is transcribed by *y* when it forms a kind of diphthong with the following vowel as in πιὸ πολύ (pyoh poh-LEE) much more.

7

A final piece of instruction concerning the vowels: Be careful to avoid pronouncing single vowel sounds as diphthongs.

THE CONSONANTS

Most Greek consonants have equivalents in English. Double consonants are pronounced as the corresponding single consonants.

GREEK SPELLING	PHONETIC SYMBOL	DESCRIPTION	EXAMPLES
β or в	v	As English v.	βάρος (VAH-rohs) weight
γ	gh or y	This sound does not occur in English. It is the voiced counterpart of Χ (see below). Before i and e, it sounds almost as y in yes and is transcribed by y. But before a, o, and u, or a consonant, it sounds like g in brag but continued.	γῆ (YEE) earth γελῶ (yeh-LOH) I laugh γάλα (GHAH-lah) milk ἀργός (ahr-GHOHS) slow
δ	th	As th in that.	δίνω (THEE-noh) I give
ζ	z	As z in zest.	ζωή (zoh-EE) life
θ	th	As th in thin.	θέλω (THEH-loh) I want
κ	k	As k in task.	κρασί (krah-SEE) wine
λ	l	Almost as l in like.	λάδι (LAH-thee) oil
μ	m	As m in man.	μάτι (MAH-tee) eye
ν	n	Almost as n in not.	νερό (neh-ROH) water
ξ	ks	As x in six.	ξύλο (KSEE-loh) wood
π	p	As p in step.	πουλί (poo-LEE) b·
ρ	r	As in British English very. It is slightly trilled.	μέρος (MEH-rohs) rt; toilet
σ (-ς)	s	As s in sea. However, it is pronounced as z in zone before m or other voiced consonants.	σῶμα (SOH-mah) body κόσμος (KOH-zmohs) people, world, cosmos

	t	Almost as *t* in *stop*.	τυρί (tee-REE) cheese
	f	As *f* in *fire*.	φῶς (FOHS) light
	kh	No English equivalent. It resembles *h* in *hue*, but is much more strongly aspirated. It is pronounced with the back of the tongue raised against the soft palate so that it will impede the breath-stream in a way that will form some friction. It is like *ch* in Scottish *loch* (lake), German *Bach* (brook) or *g* in Spanish *gente* (people) or *gitano* (gypsy).	ὄχι (OH-khee) no χέρι (KHEH-ree) hand χαρά (khah-RAH) joy χωριό (khoh-RYOH) village χρῆμα (KHREE-mah) money

| | ps | As *ps* in *rhapsody*. | ψωμί (psoh-MEE) bread |

LETTER COMBINATIONS

μπ	b	At the beginning of a word as *b* in *bet*.	μπάλα (BAH-lah) ball μπλέ (BLEH) blue
	mb	In the middle of a word as *mb* in *timber*.	τύμπανο (TEEM-bah-noh) drum
ντ	d	At the beginning of a word almost as *d* in *door*.	ντομάτες (doh-MAH-tehs) tomatoes
	nd	In the middle of a word as *nd* in *tender*.	γάντια (GHAHN-dyah) gloves
γκ	g	At the beginning of a word as *g* in *go*.	γκρί (GREE) gray
	ng	In the middle of a word as *ng* in *finger*.	πάγκος (PAHN-gohs) bench
γγ	ng	As *ng* in *finger*.	ἄγγελος (AHN-geh-lohs) angel
τσ	ts	Almost as *ts* in *sits*.	σάλτσα (SAHL-tsah) sauce
τζ	dz	As in *red zone* but pronounced as one unit.	τζίτζικας (DZEE-dzee-kahs) grasshopper

ευ	ehf	As *ef* in *chef* before voiceless consonants (π, τ, κ, φ, θ, χ, σ, ξ, ψ).	εὐχαριστῶ (ehf-khah-re STOH) [almost as th English name F. Harr Stow] (I) thank you
	ehv	As *ev* in *eleven* before all other (voiced) consonants and before vowels.	Εὖα (EHV-ah) Eve
αυ	ahf	Before voiceless consonants.	αὐτό (ahf-TOH) this that
	ahv	Before voiced consonants or vowels.	αὐγό (ahv-GHOH) egg

ACCENTUATION

The accent can fall on any one of the last three syllables.

There are two types of accent with which we have to deal: th stress accent in spoken Greek which is indicated in the phonet transcription by capitals, and the orthographical accent in writte Greek which is based on historical spelling. There are three writte accents; the acute ´ (ὀξεῖα), the circumflex ˆ (περισπωμένη) an the grave ` (βαρεῖα).

The acute is used on every accented short syllable*; on the accente third from the last syllable (antepenult); and on the accented secon from the last syllable (penult) when both the penult and the last sy lable (ultima) are long: νεότης (youth); θάλασσα (sea); πρώ (first *fem.*).

The circumflex is used on the accented penult when the last syllabl is short and the next to the last is long: πρῶτος (first *masc.*); an on the last syllable when the long vowel or diphthong of this syllabl is the result of a contraction, as τιμάω → τιμῶ (I honor).

The grave is used on the last syllable. When words, written in isc lation, take the acute, this acute becomes grave when these word are written in a sentence context and are not followed by a punctua

---

* The syllables are considered short or long on the basis of the quantity their vowels in historical orthography. Syllables with ε or ο are short; wit η or ω long; and with α, ι, υ either short or long. Syllables with orthographi dipthongs are long except those with οι or αι at the absolute end of the wor

tion mark or an enclitic*, e.g. ὁ ἀδελφὸς (the brother); ὁ ἀδελφὸς τοῦ Παύλου (Paul's brother); ὁ ἀδελφός του (his brother). Most Greeks do not observe the distinction between acute and grave, and use the acute for both.

Other orthographical marks in Greek are the breathings which are placed on the initial vowel of any Greek word beginning with a vowel, or on the second vowel of a diphthong of any Greek word beginning with a diphthong. There are two breathings: the smooth breathing or spiritus lenis ' (ψιλή) and the rough breathing or spiritus asper ' (δασεῖα).

Most words beginning with a vowel take the smooth breathing. All words beginning with υ take the rough breathing. The most important words taking the rough breathing are: ἅγιος (saint), ἁγνός (pure), αἷμα (blood), ἁλάτι (salt), ἁμάξι (coach), ἁρπάζω (I grab), ἑβδομάδα (week), ἕκαστος (each), Ἑλλάδα (Greece), ἕνας (one), ἕξ (six), ἑπτά (seven), ἑκατό (hundred), ἑορτή (holiday), ἕτοιμος (ready), εὑρίσκω (I find), ἕως (till, until), ἡλικία (age), ἡμέρα (day), ἥσυχος (quiet), ἱερός (holy, sacred), ἱκανός (able), ἱστορία (history, story), ὅλος (whole), ὅμως (however), ὥρα (hour), ὡραῖος (handsome).

PUNCTUATION

The punctuation marks in Greek are:

Period . (τελεία)   Exclamation point ! (θαυμαστικό)
Comma , (κόμμα)   Semicolon   (ἄνω τελεία)
Question mark ; (ἐρωτηματικό)   Quotes « » (εἰσαγωγικά)
Note that the Greek question mark looks like the English semicolon.

CAPITALIZATION

All common nouns, adjectives, and pronouns are written with small initial letters, except when beginning a sentence. Proper names only

---

* Enclitics are primarily one-syllable words which, losing their own accent, are attached in pronunciation to a preceding word, in which a secondary accent is caused on the final syllable, if it is accented on the third from the last syllable.

are capitalized, i.e., names of individual persons (Christian names, patronymics, surnames), institutions, inhabited places (cities, towns), provinces, countries. Names of languages and adjectives of nationality are written with a small initial letter.

THE GREEK ALPHABET

The Greek alphabet has twenty-four letters:

PRINTED		NAMES OF LETTERS		PRONUNCIATION
CAPITAL	SMALL			
A	α	Ἄλφα	Alpha	AHL-fah
B	β	Βῆτα	Veeta	VEE-tah
Γ	γ	Γάμμα	Ghamma	GHAH-mah
Δ	δ	Δέλτα	Dhelta	THEHL-tah
E	ε	Ἔψιλον	Epsilon	EH-psee-lohn
Z	ζ	Ζῆτα	Zeeta	ZEE-tah
H	η	Ἦτα	Eeta	EE-tah
Θ	θ	Θῆτα	Theeta	THEE-tah
I	ι	Ἰῶτα	Yiota	YOH-tah
K	κ	Κάππα	Kappa	KAH-pah
Λ	λ	Λάμβδα	Lamvdha	LAHM-thah
M	μ	Μῦ	Mee	MEE
N	ν	Νῦ	Nee	NEE
Ξ	ξ	Ξῦ	Ksee	KSEE
O	ο	Ὄμικρον	Omicron	OH-mee-krohn
Π	π	Πῖ	Pee	PEE
P	ρ	Ῥῶ	Rho	ROH
Σ	σ, ς	Σῖγμα	Seegma	SEEGH-mah
T	τ	Ταῦ	Taf	TAHF
Y	υ	Ὕψιλον	Eepsilon	EE-psee-lohn
Φ	φ	Φῖ	Fee	FEE
X	χ	Χῖ	Hee	KHEE
Ψ	ψ	Ψῖ	Psee	PSEE
Ω	ω	Ὠμέγα	Omegha	oh-MEH-ghah

BASIC TYPES OF SENTENCES

In each language there are a few basic types of sentences which are used more often than others in everyday speech.

On the basis of such sentences, one can form many others by substituting one or two of the words of each of these basic sentences. The sentences we selected to illustrate the basic patterns are short, easy to memorize, and useful. Learning them before you enter the main section of the book (Everyday Conversations) will automatically enable you to acquire an idea of the structure of the language. You will also learn indirectly through them some of the most important grammatical categories and their function in the construction of sentences the natural way,—the way a child absorbs them as he encounters them in actual usage.

Cross references have been supplied to establish a correlation between the basic sentence patterns and the Reference Grammar in this book. This will help you to relate the grammatical knowledge you will acquire from the basic sentences to the systematic presentation of Greek grammar.

BASIC QUESTIONS AND ANSWERS
(See Grammar 5.4; 5.1; 5.3; 2.0; 2.1; 3.1; 7.3)

Πῶς εἶσθε; or (Τί κάνετε;)
POHS EE-stheh? (TEE KAH-neh-teh?)
How are you? (*lit.*, What are you doing?)

Καλά, εὐχαριστῶ. [Καὶ] σεῖς (πῶς εἶσθε);
kah-LAH, ehf-khah-ree-STOH. [keh] SEES (POHS EE-stheh)?
Fine, thank you. And you (how are you)?

Πολὺ καλά. Εὐχαριστῶ.
poh-LEE kah-LAH. ehf-khah-ree-STOH.
Very well. Thank you.

Τί εἶναι αὐτό;
TEE EE-neh ahf-TOH?
What is that?

Εἶναι ἕνα καινούριο βιβλίο.
EE-neh EH-nah keh-NOOR-yoh vee-VLEE-oh.
It is a new book.

Ποιὸς εἶναι αὐτός;
PYOHS EE-neh ahf-TOHS?
Who is he?

[Εἶναι] ὁ πατέρας μου (ὁ θεῖος μου, ὁ παππούς μου).
EE-neh oh pah-TEH-rahz-moo (oh THEE-ohz-moo, oh pah-POOZ-moo).
He is my father (uncle, grandfather).

Ποιὰ εἶναι αὐτή;
PYAH EE-neh ahf-TEE?
Who is she?

[Εἶναι] ἡ μητέρα μου (ἡ θεία μου, ἡ γιαγιά μου).
EE-neh ee mee-TEH-rah-moo (ee THEE-ah-moo, ee yah-YAH-moo).
She is my mother (aunt, grandmother).

Ποιὸ εἶναι αὐτὸ τὸ παιδί;
PYOH EE-neh ahf-TOH toh peh-THEE?
Who is that boy?

[Εἶναι] ὁ ἀδελφός μου (ὁ ἐξάδελφός μου, ὁ ἀνεψιός μου).
EE-neh oh ah-thehl-FOHZ-moo (oh eh-KSAH-thehl-FOHZ-moo, oh ah-neh-PSYOHZ-moo).
He is my brother (cousin, nephew).

Ποιὸ εἶναι τὸ ἄλλο παιδί;
PYOH EE-neh toh AH-loh peh-THEE?
Who is the other boy?

[Εἶναι] ὁ μεγαλύτερος ἀδελφός μου.
EE-neh oh meh-ghah-LEE-teh-rohs ah-thehl-FOHZ-moo.
He is my older brother.

Ποιὸ εἶναι αὐτὸ τὸ κορίτσι;
PYOH EE-neh ahf-TOH toh koh-REE-tsee?
Who is that girl?

[Εἶναι] ἡ μικρότερή μου ἀδελφή (ἐξαδέλφη, ἀνεψιά).
EE-neh ee mee-KROH-teh-REE-moo ah-thehl-FEE (eh-ksah-THEHL-fee, ah-neh-PSYAH).
She is my younger sister (cousin, niece).

Ποιοί εἶναι αὐτοί;
PYEE EE-neh ahf-TEE?
Who are they?

[Εἶναι] ὁ παππούς μου καὶ ἡ γιαγιά μου.
EE-neh oh pah-POOZ-moo keh ee yah-YAH-moo.
They are my grandparents.

Τί εἶναι αὐτά;
TEE EE-neh ahf-TAH?
What are they?

Εἶναι ἀχλάδια καὶ μῆλα.
EE-neh ah-KHLAH-thyah keh MEE-lah.
They are pears and apples.

Αὐτὴ ἡ ψηλὴ κοπέλ(λ)α εἶναι ἡ κόρη μου (θυγατέρα μου).
ahf-TEE ee psee-LEE koh-PEH-lah EE-neh ee KOH-ree-moo (thee-ghah-TEH-rah-moo).

That tall girl is my daughter.

Ἀλήθεια;
ah-LEE-thyah?
Is that so?

Ποῦ εἶναι τὸ καπέλλο μου;
POO EE-neh toh kah-PEH-loh-moo?
Where is my hat?

Ἐδῶ εἶναι.
eh-THOH EE-neh.
Here it is.

Ποῦ εἶναι ἡ ὀμπρέλλα σας;
POO EE-neh ee ohm-BREH-lah-sahs?
Where is your umbrella?

Εἶναι ἐκεῖ (πέρα).
EE-neh eh-KEE (PEH-rah).
It's over there.

Ποῦ εἶναι ἡ τσάντα της;
POO EE-neh ee TSAHN-dah-tees?
Where's her handbag?

Εἶναι ἐδῶ.
EE-neh eh-THOH.
It's over here.

Ποῦ εἶναι ἡ κουζίνα;
POO EE-neh ee koo-ZEE-nah?
Where's the kitchen?

Εἶναι [πρὸς τὰ] δεξιά (ἀριστερά).
EE-neh [prohs tah] theh-ksee-AH (ah-ree-steh-RAH).
It's on the right (on the left).

Ποῦ εἶναι τὸ δωμάτιο τοῦ Γιάννη;
POO EE-neh toh thoh-MAH-tee-oh too YAH-nee?
Where is John's room?

Εἶναι κατ' εὐθεῖαν ἐμπρός.
EE-neh kah-tehf-THEE-ahn ehm-BROHS.
It's straight ahead.

Ποῦ εἶναι τὸ δωμάτιο τῆς Μαρίας;
POO EE-neh toh *thoh*-MAH-tee-oh tees mah-REE-ahs?
Where is Mary's room?

Εἶναι στὸ (ἐ)πάνω πάτωμα.
EE-neh stoh (eh-) PAH-noh PAH-toh-mah.
It's one flight up.

SENTENCES WITH INTERROGATIVE PRONOUNS

(See Grammar 5.4; 5.5; 10; 2)

Ποιὸς ἔχει τὰ τετράδιά μου; Ὁ Παῦλος τὰ ἔχει.
PYOHS EH-khee tah teh-TRAH-*thee*-AH-moo? oh PAHV-lohs tah EH-khee.
Who has my notebooks? Paul has them.

Μὲ ποιὸν μιλούσατε; Μὲ τὸν φίλο μου τὸν Πέτρο.
meh PYOHN mee-LOO-sah-teh? meh toh FEE-loh-moo tohm-BEH-troh.
With whom were you talking? With my friend Peter.

Ποιοὶ εἶναι αὐτοὶ οἱ νέοι; Εἶναι φίλοι τοῦ γυιοῦ μου.
PYEE EE-neh ahf-TEE ee NEH-ee? EE-neh FEE-lee too YOO-moo.
Who are those young men? They are my son's friends.

Ποιὲς εἶναι αὐτὲς οἱ κοπέλες; Εἶναι συμμαθήτριες τῆς κόρης μου.
PYEHS EE-neh ahf-TEHS ee koh-PEH-lehs? EE-neh see-mah-THEE-tree-ehs tees KOH-reez-moo.
Who are those girls? They are my daughter's schoolmates.

Τί σᾶς εἶπε (αὐτή); Μᾶς εἶπε ὅτι δὲν θὰ ἔλθη.
TEE sahs EE-peh (ahf-TEE)? mahs EE-peh OH-tee *the*hn thah EHL-thee.
What did she tell you? She told us that she will not come.

Τί εἶναι ἡ πίστη; Εἶναι τὸ θεμέλιο τῆς ζωῆς.
TEE EE-neh ee PEE-stee? EE-neh toh theh-MEH-lee-oh tees zoh-EES.
What is faith? It's life's foundation.

Ποιὸ εἶναι τὸ ἐπάγγελμά σας; Εἶμαι ράφτης.
PYOH EE-neh toh eh-PAHN-gehl-MAH-sahs? EE-meh RAHF-tees.
What is your occupation? I am a tailor.

Ποιά ἀπ' αὐτὲς τὶς εἰκόνες σᾶς ἀρέσει περισσότερο; Αὐτὴ
ἐδῶ (τούτη).

PYAH ah-pahf-TEHS tees ee-KOH-nehs sahs ah-REH-see peh-ree-SOH-
teh-roh? ahf-TEE eh-*THOH* (TOO-tee).

Which one of these pictures do you like best? This one right here.

SENTENCES WITH PERSONAL OBJECT
PRONOUNS

(See Grammar 5.2; 10.4; 10.5)

Ὁ Γιῶργος τοῦ τὸ ἔδωσε (σ'αὐτόν).

oh YOHR-ghohs too toh EH-*th*oh-seh (sahf-TOHN).

George gave it to him.

Μοῦ τὸ ἔδωσε.

mo toh EH-*th*oh-seh.

He gave it to me.

Τῆς τὸ ἔδωσα.

tees toh EH-*th*oh-sah.

I gave it to her.

(Αὐτὴ) μᾶς τὸ ἔστειλε.

ahf-TEE mahs toh EH-stee-leh.

She sent it to us.

Σᾶς τὸ δώσαμε.

sahs toh *THOH*-sah-meh.

We gave it to you.

Δὲν τοὺς τὸ δώσατε.

*th*ehn toos toh *THOH*-sah-teh.

You did not give it to them.

Δός μου το. (Δῶστε το σὲ μᾶς).

*THOH*Z-moo-toh. (*THOH*-steh-toh seh-MAHS).

Give it to me. (Give it to us).

Μὴ τοῦ τὸ δίνετε.

MEE too toh *TH*EE-neh-teh.

Don't give it to him.

Στεῖλε το σ' αὐτή(ν).

STEE-lteh-toh sahf-TEEN.

Send it to her.

Ταχυδρομῆστε το σὲ μᾶς.

tah-khee-*th*roh-MEE-steh-toh seh-MAHS.

Mail it to us.

Μὴ(ν) τοὺς τὸ στέλλετε.

MEE(N) toos toh STEH-leh-teh.

Don't mail it to them.

Δὲν τὶς τὸ στείλατε;

*TH*EHN tees toh STEE-lah-teh?

Didn't you send it to them (fem.)?

SENTENCES ON THE USE OF THE ARTICLE
(See Grammar 1.0-1.5; 2.2; 2.3; 9.2)

Ἡ φιλοξενία εἶναι ἑλληνικὴ ἀρετή.
ee fee-loh-kseh-NEE-ah EE-neh eh-lee-nee-KEE ah-reh-TEE
Hospitality is a Greek virtue.

Ἐκτιμῶ τὴν ἀλήθεια.
eh-ktee-MOH teen ah-LEE-thyah
I appreciate truth.

Ἡ ἐγκράτεια εἶναι πολὺ καλὴ γιὰ τοὺς νέους.
ee ehn-GRAH-tee-ah EE-neh poh-LEE kah-LEE yah toos NEH-oos
Restraint is very good for young people.

Ὁ ἑλληνικὸς οὐρανὸς εἶναι σχεδὸν πάντοτε γαλανός.
oh eh-lee-nee-KOHS oo-rah-NOHS EE-neh skheh-THOHN PAHN-doh-teh ghah-lah-NOHS.
The Greek sky is nearly always blue.

Ἡ Ἑλλάδα εἶναι μία ἀπὸ τὶς πιὸ ὄμορφες χῶρες τῆς Εὐρώπης.
ee eh-LAH-thah EE-neh MEE-ah ah-POH tees pyoh OH-mohr-fehs KHOH-rehs tees ehv-ROH-pees.
Greece is one of the most beautiful countries in Europe.

Μένουν στὴν Τρίτη Λεωφόρο.
MEH-noon steen TREE-tee leh-oh-FOH-roh.
They live on Third Avenue.

Ἡ Ἄννα μένει στὴν ὁδὸν Σοφοκλέους.
ee AH-nah MEH-nee steen oh-THOHN soh-foh-KLEH-oos.
Ann lives on Sophocles Street.

Ὁ κύριος Μάνος δὲν μένει στὴ Νέα Ὑόρκη.
oh KEE-ree-ohs MAH-nohs thehnn MEH-nee stee NEH-ah ee-OHR-kee.
Mr. Manos does not live in New York.

Τὸ σπίτι τοῦ Νίκου εἶναι στὴν Ἀστόρια.
toh SPEE-tee too NEE-koo EE-neh steen ah-STOH-ree-ah.
Nick's house is in Astoria.

Ὁ Κώστας εἶναι μηχανικός.
oh KOH-stahs EE-neh mee-khah-nee-KOHS.
Gus (Costas) is an engineer.

Ἡ Πόπη εἶναι ἔξυπνη κοπέλα.
ee POH-pee EE-neh EH-ksee-pnee koh-PEH-lah.
Penny is an intelligent girl.

Τί ἀνόητος! (m.) Τί ἀνόητη! (f.) Τί ἀνόητο! (n.)
TEE ah-NOH-ee-tohs. TEE ah-NOH-ee-tee. TEE ah-NOH-ee-toh.
What a fool!

Τί κρῖμα!
TEE KREE-mah.
What a pity!

Τί ὡραῖο αὐτοκίνητο!
TEE oh-REH-oh ahf-toh-KEE-nee-toh.
What a beautiful car!

SENTENCES WITH INDEFINITE PRONOUNS
(See Grammar 5.6; 7.1; 2.4; 2.5)

Ἦλθε κανένας; Κανένας δὲν ἦλθε.
EEL-theh kah-NEH-nahs? kah-NEH-nahs thehn EEL-theh.
Has anybody come? Nobody has come.

Ἦταν κανένας ἐδῶ; Ναί, κάποιος ἦταν ἐδῶ.
EE-tahn kah-NEH-nahs eh-THOH? NEH, KAH-pyohs EE-tahn eh-THOH.
Has anybody been here? Yes, somebody has been here.

Λάβατε (or πήρατε) κανένα γράμμα; Ναί, ἔλαβα μερικά.
Ὄχι, δὲν ἔλαβα κανένα.
LAH-vah-teh (PEE-rah-teh) kah-NEH-nah GHRAH-mah? NEH, EH-lah-vah meh-ree-KAH. OH-khee, thehn EH-lah-vah kah-NEH-nah.
Have you received any letters? Yes, I received some. No, I have not received any.

Ἔχετε ἀμερικανικὰ περιοδικά; Ναί, ἔχω μερικά. Ὁρίστε ἕνα.
EH-kheh-teh ah-meh-ree-kah-nee-KAH peh-ree-oh-thee-KAH? NEH, EH-khoh meh-ree-KAH. oh-REE-steh EH-nah.
Have you any American magazines? Yes, I have some. There is one.

Ἔχετε ἀγγλικὲς ἐφημερίδες; Λυποῦμαι μὰ δὲν ἔχω.
EH-kheh-teh ahn-glee-KEHS eh-fee-meh-REE-thehs? lee-POO-meh mah thehn EH-khoh.
Have you any English newspapers? I'm sorry, but I don't have any.

Ἔχετε σπίρτα; Δυστυχῶς ὄχι.
EH-kheh-teh SPEER-tah? thees-tee-KHOHS OH-khee.
Have you got a match? Sorry. No. (Lit. unfortunately not).

Πωλεῖτε γάλα; Μάλιστα. Σᾶς παρακαλῶ, δῶστε μου ἕνα
μπουκάλι.
poh-LEE-teh GHAH-lah? MAH-lee-stah. sahs pah-rah-kah-LOH THOH-
steh-moo EH-nah boo-KAH-lee.
Do you sell milk? Yes. We do. Please give me a bottle.

Ἔχετε λεφτά (or χρήματα); Ὄχι, δὲν ἔχω (χρήματα).
EH-kheh-teh leh-FTAH(KHREE-mah -tah)? OH-khee, thehn EH-khoh
KHREE-mah-tah.
Have you got any money? No, I have no money.

Τί φάγατε; Ἔφαγα σούπα, ψάρι, τυρὶ καὶ ψωμί.
TEE FAH-ghah-teh? EH-fah-ghah SOO-pah, PSAH-ree, tee-REE keh
psoh-MEE.
What did you eat? I ate soup, fish, cheese and bread.

Τί ἀγοράσατε; Ἀγόρασα μερικὰ φορέματα κι' ἕνα καπέλλο.
TEE ah-ghoh-RAH-sah-teh? ah-GHOH-rah-sah meh-ree-KAH foh-REH-
mah-tah KYEH-nah kah-PEH-loh.
What did you buy? I bought some dresses and a hat.

Τί κοιτά(ζε)τε (or κυττάτε); Κοιτάζω μερικὲς εἰκόνες.
TEE kee-TAH-teh? kee-TAH-zoh meh-ree-KEHS ee-KOH-nehs.
What are you looking at? I am looking at some pictures.

SENTENCES ON ADJECTIVES
(See Grammar 3.2-3.53; 7.2)

Ἡ Ἑλένη εἶναι ψηλότερη ἀπὸ τὴν Μαρία.
ee eh-LEH-nee EE-neh psee-LOH-teh-ree ah-POH teen mah-REE-ah.
Helen is taller than Mary.

Ἡ Ἀλίκη εἶναι λιγώτερο ἐπιμελὴς ἀπὸ τὴ Βαρβάρα.
ee ah-LEE-kee EE-neh lee-GHOH-teh-roh eh-pee-meh-LEES ah-POH
tee vahr-VAH-rah.
Alice is less diligent than Barbara.

Ἡ Κατίνα εἶναι τόσο ψηλὴ ὅσο (καὶ) ἡ Μαρία.
ee kah-TEE-nah EE-neh TOH-soh psee-LEE OH-soh (keh) ee mah-
REE-ah.
Kate is as tall as Mary.

Ή Ρίτα δὲν εἶναι τόσο ψηλὴ ὅσο (καὶ) ἡ Σοφία.
ee REE-tah *th*ehn EE-neh TOH-soh psee-LEE OH-soh (keh) ee soh-
FEE-ah.
Rita is not so tall as Sophie.

Ή ᾽Άννα εἶναι ἡ ψηλότερη ἀπὸ τὰ κορίτσια.
ee AH-nah EE-neh ee psee-LOH-teh-ree ah-POH tah koh-REE-tsyah.
Ann is the tallest of the girls.

Θὰ πάρω ἀκόμη λίγο κρέας.
thah PAH-roh ah-KOH-mee LEE-ghoh KREH-ahs.
I will take a little more meat.

Παρακαλῶ, πάρτε καὶ ἄλλο.
pah-rah-kah-LOH, PAH-rteh keh AH-loh.
Please have some more.

Δὲ θέλω ἄλλο.
*TH*EH THEH-loh AH-loh.
I don't want any more.

Δὲ θέλουν νὰ καθήσουν ἐδῶ πιά.
*TH*EH THEH-loon nah kah-THEE-soon eh-*TH*OH PYAH.
They don't want to stay here any longer.

Δὲν μπορεῖ νὰ πάη πιὰ ἐκεῖ.
*TH*EHN boh-REE nah PAH-ee PYAH eh-KEE.
He can no longer go there.

Ή κοπέλα μὲ τὰ μεγάλα καστανὰ μάτια ἐξελέγη βασίλισσα
τοῦ χοροῦ.
ee koh-PEH-lah meh tah meh-GHAH-lah kah-stah-NAH MAH-tyah
eh-kseh-LEH-yee vah-SEE-lee-sah too khoh-ROO.
The girl with the big brown eyes was elected the queen of the
ball.

᾽Ο κουνιάδος μου ἔχει ἕνα καινούργιο φορτηγό (αὐτοκίνητο).
oh koo-NYAH-*TH*ohz-moo EH-khee EH-nah keh-NOO-ryoh fohr-tee-
GHOH (ahf-toh-KEE-nee-toh).
My brother-in-law has a new truck.

Ή ὄμορφη ῾Ελληνίδα δὲν ἦλθε νὰ μᾶς ἰδῆ (νὰ μᾶς
ἐπισκεφθῆ).
ee OH-mohr-fee eh-lee-NEE-*th*ah *TH*EHN EEL-theh nah mahs ee-
*TH*EE (nah mahs eh-pee-skeh-FTHEE).
The beautiful Greek girl didn't come to see us (to visit us).

BASIC TYPES OF SENTENCES
(See Grammar 10.1-10.15; 5.7; 8.1-2)

Affirmative: Αὐτὸ τὸ μάθημα εἶναι εὔκολο.
ahr-TOH toh MAH-thee-mah EE-neh EHF-koh-loh
This lesson is easy.

Negative: Αὐτὸ τὸ μάθημα δὲν εἶναι δύσκολο.
ahf-TOH toh MAH-thee-mah *th*ehn EE-neh THEN-
koh-loh.
This lesson is not difficult.

Interrogative: Εἶναι αὐτὸ τὸ μάθημα εὔκολο;   (or Εἶναι
εὔκολο αὐτὸ τὸ μάθημα;)
EE-neh ahf-TOH toh MAH-thee-mah EHF-koh-loh
(EE-neh EHF-koh-loh ahf-TOH toh-MAH-
thee-mah?)
Is this lesson easy?

Εἶναι εὔκολο.
EE-neh EHF-koh-loh.
It's easy.

Δὲν εἶναι αὐτὸ τὸ δωμάτιο μεγάλο;
*th*ehn EE-neh ahf-TOH toh *th*oh-MAH-tee-on meh-
GHAH-loh?
Isn't this room large?

Ναί, εἶναι μεγάλο.
NEH, EE-neh meh-GHAH-loh.
Yes, it's large.

Τί μέρα εἶναι σήμερα;
TEE MEH-rah EE-neh SEE-meh-rah?
What day is today?

Σήμερα εἶναι Σάββατο.
SEE-meh-rah EE-neh SAH-
Today is Saturday.

Χθὲς ἦταν Παρασκευή.
KHTES EE-tahn pah-rah-skehv-EE.
Yesterday was Friday.

Αὔριο (θὰ) εἶναι Κυριακή.
AHV-ree-oh (thah) EE-neh kee-ryah-KEE.
Tomorrow will be Sunday.

Ἔδωσα τὸ βιβλίο στὴ Μαρία.
EH-_thoh_-sah toh vee-VLEE-oh stee mah-REE-ah.
I gave Mary the book.

Τὸ ἔδωσα στὴ Μαρία.
toh EH-_thoh_-sah stee mah-REE-ah.
I gave it to Mary.

Τοῦ (τῆς) τὸ ἔδωσα.
TOO (TEES) toh EH-_thoh_-sah.
I gave it to him (her).

(Αὐτὴ) (ἐ)πῆγε ἐκεῖ.
(ahf-TEE) (eh-) PEE-yeh eh-KEE.
She went there.

(Ἐ)πῆγε (αὐτὸς) ἐκεῖ;
(eh-) PEE-yeh (ahf-TOHS) eh-KEE?
Did he go there?

(Αὐτὸς) δὲν (ἐ)πῆγε ἐκεῖ.
(ahf-TOHS) _the_hn (eh-) PEE-yeh eh-KEE.
He didn't go there.

Δὲν (ἐ)πῆγαν (αὐτοὶ) ἐκεῖ;
_the_hn (eh-) PEE-ghahn (ahf-TEE) eh-KEE?
Didn't they go there?

Ναί, (ἐ)πῆγαν.
NEH, (eh-) PEE-ghahn.
Yes, they did.

Θέλω νὰ πάω στὸ σχολεῖο.
THEH-loh nah PAH-oh stoh skhoh-LEE-oh.
I want to go to school.

Δὲν θέλετε νὰ πᾶτε στὸ σχολεῖο;
_the_hn THEH-leh-teh nah PAH-teh stoh skhoh-LEE-oh?
Don't you want to go to school?

Ποιὸς θέλει νὰ πάῃ στὸ σχολεῖο;
PYOHS THEH-lee nah PAH-ee stoh skhoh-LEE-oh?
Who wants to go to school?

Θέλουν πράγματι νὰ πᾶν(ε) στὸ σχολεῖο;
THEH-loon PRAH-ghmah-tee nah PAH-n(eh) stoh skhoh-LEE-oh?
Do they really want to go to school?

Ποιὰ ἦταν ἡ κυρία μὲ τὴν ὁποία σᾶς εἶδα χθὲς τὸ βράδυ
(or ψές);
PYAH EE-tahn ee kee-REE-ah meh teen oh-PEE ah sahs EE-_tha_h
KHTEHS toh VRAH-_the_e (PSEHS)?
Who was the lady with whom I saw you last night?

⁷Ηταν ἡ θεία μου, ποὺ μόλις ἦλθε ἀπὸ τὴν Εὐρώπη.
EE-tahn ee THEE-ah-moo poo MOH-lees EEL-theh ah-POH teen ehv-
ROH-pee.
She was my aunt who just came from Europe.

Ἡ κοπέλα μὲ τὴν ὁποία μιλοῦσα εἶναι ἡ ἀρραβωνιαστικιά μου.
ee koh-PEH-lah meh teen oh-PEE-ah mee-LOO-sah EE-neh ee ah-rah-
voh-nyah-stee-KYAH-moo.
The girl to whom I was speaking is my fiancee.

Τὸ ἀγόρι ποὺ ἡ μητέρα του εἶναι ἡ δασκάλα μου μένει ἐδῶ.
toh ah-GHOH-ree poo ee mee-TEH-rah-too EE-neh ee thah-SKAH-
lah-moo MEH-nee eh-THOH.
The boy whose mother is my teacher lives here.

Μὴ μοῦ λέτε, ὅτι αὐτὸ τὸ γαλάζιο βιβλίο δὲν εἶναι δικό μου.
MEE moo LEH-teh OH-tee ahf-TOH toh ghah-LAH-zyoh vee-VLEE-
oh thehn EE-neh thee-KOH-moo.
Don't tell me that this blue book is not mine.

Ὅταν ἡ Μαρία ἦλθε, ὁ Γιῶργος ἔφυγε.
OH-tahn ee mah-REE-ah EEL-theh, oh YOHR-ghohs EH-fee-yeh.
When Mary came, George left.

Ἂν ἔλθη ὁ Χρῖστος, θὰ τοῦ μιλήσω γιὰ (τὸ ζήτημα) αὐτό.
AHN EHL-thee oh KHREE-stohs, thah too mee-LEE-soh yah toh ZEE-
tee-mah ahf-TOH.
If Chris comes, I will tell him about that.

Ἂν ἐρχόταν ὁ Χρῖστος, θὰ τοῦ ἔλεγα γι' αὐτὸ (τὸ ζήτημα).
AHN ehr-KHOH-tahn oh KHREE-stohs, thah too EH-leh-ghah
yahf-TOH toh ZEE-tee-mah.
If Chris came, I would tell him about that.

Ἐὰν εἶχε ἔλθει ὁ Χρῖστος, θὰ τοῦ (τὸ) εἶχα πεῖ γι' αὐτό.
eh-AHN EE-kheh EHL-thee oh KHREE-stohs, thah too (toh) EE-
khah PEE yahf-TOH.
If Chris had come, I would have told him about it.

Ὅταν ἔλθη ὁ Χρῖστος, θὰ τοῦ (τὸ) πῶ γι' αὐτό.
OH-tahn EHL-thee oh KHREE-stohs, thah too (toh) POH yahf-TOH.
When Chris comes, I will tell him about it.

Ὅταν ἦλθε ὁ Χρῖστος, τοῦ εἶπα τὰ νέα.
OH-tahn EEL-theh oh KHREE-stohs, too EE-pah tah NEH-ah.
When Chris came, I told him the news.

EVERYDAY CONVERSATIONS

BASIC EXPRESSIONS

Καλημέρα.
kah-lee-MEH-rah.
Good morning.

Καλησπέρα.
kah-lee-SPEH-rah.
Good evening.

Καληνύχτα.
kah-lee-NEE-khtah.
Good night.

Χαίρετε or **'Αντίο.**
KHEH-reh-teh or ahn-DEE-oh.
Goodbye.

Γειά σου.
YAH-soo.
Hello.

Εὐχαριστῶ.
ehf-khah-ree-STOH.
Thank You.

Παρακαλῶ or **τίποτε**
pah-rah-kah-LOH or TEE-poh-teh.
You're welcome.

Συγγνώμη or **Μὲ συγχωρεῖτε.**
see-GNOH-mee or meh-seegh-khoh-REE-teh.
Excuse me.

Λυποῦμαι (πολύ).
lee-POO-meh (poh-LEE).
I'm (very) sorry.

Παρακαλῶ.
pah-rah-kah-LOH.
Please.

Μάλιστα or **ναί.**
MAH-lee-stah or NEH.
Yes.

Ὄχι.
OH-khee.
No.

Πόσο;
POH-soh?
How much?

Ποῦ;
POO?
Where?

Πότε;
POH-teh?
When?

Πῶς;
POHS?
How?

Γιατί;
yah-TEE?
Why?

25

Θέλω.
THEH-loh.
I want.

Δός μου *or* Δῶστε μου.
THOHZ-moo or THOH-steh-moo.
Give me.

Ποῦ εἶναι . . . ;
POO EE-neh...?
Where is (*or* are) . . . ?

Πῶς σᾶς λένε;
POHS sahz-LEH-neh?
What's your name?

Μὲ λένε Γιάννη.
meh-LEH-neh YAH-nee.
My name is John.

Τί εἴπατε;
TEE EE-pah-teh?
What did you say?

Μιλᾶτε ἀγγλικά;
mee-LAH-teh ahn-glee-KAH?
Do you speak English?

Δὲν καταλαβαίνω.
(*THEHN*) kah-tah-lah-VEH-noh.
I don't understand.

Μιλᾶτε πιὸ ἀργά.
mee-LAH-teh PYOH ahr-GHAH.
Speak more slowly.

Μοῦ ἀρέσει αὐτό.
moo-ah-REH-see ahf-TOH.
I like this.

Δὲν μοῦ ἀρέσει τὸ ἄλλο.
THEHN moo-ah-REH-see toh-AH-loh.
I don't like the other.

Πῶς εἶστε; *or* Τί κάνετε;
POHS EE-steh *or* TEE KAH-neh-teh?
How do you do?

GETTING ACQUAINTED

Μπορῶ νὰ σᾶς συστήσω τὸν κύριο Παπαδόπουλο (τὴν κυρ
    Παπαδοπούλου, τὴ δεσποινίδα Παπαδοπούλου);
boh-ROH nah-sahs-see-STEE-soh tohn-GEE-ree-oh pah-pah-*THOH*-p
    loh (teen-gee-REE-ah pah-pah-*thoh*-POO-loo, tee *theh*-spee-NE
    thah pah-pah-*thoh*-POO-loo)?
May I present (or introduce) Mr. (Mrs., Miss) Papadopoulo

Ἡ Κυρία μου (ἡ συζυγός μου *or* ἡ γυναίκα μου)
ee-kee-REE-ah-moo (*or* ee-see-zee-GHOHZ-moo *or* ee-yee-NEH-kah-mo
This is my wife.

Καὶ ἐδῶ εἶναι] ὁ γυιός μου (ἡ κόρη μου).
kyeh-*THOH* EE-neh] oh-YOHZ-moo (ee-KOH-ree-moo).
And this is my son (daughter).

Μιλᾶτε ἑλληνικά, βλέπω.
nee-LAH-teh eh-lee-nee-KAH, VLEH-poh.
You speak Greek, I see.

Πολὺ λίγο, φοβοῦμαι.
oh-LEE LEE-ghoh, foh-VOO-meh.
Very little, I'm afraid.

Μπορεῖτε νὰ καταλάβετε τί λέγω;
oh-REE-teh nah-kah-tah-LAH-veh-teh TEE LEH-ghoh?
Can you understand what I'm saying?

Ὄχι τόσο καλά.
OH-khee TOH-soh kah-LAH.
Not so well.

Αὐτὸ εἶναι τὸ πρῶτο σας ταξίδι στὴν Ἑλλάδα;
hf-TOH EE-neh toh-PROH-toh-sahs tah-KSEE- *thee* steen-eh-LAH-*thah*?
Is this your first trip to Greece?

Μάλιστα, τὸ πρῶτο μου ταξίδι.
MAH-lee-stah, toh-PROH-toh-moo tah-KSEE-*thee*.
Yes, my first trip.

Περνᾶτε εὐχάριστα;
pehr-NAH-teh ehf-KHAH-ree-stah?
Are you enjoying yourself?

Γιὰρα πολύ. Μοῦ ἀρέσει ἡ χώρα σας.
ah-rah-poh-LEE. moo-ah-REH-see ee-KHOH-rah-sahs.
Very much. I like your country.

Ποῦ μένετε στὶς Ἡνωμένες Πολιτεῖες;
POO MEH-neh-teh stees ee-noh-MEH-nehs poh-lee-TEE-ehs?
Where do you live in the United States?

Μένω στὴ Νέα Ὑόρκη.
MEH-noh stee-NEH-ah-ee-OHR-kee.
. live in New York.

῀Αν ἔλθετε κάποτε, περάστε νὰ μὲ ἰδῆτε.
ahn-EHL-theh-teh KAH-poh-teh, peh-RAH-steh nah-meh-ee-THEE-teh.
If you ever come my way, call upon me.

Θὰ χαρῶ πολὺ (νὰ περάσω).
thah-khah-ROH poh-LEE (nah-peh-RAH-soh).
I'll be very glad to do so.

῀Ισως μποροῦμε νὰ φᾶμε μαζί.
EE-sohs boh-ROO-meh nah-HAH-meh mah-ZEE.
Perhaps we can have lunch together.

῀Η νὰ πάρωμε ἕνα ποτό, πρὶν φύγετε.
EE nah PAH-roh-meh EH-nah poh-TOH PREEN FEE-yeh-teh.
Or have a drink before you leave.

Πόσον καιρὸ θὰ μείνετε στὴν ᾿Αθήνα;
POH-sohn-geh-ROH   thah-MEE-neh-teh   steen-ah-THEE-nah?
How long will you stay in Athens?

Θὰ μείνω στὴν ᾿Αθήνα δέκα μέρες.
thah-MEE-noh steen-ah-THEE-nah THEH-kah MEH-rehs.
I'll be in Athens for ten days.

STRANGER IN TOWN

Μιλᾶτε ἀγγλικά;
mee-LAH-teh ahn-glee-KAH?
Do you speak English?

Εἶναι κανένας ἐδῶ ποὺ ὁμιλεῖ (or μιλᾶ) ἀγγλικά;
EE-neh kah-NEH-nahs eh-THOH poo-oh-mee-LEE (or mee-LAH) ahn
glee-KAH?
Is there anyone here who speaks English?

῀Εχασα τὸ δρόμο.
EH-khah-sah toh-THROH-moh.
I've lost my way.

Ποῦ θέλετε νὰ πᾶτε;
POO THEH-leh-teh nah-PAH-teh?
Where do you want to go?

Μὲ καταλαβαίνετε;
meh-kah-tah-lah-VEH-neh-teh?
Do you understand me?

Ὄχι, δὲ(ν) σᾶς καταλαβαίνω.
OH-khee, *THEH*(N) sahs-kah-tah-lah-VEH-noh.
No, I don't understand you.

Παρακαλῶ, μιλᾶτε ἀργά.
pah-rah-kah-LOH, mee-LAH-teh ahr-GHAH.
Please, speak slowly.

Τί λέτε;
TEE LEH-teh?
What are you saying?

Πέστε το πάλι, παρακαλῶ.
PEH-steh-toh PAH-lee, pah-rah-kah-LOH.
Please, repeat.

Δὲν μπορῶ νὰ βρῶ τὸ πορτοφόλι μου.
*THEH*N boh-ROH nah-VROH toh-pohr-toh-FOH-lee-moo,
I can't find my wallet.

Μὲ ἔκλεψαν.
meh-EH-kleh-psahn.
I've been robbed.

Παρακαλῶ, φωνάξετε τὴν ἀστυνομία.
pah-rah-kah-LOH, foh-NAH-ks(eh)-teh teen-ah-stee-noh-MEE-ah.
(Please) call the police.

Ποῦ εἶναι τὸ Ἀστυνομικὸ Τμῆμα;
POO EE-neh toh-ah-stee-noh-mee-KOH TMEE-mah?
Where is the Police Station?

Ἀπὸ (ἐ)κεῖ.
ah-POH (eh)-KEE.
That way.

Ἀστυνομία!
ah-stee-noh-MEE-ah!
Police!

Βοήθεια!
voh-EE-thee-ah!
Help!

Εἶμαι Ἀμερικανός.
EE-meh ah-meh-ree-kah-NOHS.
I am an American.

Ὁδηγῆστε με στὸ Ἀμερικανικὸ Προξενεῖο.
oh-*thee*-YEE-steh-meh stoh-ah-meh-ree-kah-nee-KOH proh-kseh-NEE-oh.
Take me to the American Consulate.

Ξέχασα τὸ παλτό μου στὸ τραῖνο.
KSEH-khah-sah toh-pahl-TOH-moo stoh-TREH-noh.
I've left my overcoat in the train.

Πῶς μπορῶ νὰ τὸ βρῶ;
POHS boh-ROH nah-toh-VROH?
How can I get it back?

Δὲν μπορῶ νὰ βρῶ τὸ ξενοδοχεῖο (μου).
THEHN boh-ROH nah-VROH toh-kseh-noh-*th*oh-KHEE-oh(-moo).
I cannot find my hotel.

Μπορεῖτε νὰ μὲ βοηθήσετε;
boh-REE-teh nah-meh-voh-ee-THEE-seh-teh?
Can you help me?

Θὰ ἤθελα νὰ τηλεφωνήσω.
thah-EE-theh-lah nah-tee-leh-foh-NEE-soh.
I would like to use the phone.

Ἔχασα τὴν ὀμπρέλ(λ)α μου.
EH-khah-sah teen-ohm-BREH-lah-moo.
I've lost my umbrella.

Ἔχασα μιὰ βαλίτσα.   Ἔχει τὰ ἀρχικά: G. P.
EH-khah-say MYAH vah-LEE-tsah. EH-khee tah-ahr-khee-KAH: G. P.
I've lost a suitcase.   It carries the initials G. P.

Μοῦ δίνετε, σᾶς παρακαλῶ, τὸ ὄνομα καὶ τὴ διεύθυνσή σας;
moo-*THEE*-neh-teh, sahs-pah-rah-kah-LOH toh-OH-noh-mah keh tee-*th*ee-EHF-theen-SEE-sahs?
Will you please give your name and address?

Μοῦ δείχνετε, σᾶς παρακαλῶ, τὸ διαβατήριό σας;
moo-*THEE*-khneh-teh, sahs-pah-rah-kah-LOH, toh-*th*ee-ah-vah-TEE-ree-OH-sahs?
Will you please show me your passport?

Ἂν βρεθῆ ἡ βαλίτσα μου, τηλεφωνῆστε μου στὸν ἀριθμὸ
    35-1438.
ahn-vreh-*THEE* ee-vah-LEE-tsah-moo, tee-leh-foh-NEE-steh-moo stohn-ah-reeth-MOH tree-AHN-dah-PEHN-deh — KHEE-lyah-teh-trah-KOH-syah — tree-AHN-dah-oh-KTOH.
If my suitcase is found call me at 35-1438.

COUNTING

Cardinal Numbers

ένα EH-nah One	**δύο** (or **δυό**) *THEE-oh (or THYOH)* two	**τρία** TREE-ah three
τέσσερα TEH-seh-rah four	**πέντε** PEHN-deh five	**έξι** EH-ksee six
επτά (or **εφτά**) eh-PTAH (or eh-FTAH) seven		**οκτώ** (or **οχτώ**) oh-KTOH (or oh-KHTOH) eight
εννέα (or **εννιά**) eh-NEH-ah (or eh-NYAH) nine		**δέκα** THEH-kah ten
ένδεκα (or **έντεκα**) EHN-theh-kah (or EHN-deh-kah) eleven		**δώδεκα** THOH-theh-kah twelve
δεκατρία theh-kah-TREE-ah thirteen	**δεκατέσσερα** theh-kah-TEH-seh-rah fourteen	**δεκαπέντε** theh-kah-PEHN-deh fifteen
δεκαέξι theh-kah-EH-ksee sixteen	**δεκαεπτά** theh-kah-eh-PTAH seventeen	**δεκαοκτώ** theh-kah-oh-KTOH eighteen
δεκαεννέα theh-kah-eh-NEH-ah nineteen	**είκοσι** EE-koh-see twenty	**εικοσιένα** ee-koh-see-EH-nah twenty-one
εικοσιδύο ee-koh-see-*THEE*-oh twenty-two	**εικοσιτρία** ee-koh-see-TREE-ah twenty-three	**τριάντα** tree-AHN-dah thirty

σαράντα
sah-RAHN-dah
forty

πενήντα
peh-NEEN-dah
fifty

ἑξήντα
eh-KSEEN-dah
sixty

ἑβδομήντα
ehv-thoh-MEEN-dah
seventy

ὀγδόντα
ohgh-THOHN-dah
eighty

ἐνενήντα
eh-neh-NEEN-dah
ninety

ἑκατό   χίλια
eh-kah-TOH   KHEE-lyah
one hundred one thousand

ἕνα ἑκατομμύριο
EH-nah eh-kah-toh-MEE-ree-oh
one million

ἕνα δισεκατομμύριο
EH-nah thee-seh-kah-toh-MEE-ree-oh
one billion

Ordinal Numbers

(See Grammar 4.3)

πρῶτος, πρώτη, πρῶτο
PROH-tohs, PROH-tee, PROH-toh
first

δεύτερος, δεύτερη, δεύτερο
THEHF-teh-rohs, THEHF-teh-ree, THEHF-teh-roh
second

τρίτος, τρίτη, τρίτο
TREE-tohs, TREE-tee, TREE-toh
third

τέταρτος, τέταρτη, τέταρτο
TEH-tahr-tohs, TEH-tahr-tee, TEH-tahr-toh
fourth

πέμπτος, πέμπτη, πέμπτο
PEHM-ptohs, PEHM-ptee, PEHM-ptoh
fifth

ἕκτος, ἕκτη, ἕκτο
EH-ktohs, EH-ktee, EH-ktoh
sixth

ἕβδομος, ἕβδομη, ἕβδομο
EHV-*thoh*-mohs, EHV-*thoh*-mee, EHV-*thoh*-moh
seventh

ὄγδοος, ὄγδοη, ὄγδοο
OHGH-*thoh*-ohs, OHGH-*thoh*-ee, OHGH-*thoh*-oh
eighth

ἔνατος, ἔνατη, ἔνατο
EH-nah-tohs, EH-nah-tee, EH-nah-toh
ninth

δέκατος, δέκατη, δέκατο
THEH-kah-tohs, *THEH*-kah-tee, *THEH*-kah-toh
tenth

ἑνδέκατος, ἑνδέκατη, ἑνδέκατο
ehn-*THEH*-kah-tohs, ehn-*THEH*-kah-tee, ehn-*THEH*-kah-toh
eleventh

δωδέκατος, δωδέκατη, δωδέκατο
thoh-*THEH*-kah-tohs, thoh-*THEH*-kah-tee, thoh-*THEH*-kah-toh
twelfth

δέκατος τρίτος, δέκατη τρίτη, δέκατο τρίτο
THEH-kah-tohs-TREE-tohs, *THEH*-kah-tee-TREE-tee, *THEH*-*kah*-*toh*-
TREE-toh
thirteenth

δέκατος τέταρτος, δέκατη τέταρτη, δέκατο τέταρτο
THEH-kah-tohs TEH-tahr-tohs, *THEH*-kah-tee teh-TAHR-tee, *THEH*-
kah-toh TEH-tahr-toh
fourteenth

εἰκοστός, εἰκοστή, εἰκοστό
ee-koh-STOHS, ee-koh-STEE, ee-koh-STOH
twentieth

εἰκοστός πρῶτος, εἰκοστή πρώτη, εἰκοστό πρῶτο
ee-koh-STOHS PROH-tohs, ee-koh-STEE PROH-tee, ee-koh-STOH PROH
-toh
twenty-first

μισός, μισή, μισό
mee-SOHS, mee-SEE, mee-SOH
half *or* a half

ἕνα τρίτο
EH-nah TREE-toh
one third

ἕνα τέταρτο
EH-nah TEH-tahr-toh
one fourth

τρία τέταρτα
TREE-ah TEH-tahr-tah
three quarters

ἕνα ὄγδοο
EH-nah OHGH-*thoh*-oh
one eighth

ἕνα δέκατο πέμπτο
EH-nah *TH*EH-kah-toh-PEHM-toh
one fifteenth

THE CLOCK AND THE CALENDAR

Τί ὥρα εἶναι;
TEE-oh-rah EE-neh?
What time is it?

Εἶναι δέκα.
EE-neh *TH*EH-kah.
It is ten o'clock

Εἶναι τρεῖς καὶ τέταρτο.
EE-neh TREES-keh-TEH-tahr-toh.
It is a quarter past three.

Εἶναι ἑπτὰ καὶ μισή.
EE-neh eh-PTAH-keh-mee-SEE.
It is half past seven.

Εἶναι ἐννέα παρὰ τέταρτο.
EE-neh eh-NEH-ah-pah-RAH-TEH-tahr-toh.
It is a quarter to nine.

Εἶναι ἕξι παρὰ εἴκοσι.
EE-neh EH-ksee-pah-RAH-EE-koh-see.
It is twenty to six.

Οἱ ἡμέρες τῆς Ἑβδομάδος εἶναι: ἡ Κυριακή, ἡ Δευτέρα, ἡ Τρίτη, ἡ Τετάρτη, ἡ Πέμπτη, ἡ Παρασκευή, τὸ Σάββατο.
ee-ee-MEH-rehs tees-ehv-*thoh*-MAH-*thohs* EE-neh: ee-kee-ryah-KEE, ee-
thehf-TEH-rah, ee-TREE-tee, ee-teh-TAHR-tee, ee-PEHM-tee, ee-
pah-rah-skeh-VEE, toh-SAH-vah-toh.
The days of the week are: Sunday, Monday, Tuesday, Wednesday, Thursday, Friday, Saturday.

Οἱ μῆνες τοῦ ἔτους (χρόνου) εἶναι: Ἰανουάριος, Φεβρουάριος, Μάρτιος, Ἀπρίλιος, Μάϊος, Ἰούνιος, Ἰούλιος, Αὔγουστος, Σεπτέμβριος, Ὀκτώβριος, Νοέμβριος, Δεκέμβριος.
ee-MEE-nehs too-EH-toos (or KHROH-noo) EE-neh: ee-ah-noo-AH-ree-ohs, feh-vroo-AH-ree-ohs, MAHR-tee-ohs, ah-PREE-lee-ohs, MAH-ee-ohs, ee-OO-nee-ohs, ee-OO-lee-ohs, AHV-ghoo-stohs, seh-PTEHM-vree-ohs, oh-KTOH-vree-ohs, noh-EHM-vree-ohs, theh-KEHM-vree-ohs.

The months of the year are: January, February, March, April, May, June, July, August, September, October, November, December.

Οἱ ἐποχὲς τοῦ ἔτους (or χρόνου) εἶναι: ἡ ἄνοιξη, τὸ καλοκαίρι, τὸ φθινόπωρο, ὁ χειμώνας.
ee-eh-poh-KHEHS too-EH-toos (or KHROH-noo) EE-neh: ee-AH-nee-ksee, toh-kah-loh-KEH-ree, toh-fthee-NOH-poh-roh, oh khee-MOH-nahs.

The seasons of the year are: Spring, Summer, Autumn, Winter.

Σήμερα τὸ πρωῒ (τὸ ἀπόγευμα) εἴχαμε ἥλιο.
SEE-meh-rah toh-proh-EE (toh-ah-POH-yehv-mah) EE-khah-meh EE-lyoh.

This morning (afternoon) the sun was shining.

Πῶς εἶναι ὁ καιρός;
POHS EE-neh oh keh-ROHS?

How is the weather?

Εἶναι πολὺ καλός.
EE-neh poh-LEE kah-LOHS.

It is fine.

Εἶναι ὡραία μέρα.
EE-neh oh-REH-ah MEH-rah.

It is a beautiful day.

Βρέχει (χιονίζει).
VREH-khee (khyoh-NEE-zee).

It is raining (snowing).

Βρέχει ραγδαία (ψιχαλίζει).
VREH-khee rahgh-THEH-ah (psee-khah-LEE-zee).

It is showering (drizzling).

Ποιὲς εἶναι οἱ πιὸ σπουδαῖες γιορτὲς στὴν Ἑλλάδα;
PYEHS EE-neh ee-PYOH-spoo-THEH-ehs yohr-TEHS steen-eh-LAH-thah?

What are the most important holidays in Greece?

Ἡ Πρωτοχρονιά, τὰ Χριστούγεννα, τὸ Πάσχα, ἡ Ἀνάληψη, ἡ Κοίμηση (15 Αὐγούστου **or** Δεκαπενταύγουστος).

ee-proh-toh-khroh-NYAH, tah-khree-STOO-yeh-nah, toh-PAHS-khah, ee-ah-NAH-lee-psee, ee-KEE-mee-see (theh-KAH-tee-PEHM-tee ahv-GHOO-stoo **or** theh-kah-pehn-DAHV-ghoo-stohs).

New Year's Day, Christmas, Easter, Ascension, Assumption (August 15).

Οἱ ἐθνικὲς ἑορτὲς εἶναι: ἡ 25η Μαρτίου καὶ ἡ 28η Ὀκτωβρίου.

ee-eh-thnee-KEHS yohr-TEHS EE-neh: ee-ee-koh-STEE-PEHM-tee mahr-TEE-oo keh ee-ee-koh-STEE-ohgh-THOH-ee oh-ktoh-VREE-oo.

The National Holidays are: Greek Independence Day (March 25th), and October 28th.

ABOARD SHIP

Ταξιδεύω πρώτη θέση. Καμπίνα ἀριθμὸς 87.

tah-ksee-THEH-oh PROH-tee THEH-see. kahm-BEE-nah ah-reeth-MOHS ohgh-THOHN-dah-eh-FTAH.

I am traveling first class. Stateroom No. 87.

Μπορεῖτε νὰ μὲ ὁδηγήσετε;

boh-REE-teh nah-meh-oh-thee-YEE-seh-teh?

Can you please direct me?

Εἶστε στὸ τρίτο κατάστρωμα.

EE-steh stoh-TREE-toh-kah-TAH-stroh-mah.

You are on deck C.

Πρὸς ποιά διεύθυνση (or κατεύθυνση) εἶναι;

prohs PYAH thee-EHF-theen-see (or kah-TEHF-theen-see) EE-neh?

In what direction is it?

Παίρνετε τὰ πράγματά μας στὴν καμπίνα, παρακαλῶ;

PEHR-neh-teh tah PRAHGH-mah-TAH-mahs steen-gahm-BEE-nah, pah-rah-kah-LOH?

Will you take our bags to our cabin, please?

Τί ὥρα σερβίρουν γεῦμα (δεῖπνο);

TEE OH-rah sehr-VEE-roon YEHV-mah (THEE-pnoh)?

At what time is lunch (dinner) served?

Τὸ γεῦμα σερβίρεται στὶς δώδεκα.

toh YEHV-mah sehr-VEE-reh-teh stees-THOH-theh-kah.

Lunch is served at twelve.

Θὰ ἤθελα νὰ νοικιάσω ἕνα κάθισμα στὸ κατάστρωμα.
thah-EE-theh-lah nah-nee-KYAH-soh EH-nah-KAH-thee-zmah stoh-kah-TAH-stroh-mah.

I would like to rent a deck chair.

Πόσο κοστίζει νὰ νοικιάσω ἕνα κάθισμα στὸ κατάστρωμα;
POH-soh koh-STEE-zee nah-nee-KYAH-soh E H-nah-K A H-thee-zmah stoh-kah-TAH-stroh-mah?

How much does it cost to rent a deck chair?

Κοστίζει 60 δραχμές.
koh-STEE-zee eh-KSEEN-dah *th*rakh-MEHS.

It costs 60 drachmas.

῎Εχετε τίποτε (or κάτι) γιὰ τὴ ναυτία;
EH-kheh-teh TEE-poh-teh (*or* KAH-tee) yah-tee-nah-FTEE-ah?

Do you have anything for seasickness?

Τί ὥρα φθάνει αὔριο τὸ πλοῖο;
TEE OH-rah FTHAH-nee AHV-ree-oh toh-PLEE-oh?

At what time does the boat dock tomorrow?

Θὰ φθάσωμε στὸν Πειραιᾶ στὶς ὀκτώ.
thah-FTHAH-soh-meh stohm-bee-reh-AH stees-oh-KTOH.

We will dock at Piraeus at eight o'clock.

Προσέξετε νὰ βγάλετε τὰ πράγματά μου ἐγκαίρως.
proh-SEH-ks(eh)-teh nah-VGHAH-l(eh)-teh tah-PRAHGH-mah-TAH-moo ehn-GEH-rohs.

See that my bags are off in time.

PLANE TRAVEL

῎Εχει ἀεροπλάνο γιὰ τὴ Θεσσαλονίκη;
EH-khee ah-eh-roh-PLAH-noh yah-tee-theh-sah-loh-NEE-kee?

Is there a plane to Salonica?

Θὰ ἤθελα νὰ κρατήσω μιὰ θέση γιὰ τὸ ἑπόμενο ἀεροπλάνο.
thah-EE-theh-lah nah-krah-TEE-soh MYAH-THEH-see yah-toh-eh-POH-meh-noh ah-eh-roh-PLAH-noh.

I would like to reserve a seat on the next flight.

Πόσο ἔχει τὸ εἰσιτήριο;
POH-soh EH-khee toh-ee-see-TEE-ree-oh?

What is the fare?

῍Ενα εἰσιτήριο γιὰ τὴ Θεσσαλονίκη, παρακαλῶ. Θὰ ἤθελα
        μιὰ θέση κοντὰ στὸ παράθυρο.

EH-nah-ee-see-TEE-ree-oh   yah-tee-theh-sah-loh-NEE-kee,   pah-rah-kah-
    LOH.   thah-EE-theh-lah   MYAH-THEH-see   kohn-DAH-stoh-pah-
    RAH-thee-roh.

A ticket to Salonica, please. I would like a seat next to the
        window.

Πότε φεύγει τὸ λεωφορεῖο γιὰ τὸ ἀεροδρόμιο;

POH-teh   FEHV-yee   toh-leh-oh-foh-REE-oh   yah-toh-ah-eh-roh-THROH-
    mee-oh?

When does the bus leave for the airport?

Σερβίρεται γεῦμα (δεῖπνο) στὸ ἀεροπλάνο;

schr-VEE-reh-teh   YEHV-mah   (THEE-pnoh)   stoh-ah-eh-roh-PLAH-noh

Is lunch (dinner) served on this flight?

Οἱ ἀποσκευές μου μεταφέρονται δωρεάν;

ee-ah-poh-skeh-VEHZ-moo   meh-tah-FEH-rohn-deh   thoh-reh-AHN?

Is my luggage carried free?

Εἶναι δυὸ κιλὰ περισσότερο ἀπὸ τὸ κανονικό. Πρέπει νὰ πλη
        ρώσετε 300 δραχμές.

EE-neh   THYOH-kee-LAH   peh-ree-SOH-teh-roh   ah-POH-toh-kah-noh-
    nee-KOH.   PREH-pee   nah-plee-ROH-seh-teh   tree-ah-KOH-see-eh
    thrahkh-MEHS.

It is two kilos overweight. You must pay 300 drachmas.

Πῶς λέγεται τὸ ἀεροδρόμιο τῶν ᾿Αθηνῶν;

pohs   LEH-yeh-teh   toh-ah-eh-roh-THROH-mee-oh   tohn-ah-thee-NOHN

What is the name of the Athens airport?

Τὸ ἀεροδρόμιο τῶν ᾿Αθηνῶν λέγεται «᾿Ελληνικό».

toh-ah-eh-roh-THROH-mee-oh   tohn   ah-thee-NOHN   LEH-yeh-teh   "eh
    lee-nee-KOH".

The Athens airport is called Hellenico.

Τὸ ἀεροπλάνο μόλις προσγειώθηκε.

toh-ah-eh-roh-PLAH-noh   MOH-lees   prohs-yee-OH-thee-keh.

The plane has just landed.

Μπορῶ νὰ ἰδῶ τὸ εἰσιτήριό σας;

boh-ROH   nah-ee-THOH   toh-ee-see-TEE-ree-OH-sahs?

May I see your ticket?

Δεσποινίς (συνοδός), τὸ ἀεροπλάνο θὰ φθάση στὴν ὥρα του;
*th*ehs-pee-NEES   (see-noh-*THOHS*),   toh-ah-eh-roh-PLAH-noh   thah-
    FTHAH-see steen-OH-rah-too?
Stewardess, will the plane arrive on time?

TRAVEL BY RAIL

Ποῦ εἶναι τὸ γραφεῖο εἰσιτηρίων;
POO EE-neh toh-ghrah-FEE-oh ee-see-tee-REE-ohn?
Where is the ticket office?

Ἕνα εἰσιτήριο γιὰ τὴ Λάρισα.
EH-nah ee-see-TEE-ree-oh yah-tee-LAH-ree-**sah**.
One ticket to Larisa.

Πρώτη (δεύτερη, τρίτη) θέση.
PROH-tee (*THEHF*-teh-ree, TREE-tee) THEH-**see**.
First (second, third) class.

ʿΑπλό.   Μετ᾿ ἐπιστροφῆς.
ah-PLOH.   meh-teh-pee-stroh-FEES.
One way.   Round trip.

Εἶναι ἡ «ταχεῖα» ἢ τὸ «τοπικό»;
EE-neh ee-tah-KHEE-ah ee toh-toh-pee-KOH?
Is it an express or a local?

Αὐτὸ τὸ κάθισμα εἶναι πιασμένο;
ahf-TOH toh-KAH-thee-zmah EE-neh pyah-ZMEH-noh?
Is this seat taken?

Ἐπιτρέπεται τὸ κάπνισμα ἐδῶ;
eh-pee-TREH-peh-teh toh-KAH-pnee-zmah eh-*THOH*?
Is smoking permitted here?

Πότε φεύγει αὐτὸ τὸ τραῖνο;   Πότε φθάνει;
POH-teh FEHV-yee ahf-TOH-toh-TREH-noh?   POH-teh FTHAH-nee?
What time does this train leave?   When does it arrive?

Εἰσιτήρια, παρακαλῶ.
e-see-TEE-ree-ah, pah-rah-kah-LOH.
Tickets, please.

Ποῦ εἶναι τὸ «βαγκόν-ρεστωράν»;
POO EE-neh toh-vah-GOHN-reh-stoh-RAHN?
Which way is the dining-car?

Πότε φθάνομε;
POH-teh FTHAH-noh-meh?
How soon do we arrive?

Τὸ τραῖνο ἔχει δέκα λεπτὰ καθυστέρηση.
toh-TREH-noh EH-khee *THEH*-kah leh-PTAH kah-thee-STEH-ree-see
The train is ten minutes late.

Σὲ ποιὰ πόλη πλησιάζομε;
seh-PYAH-POH-lee plee-see-AH-zoh-meh?
What town are we coming to?

GOING THROUGH CUSTOMS

Ἀνοῖξτε τὴ βαλίτσα σας, παρακαλῶ.
ah-NEE-ksteh tee-vah-LEE-tsah-sahs, pah-rah-kah-LOH.
Open your baggage, please.

Ἔχετε κάτι (*or* τίποτε) ἄλλο ἐκτὸς ἀπὸ τὰ ροῦχα σας;
EH-kheh-teh KAH-tee (*or* TEE-poh-teh) AH-loh eh-KTOHS-ah-**POH**
    tah-ROO-khah-sahs?
Do you have anything besides personal wearing apparel?

Μάλιστα, μερικὰ δῶρα.
MAH-lee-stah, meh-ree-KAH *THOH*-rah.
Yes, a few presents.

Καὶ τὴ φωτογραφική μου μηχανή.
keh tee-foh-toh-ghrah-fee-KEE-moo mee-khah-NEE.
And my camera.

Ἡ φωτογραφικὴ μηχανὴ εἶναι γιὰ ἀτομικὴ (*or* προσωπικὴ)
        χρήση;
ee-foh-toh-ghrah-fee-KEE mee-khah-NEE EE-neh yah-ah-toh-mee-KEE
    (*or* proh-soh-pee-KEE) KHREE-see?
Is the camera for personal use?

Μάλιστα[, εἶναι].
MAH-lee-stah[, EE-neh].
Yes, it is.

Πόσα κουτιά τσιγάρα ἔχετε;
POH-sah koo-TYAH tsee-GHAH-rah EH-kheh-teh?
How many cigarettes do you have?

Ἔχω δύο πακέτα.
EH-khoh *THEE*-oh pah-KEH-tah.
I have two packs.

Ποῦ εἶναι τὰ χαρτιά (or πιστοποιητικά) σας, παρακαλῶ;
POO EE-neh tah-khahr-TYAH *(or* pee-stoh-pee-ee-tee-KAH)-sahs, pah-
rah-kah-LOH?
Where are your papers, please?

Ὁρίστε τὰ χαρτιά μου.
oh-REE-steh tah-khahr-TYAH-moo.
Here are my papers.

Παρακαλῶ, φωνάζετε ἕναν ἀχθοφόρο;
pah-rah-kah-LOH, foh-NAH-zeh-teh EH-nahn-ahkh-thoh-FOH-roh?
Will you please get a porter?

Παρακαλῶ, πάρτε τὰ πράγματά μου σὲ ἕνα ταξί (στὸ λεωφορεῖο).
pah-rah-khah-LOH, PAHR-teh tah-PRAHGH-mah-TAH-moo s(eh)-EH-
nah-tah-KSEE (stoh-leh-oh-foh-REE-oh).
Will you please take my bags to a taxi (to the bus).

Πόσο θὰ μοῦ κοστίση;   Εἶναι πολλά!
POH-soh thah-moo-koh-STEE-see?   EE-neh poh-LAH!
How much do you charge?   That is too much!

Θὰ σᾶς πληρώσω (or δώσω) 30 δραχμές.
thah-sahs-plee-ROH-soh *(or THOH*-soh) tree-AHN-dah-*th*rahkh-MEHS.
I will pay you 30 drachmas.

Ἀκολουθῆστε με, παρακαλῶ.
ah-koh-loo-THEE-steh-meh, pah-rah-kah-LOH.
Follow me, please.

GETTING AROUND TOWN

Taxis

Ταξί!   Εἶστε ἐλεύθερος;
tah-KSEE!   EE-steh eh-LEHF-theh-rohs?
Taxi!   Are you free?

[Μὲ πηγαίνετε] στὴν Ἀκρόπολη.
[meh-pee-YEH-neh-teh]   steen-ah-KROH-poh-lee.
Take me to the Acropolis.

Ποιὸ εἶναι αὐτὸ τὸ κτίριο δεξιά (ἀριστερά);
PYOH   EE-neh   ahf-TOH-toh-KTEE-ree-oh   theh-ksee-AH   (ah-ree-ste
RAH)?
What's this building on the right (left)?

Σταματῆστε στὴ γωνία.
stah-mah-TEE-steh   stee-ghoh-NEE-ah.
Stop at the corner.

Ἀφῆστε μας στὸ ἄλλο μέρος τῆς πλατείας.
ah-FEE-steh-mahs   stoh-AH-loh   MEH-rohs   tees-plah-TEE-ahs.
Let us out at the other side of the square.

Τί σᾶς χρεωστῶ;
TEE   sahs-khr(eh-) oh-STOH?
What's the charge?

Ποῦ εἶναι ἡ στάση τῶν λεωφορείων;
POO   EE-neh   ee-STAH-see   tohn-leh-oh-foh-REE-ohn?
Where is the bus stop?

Σταματάει ἐδῶ τὸ λεωφορεῖο τῆς Βουλιαγμένης;
stah-mah-TAH(-ee)   eh-THOH   toh-leh-oh-fo-REE-oh   teez-voo-lyah
MEH-nees?
Does the bus to Vouliagmeni stop here?

Buses

Κάθε πόση ὥρα ἔχει λεωφορεῖο;
KAH-theh   POH-see   OH-rah   EH-khee   leh-oh-foh-REE-oh?
How often do the buses run?

Πότε φεύγει τὸ ἐπόμενο λεωφορεῖο γιὰ τὴν Κηφισιά;
POH-teh   FEHV-yee   toh-eh-POH-meh-noh   leh-oh-foh-REE-oh   yah-te
gee-fee-SYAH?
When does the next bus leave for Kifisia?

Πόσο ἔχει τὸ εἰσιτήριο;
POH-soh   EH-khee   toh-ee-see-TEE-ree-oh?
How much is the fare?

Ἕνα εἰσιτήριο, παρακαλῶ.

EH-nah ee-see-TEE-ree-oh, pah-rah-kah-LOH.

One ticket, please.

Ὅταν φθάσωμε στὸ Ψυχικό, πέστε μου, παρακαλῶ.

OH-tahn-FTHAH-soh-meh stoh-psee-khee-KOH, PEH-steh-moo, pah-rah-kah-LOH.

When we reach Psychico, let me know, please.

Ὁδηγέ (ἢ σωφέρ), σταματῆστε νὰ κατεβῶ, παρακαλῶ.

oh-thee-YEH (or soh-FEHR), stah-mah-TEE-steh nah-kah-teh-VOH, pah-rah-kah-LOH.

Driver, please, let me off.

Μέχρι (or "Ὡς) ποιὰ ὥρα κυκλοφοροῦν τὰ λεωφορεῖα τῆς γραμμῆς αὐτῆς;

MEH-khree (or OHS)-PYAH-OH-rah kee-kloh-foh-ROON tah-leh-oh-foh-REE-ah tees-ghrah-MEES-ahf-TEES?

How late do the buses run on this line?

MOTORING THROUGH GREECE

Ποῦ εἶναι τὸ πλησιέστερο γκαράζ;

POO EE-neh toh-plee-see-EH-steh-roh gah-RAHZ?

Where is the nearest gas station?

Παρακαλῶ, γεμίστε τὸ ντεπόζιτο (βενζίνης).

pah-rah-kah-LOH, yeh-MEE-steh toh-deh-POH-zee-toh (vehn-ZEE-nees).

Fill the tank, please.

Δῶστε μου δέκα γαλ(λ)όνια βενζίνη.

THOH-steh-moo THEH-kah ghah-LOH-nyah vehn-ZEE-nee.

Give me ten gallons of gas.

Αὐτὸς εἶναι ὁ δρόμος πρὸς τὴ Λαμία;

ahf-TOHS EE-neh oh-THROH-mohs prohs-tee-lah-MEE-ah?

Is this the road to Lamia?

Προχωρῆστε [κατ' εὐθεῖαν], 20 χιλιόμετρα.

proh-khoh-REE-steh [kah-tehf-THEE-ahn], EE-koh-see khee-lee-OH-meh-trah.

Straight ahead 20 kilometers.

Γυρίστε ἀριστερὰ (δεξιὰ) στὴν πρώτη διασταύρωση.
yee-REE-steh ah-ree-steh-RAH (theh-ksee-AH) steem-BROH-tee thee-ah
STAH-vroh-see.
Turn left (right)at the next crossroad.

Μποροῦμε νὰ φθάσωμε στὰ Μετέωρα πρὶν νυχτώση;
boh-ROO-meh   nah-FTHAH-soh-meh   stah-meh-TEH-oh-rah   PREEN
nee-KHTOH-see?
Can we reach Meteora before nightfall?

Ποιὰ πόλη εἶναι αὐτή;
PYAH POH-lee EE-neh ahf-TEE?
What town is this?

Ποῦ ὁδηγεῖ αὐτὸς ὁ δρόμος;
POO oh-thee-YEE ah-FTOHS-oh-THROH-mohs?
Where does this road go?

Ἔσπασε τὸ λάστιχο.
EH-spah-seh toh-LAH-stee-khoh.
I have a flat tire.

Παρακαλῶ, δεῖξτε μου τὸ πλησιέστερο γκαράζ.
pah-rah-kah-LOH, THEE-ksteh-moo toh-plee-see-EH-steht-roh-gah-RAHZ
Please take me to the nearest garage.

Παρακαλῶ, μπορῶ νὰ ἔχω λίγο νερὸ γιὰ τὸ αὐτοκίνητο;
pah-rah-kah-LOH, boh-ROH-nah EH-khoh LEE-ghoh-neh-ROH yah-toh
ahf-toh-KEE-nee-toh?
May I have some water for my car, please?

Μπορεῖτε νὰ σπρώξετε τὸ αὐτοκίνητό μου;
boh-REE-teh nah-SPROH-kseh-teh toh-ahf-toh-KEE-nee-TOH-moo?
Can you give my car a push?

Μπορεῖτε νὰ μὲ πάρετε ὡς τὴ Γλυφάδα;
boh-REE-teh nah-meh-PAH-reh-teh ohs-tee-ghlee-FAH-thah?
Can you give me a lift to Glyfada?

AUTO CARE

Τὸ αὐτοκίνητό μου χάλασε.
toh-ahf-toh-KEE-nee-TOH-moo KHAH-lah-seh.
My car has broken down.

Παρακαλῶ, κοιτάξτε τὰ λάστιχα.
pah-rah-kah-LOH, kee-TAHKS-teh tah-LAH-stee-khah.
Please, check the tires.

Πόσο?

Πόσο κοστίζει τὸ γαλόνι ἡ βενζίνη;
POH-soh koh-STEE-zee toh-ghah-LOH-nee ee-vehn-ZEE-nee?
What is the price of gasoline per gallon?

Παρακαλῶ, γεμίστε το.
pah-rah-kah-LOH, yeh-MEE-steh-toh.
Please, fill'er up.

Παρακαλῶ, ἀλλάξτε τὸ μηχανέλαιο (or τὰ λάδια).
pah-rah-kah-LOH, ah-LAHKS-teh toh-mee-khah-NEH-leh-oh (or tah-LAH-thyah).
Please, change the oil.

Δῶστε μου ἕνα κιλὸ μηχανέλαιο (or λάδι).
THOH-steh-moo EH-nah kee-LOH mee-khah-NEH-leh-oh (or LAH-thee).
Give me a kilo of oil.

Παρακαλῶ, γρασάρετε τὸ αὐτοκίνητο.
pah-rah-kah-LOH, ghrah-SAH-reh-teh toh-ahf-toh-KEE-nee-toh.
Please, grease the car.

Παρακαλῶ, διορθώσετε τὰ φρένα.
pah-rah-kah-LOH, thee-ohr-THOH-s(es)-teh tah-FREH-nah.
Please, adjust the brakes.

Παρακαλῶ, βάλτε νερὸ στὸ ψυγεῖο.
pah-rah-kah-LOH, VAHL-teh neh-ROH stoh-psee-YEE-oh.
Please, put water in the radiator.

Εἶναι κάποια βλάβη στὶς ταχύτητες.
EE-neh- KAH-pyah VLAH-vee stees-tah-KHEE-tee-tehs.
There is something wrong with the gears.

Παρακαλῶ, στεῖλτε μου ἕνα ρυμουλκό.
pah-rah-kah-LOH, STEEL-teh-moo EH-nah-ree-mool-KOH.
Please send a tow car.

Εἶναι ἐδῶ κανένας μηχανικὸς ποὺ γνωρίζει ἀπὸ ἀμερικάνικα
αὐτοκίνητα;
EE-neh-eh-*THOH* kah-NEH-nahs mee-khah-nee-KOHS poo-ghnoh-REE-
zee ah-POH-ah-meh-ree-KAH-nee-kah-ahf-toh-KEE-nee-tah?
Is there a mechanic here who knows American cars?

Πόσον καιρὸ θὰ πάρη ἡ ἐπισκευή;
POH-sohn-geh-ROH thah-sahs-PAH-ree ee-eh-pee-skeh-VEE?
How long will the repairs take?

Γκάζ (τροφοδότης βενζίνης)
GAHZ (troh-foh-*THOH*-tees vehn-ZEE-nees)
Accelerator.

Μεγάλα φῶτα
meh-GHAH-lah FOH-tah
Headlights.

Προφυλαχτήρας.
proh-fee-lahkh-TEE-rahs
Bumper.

Ντεμπραγιάζ (Συμπρέκτης)
dehm-brah-YAHZ (seem-BREH-ktees)
Clutch.

Τιμόνι
tee-MOH-nee
Steering Wheel.

Μηχανή
mee-khah-NEE
Engine.

Κλάξον.
KLAH-ksohn
Horn.

TRAFFIC SIGNS AND DIRECTIONS

ΑΠΑΓΟΡΕΥΕΤΑΙ Η ΣΤΑΣΙΣ
ah-pah-ghoh-REV-veh-teh ee-STAH-sees
No parking.

ΣΙΔΗΡΟΔΡΟΜΟΣ
see-*thee*-ROH-*th*roh-mohs
Railroad.

ΔΙΑΣΤΑΥΡΩΣΙΣ ΟΔΩΝ
thee-ah-STAH-vroh-sees oh-*THOH*N
Crossroads.

ΥΠΟ ΕΠΙΣΚΕΥΗΝ
ee-POH eh-pee-skeh-VEEN
Under repair.

ΑΠΑΓΟΡΕΥΕΤΑΙ Η ΔΙΑΒΑΣΙΣ
ah-pah-ghoh-REH-veh-teh ee-*thee*-AH-vah-sees
No thoroughfare.

ΔΗΜΟΣΙΑ ΕΡΓΑ
thee-MOH-see-ah EHR-ghah
Work in progress *or* Men working.

ΠΡΟΣΟΧΗ
proh-soh-KHEE
Caution *or* Attention.

ΝΟΣΟΚΟΜΕΙΟΝ, ΗΣΥΧΙΑ
noh-soh-koh-MEE-ohn, ee-see-KHEE-ah
Hospital, quiet.

ΣΧΟΛΕΙΟΝ
skhoh-LEE-ohn
School.

ΑΔΙΕΞΟΔΟΣ
ah-thee-EH-ksoh-thohs
Dead end.

ΜΗ ΣΤΡΕΦΕΤΕ ΔΕΞΙΑ (ΑΡΙΣΤΕΡΑ)
MEE-STREH-feh-teh theh-ksee-AH (ah-ree-steh-RAH)
No right (left) turn.

ΠΛΗΡΟΦΟΡΙΑΙ
plee-roh-foh-REE-eh
Inquire here or information.

ΚΛΕΙΣΤΟΣ ΔΡΟΜΟΣ
klee-STOHS THROH-mohs
Road closed.

ΜΕΓΙΣΤΗ ΤΑΧΥΤΗΣ
meh-YEE-stee tah-KHEE-tees
Maximum speed.

ΚΑΜΠΗ
kahm-BEE
Curve.

ΕΙΣΟΔΟΣ
EE-soh-thohs
Entrance.

ΑΠΑΓΟΡΕΥΕΤΑΙ Η ΕΙΣΟΔΟΣ
ah-pah-ghoh-REH-veh-teh ee-EE-soh-thohs
Keep out.

ΕΞΟΔΟΣ
EH-ksoh-thohs
Exit.

ΑΠΟΤΟΜΟΣ ΚΛΙΣΙΣ
ah-POH-toh-mohs KLEE-sees
Steep grade.

ΑΝΩΜΑΛΟΣ ΟΔΟΣ
ah-NOH-mah-lohs OH-thohs
Uneven road.

ΕΛΑΤΤΩΣΑΤΕ ΤΑΧΥΤΗΤΑ
eh-lah-TOH-sah-teh tah-KHEE-tee-tah
Slow down.

ΚΙΝΔΥΝΟΣ
KEEN-thee-nohs
Danger.

ΕΜΠΟΔΙΟΝ
ehm-BOH-thee-ohn
Obstruction.

AT THE HOTEL

Μοῦ κρατήσατε δωμάτιο;
moo-krah-TEE-sah-teh thoh-MAH-tee-oh?
Do you have a room reserved for me?

Σᾶς εἰδοποίησα ταχυδρομικῶς (τηλεφωνικῶς).
sahs-ee-thoh-P E E-ee-sah tah-khee-throh-mee-K O H S (tee-leh-foh-nee-
K O H S).
I made a reservation by letter (by phone).

Θέλω μοναχικὸ δωμάτιο μὲ (χωρὶς) μπάνιο.
THEH-loh   moh-nah-khee-KOH   thoh-MAH-tee-oh   meh-(khoh-REES)-
    BAH-nyoh.

I want a single room with (without) bath.

῎Εχετε ἕνα δωμάτιο μὲ διπλὸ κρεβάτι (δυὸ κρεβάτια);
EH-kheh-teh   EH-nah-thoh-MAH-tee-oh   meh-thee-PLOH   kreh-VAH-tee
    (THYOH kreh-VAH-tyah)?

Do you have a room with a double bed (twin beds)?

Πόσο κοστίζει τὸ δωμάτιο αὐτό;
POH-soh koh-STEE-zee toh-thoh-MAH-tee-oh ahf-TOH?

What is the price of this room?

Πόσον καιρὸ σκέπτεσθε νὰ μείνετε;
POH-sohn-geh-ROH SKEH-pteh-stheh nah-MEE-neh-teh?

How long are you planning to stay?

Σκέπτομαι νὰ μείνω δέκα μέρες.
SKEH-ptoh-meh nah-MEE-noh THEH-kah-MEH-rehs.

I am planning to stay ten days.

῾Η τιμὴ εἶναι 270 δραχμὲς τὴν ἡμέρα.
ee-tee-MEE   EE-neh   thyah-KOH-syehs ehv-thoh-M E E N-dah   thrahkh-
    MEHS teen-ee-MEH-rah.

The price for a single day is 270 drachmas.

Γιὰ μιὰ ἑβδομάδα ἔχομε εἰδικὴ (or ἐλαττωμένη) τιμή.
yah-MYAH-ehv-thoh-MAH-thah   EH-khoh-meh   ee-thee-KEE   (or eh-lah-
    toh-MEH-nee)   tee-MEE.

For a week we have a special rate.

Συμπεριλαμβάνεται ἡ ὑπηρεσία;
seem-beh-ree-lahm-VAH-neh-teh ee-ee-pee-reh-SEE-ah?

Does that include service?

Τὸ φαγητὸ συμπεριλαμβάνεται;
toh-fah-yee-TOH seem-beh-ree-lahm-VAH-neh-teh?

Are meals included?

Μόνο τὸ πρωϊνὸ περιλαμβάνεται.
MOH-noh toh-proh-ee-NOH peh-ree-lahm-VAH-neh-teh.

Only breakfast is included.

Μάλιστα, θὰ κρατήσω αὐτὸ τὸ δωμάτιο.
MAH-lee-stah, thah-krah-TEE-soh ahf-TOH-toh-thoh-MAH-tee-oh.

Yes, this room will do.

Παρακαλῶ, φέρτε μου τὶς βαλίτσες ἐπάνω.
pah-rah-kah-LOH, FEHR-teh-moo tees-vah-LEE-tsehs eh-POH-noh.
Please have my bags carried up.

Παρακαλῶ, συμπληρῶστε (or ὑπογράψτε) τὸ δελτίο διαμονῆς.
pah-rah-kah-LOH, seem-blee-ROH-steh (or ee-poh-GHRAH-psteh) toh-
thehl-TEE-oh-thee-ah-moh-NEES.
Would you please sign the registration blank?

Ποῦ εἶναι τὸ μπάνιο;
POO EE-neh toh-BAH-nyoh?
Where is the bathroom?

Θέλω νὰ κάμω ἕνα λουτρό.
THEH-loh nah-KAH-noh EH-nah-loo-TROH.
I wish to take a bath.

Μοῦ σιδηρώνετε αὐτὸ τὸ κουστούμι;
moo-see-thee-ROH-neh-teh ahf-TOH-toh-koo-STOO-mee?
Could you have this suit pressed for me?

Τὸ θέλω πίσω στὶς ἕξι ἢ ὥρα.
toh-THEH-loh-PEE-soh stees-EH-ksee-ee-OH-rah.
I'll need it back at six o'clock.

Στεῖλτε μου τὸ πρωϊνὸ στὶς ὀκτὼ ἢ ὥρα.
STEE-lteh-moo toh-proh-ee-NOH stees-ah-KTOH-ee-OH-rah.
Have breakfast sent up at eight o'clock.

Θέλω νὰ ἔχω καφὲ καὶ μπισκότα.
THEH-loh nah-EH-khoh kah-FEH-keh-bee-SKOH-tah.
I wish to have coffee and biscuits.

Σκέπτομαι νὰ φύγω αὔριο.
SKEH-ptoh-meh nah-FEE-ghoh AH-vree-oh.
I am planning to leave tomorrow.

Θὰ κάμω ἕνα ταξίδι στὴ Ρόδο.
thah-KAH-moh EH-nah-tah-KSEE-thee stee-ROH-thoh.
I am going on a trip to Rhodes.

Μπορῶ νὰ ἀφήσω μερικὰ ἀπὸ τὰ πράγματά μου ἐδῶ;
boh-ROH n(ah)-ah-FEE-soh meh-ree-KAH ah-POH-tah-PRAHGH-mah-
TAH-moo eh-THOH?
May I leave some of my baggage here?

Θὰ γυρίσω τὴ Δευτέρα.
thah-yee-REE-soh tee-*theh*f-TEH-rah.
I will be back on Monday.

Παρακαλῶ, ἑτοιμάσετε τὸ λογαριασμό μου.
pah-rah-kah-LOH, eh-tee-MAH-s(eh-)teh toh-loh-ghah-ryah-ZMOH-moo.
Please have my bill ready.

Παρακαλῶ, στεῖλτε μου ἕνα παιδὶ γιὰ τὶς βαλίτσες μου.
pah-rah-kah-LOH, STEE-lteh-moo EH-nah-peh-*THEE* yah-tees-vah-LEE-
tsehz-moo.
Please send a boy for my bags.

Παρακαλῶ, καλέστε (or φωνάξετε) ἕνα ταξί.
pah-rah-kah-LOH, kah-LEH-steh (*or* foh-NAH-ks(eh)-teh) EH-nah-tah-
KSEE.
Will you please call a taxi for me?

RENTING A ROOM

Θέλετε δωμάτιο ἐπιπλωμένο ἢ χωρὶς ἔπιπλα;
THEH-leh-teh *thoh*-MAH-tee-oh eh-pee-ploh-MEH-noh EE khoh-REES-
EH-pee-plah?
Do you want a furnished or unfurnished room?

Θέλω ἕνα ἐπιπλωμένο δωμάτιο μὲ μπάνιο καὶ πρωϊνό.
THEH-loh EH-nah-eh-pee-ploh-MEH-noh *thoh*-MAH-tee-oh meh-BAH-
nyoh keh proh-ee-NOH.
I want a furnished room with a bath and breakfast.

Θὰ τρώγω ἀλλοῦ τὸ μεσημέρι.
thah-TROH-(gh)oh ah-LOO toh-meh-see-MEH-ree.
I will take my noon meals elsewhere.

**Θὰ προτιμούσατε ἕνα δωμάτιο μὲ παράθυρα πρὸς τὸ δρόμο ἢ
πρὸς τὴ θάλασσα;**
thah-proh-tee-MOO-sah-teh EH-nah-*thoh*-MAH-tee-oh meh-pah-R A H-
thee-rah prohs-toh-*TH*ROH-moh EE prohs-tee-THAH-lah-sah?
Would you prefer a room which looks out on the street or on
the sea?

Θὰ πάρω αὐτὸ μὲ τὴ θέα πρὸς τὴ θάλασσα.
thah-PAH-roh ahf-TOH-meh-tee-THEH-ah prohs-tee-THAH-lah-sah.
I shall take the one with the view on the sea.

Τί θὰ μὲ χρεώσετε μαζὶ μὲ τὴν ὑπηρεσία;
TEE   thah--meh-khreh-OH-s(eh)-teh   mah-ZEE-meh-teen-ee-pee-reh-SEE-
ah?

What price will you charge, including service?

Θὰ μπορούσατε νὰ κατεβάσετε λίγο τὴν τιμή;
thah-boh-ROO-sah-teh   nah-kah-teh-VAH-seh-teh   LEE-ghoh   teen-dee-
MEE?

Could you give me a slightly lower price?

Ἀφοῦ μάλιστα θὰ μείνω ἐδῶ ἕξι ἑβδομάδες.
ah-FOO MAH-lee-stah thah-MEE-noh eh-*THOH* EH-ksee ehv-*thoh*-MAH-
*the*hs.

After all I will be here for six weeks.

Κρατῆστε ὅλα τὰ σημειώματα καὶ προσέξτε τὸ ταχυδρομεῖο
μου.
krah-TEE-steh OH-lah-tah-see-mee-OH-mah-tah keh proh-SEHKS-teh toh-
tah-khee-*throh*-MEE-oh-moo.

Take all the messages and look after my mail.

Ἂν μὲ ζητήσουν φίλοι, φέρτε τους ἐπάνω [στὸ δωμάτιο].
ahn-meh-zee-TEE-soon FEE-lee, FEHR-teh-toos eh-PAH-noh [stoh-*thoh*-
MAH-tee-oh].

If friends call show them up.

DINING OUT

Ξέρετε κανένα καλὸ ἐστιατόριο;
KSEH-reh-teh kah-NEH-nah kah-LOH eh-stee-ah-TOH-ree-oh?

Can you recommend a good restaurant?

Ἕνα τραπέζι γιὰ δύο, παρακαλῶ.
EH-nah trah-PEH-zee yah-*THEE*-oh, pah-rah-kah-LOH.

A table for two, please.

Σερβίρετε «ἀλα-κάρτ» ἢ «ταμπλ-ντότ»;
sehr-VEE-reh-teh "ah-lah-KAHRT" EE "tahmbl-DOHT"?

Do you serve a la carte or table d' hote?

Παρακαλῶ, μοῦ δίνετε τὸν κατάλογο (or τὸ μενού).
pah-rah-kah-LOH, moo-*THEE*-neh-teh tohn-gah-TAH-loh-ghoh (or toh-
meh-NOO) .

May I have a menu, please?

Τί μὲ συμβουλεύετε σεῖς;
TEE meh-seem-voo-LEH-veh-teh SEES?
What do you recommend?

Σᾶς συμβουλεύω νὰ πάρετε ἀρνὶ ψητό.
sahs-seem-voo-LEH-voh nah-PAH-reh-teh ahr-nee-psee-TOH.
I suggest that you have roast lamb.

Θὰ ἀρχίσω μὲ ντολμαδάκια.
th(ah)-ahr-KHEE-soh meh-dohl-mah-*THAH*-kyah.
I will start with some stuffed grapeleaves.

Ἡ γυναίκα μου θὰ ἔχῃ τυρόπητ(τ)α.
ee-yee-NEH-kah-moo thah-EH-khee tee-ROH-pee-tah.
My wife will have (Greek) cheese-pie.

Θὰ πάρωμε σούπα αὐγολέμονο.
thah-PAH-roh-meh SOO-pah-ahv-ghoh-LEH-moh-noh.
For soup we will have egg-lemon rice soup.

Κύριο πιάτο, θὰ ἤθελα λαγὸ (κουνέλι) στιφάδο.
KEE-ree-oh PYAH-toh, thah-EE-theh-lah lah-GHOH (koo-NEH-lee)
    stee-FAH-*th*oh.
For the main course I would like hare (rabbit) stew.

Θὰ θέλατε νὰ πιῆτε κάτι, κύριε;
thah-THEH-lah-teh nah-PYEE-teh KAH-tee, KEE-ree-eh?
Would you like something to drink, sir?

Μπορῶ νὰ δῶ τὸν κατάλογο κρασιῶν;
boh-ROH nah-*TH*OH tohn-gah-TAH-loh-ghoh krah-SYOHN?
May I see the wine list?

Ποιὸ κρασὶ πηγαίνει μὲ αὐτὸ τὸ φαγητό;
PYOH krah-SEE pee-YEH-nee m(eh) -ahf-TOH-toh-fah-yee-TOH?
Which wine goes with this dish?

Φέρτε μας μισὴ καράφα κοκκινέλι.
FEHR-teh-mahs mee-SEE-kah-RAH-fah koh-kee-NEH-lee.
Bring us a half carafe of red wine.

Γκαρσόν, ξεχάσατε νὰ μοῦ δώσετε πετσέτα.
gahr-SOHN, kseh-KHAH-sah-teh nah-moo-*TH*OH-s (eh) -teh peh-TSEH-
    tah.
Waiter, you forgot to give me a napkin.

Λίγο ψωμί, παρακαλῶ.
LEE-ghoh-psoh-MEE, pah-rah-kah-LOH.
Some bread, please.

Μερικὰ φροῦτα.
Let us have some fruit.
meh-ree-KAH FROO-tah.

Νομίζω ὅτι κάνατε λάθος στὸ λογαριασμό.
noh-MEE-zoh O H-tee KAH-nah-teh LAH-thohs stoh-loh-ghah-ryah-ZMOH.
I think you've added up this bill incorrectly.

῎Εχετε δίκαιο. ῎Εκανα λάθος.
EH-kheh-teh THEE-keh-oh. EH-kah-nah LAH-thohs.
You are right. I've made an error.

᾿Απολαύσαμε τὸ φαγητό [σας].
ah-poh-LAHF-sah-meh toh-fah-yee-TOH-[sahs].
We enjoyed the meal very much.

῾Η ἐξυπηρέτηση ἦταν ἐξαιρετική.
ee-eh-ksee-pee-REH-tee-see EE-tahn eh-kseh-reh-tee-KEE.
The service was excellent.

FOOD

Πρωϊνό
proh-ee-NOH
Breakfast

Γεῦμα
YEHV-mah
Lunch

Δεῖπνο
THEE-pnoh
Dinner

Χυμὸς πορτοκαλλιοῦ
khee-MOHS pohr-toh-kah-LYOO
Orange juice

Αὐγὰ μελάτα (σφιχτά, τηγανητά)
ahv-GHAH meh-LAH-tah (sfeekh-TAH, tee-ghah-nee-TAH)
Soft boiled eggs (hard boiled, fried)

Φρυγανιά
free-ghah-NYAH
Toasted bread

Βούτυρο
VOO-tee-roh
Butter

Καφὲ μὲ γάλα
kah-FEH meh-GHAH-lah
Coffee with milk

Τσάϊ μὲ λεμόνι
TSAH-ee meh-leh-MOH-nee
Tea with lemon

Ζάχαρη
ZAH-khah-ree
Sugar

Ἕνα φλυτζάνι καφέ
EH-nah flee-DZAH-nee kah-FEH
A cup of coffee

Γλυκό (τοῦ κουταλιοῦ)
ghlee-KOH   (too-koo-tah-LYOO)
Jam or Fruits preserved
    in heavy syrup.

Σούπα αὐγολέμονο
SOO-pah ahv-ghoh-LEH-moh-noh
Egg and lemon soup

Ψαρόσουπα
psah-ROH-soo-pah
Fish soup

Σουπα φασόλια
SOO-pah fah-SOH-lyah
Bean soup

Σούπα φακές
SOO-pah fah-KEHS
Lentil soup

Ἕνα ποτήρι νερό
EH-nah poh-TEE-ree neh-ROH
A glass of water

Σαλάτα μὲ λάδι καὶ ξύδι
sah-LAH-tah   meh-LAH-thee-keh-KSEE-thee
A green salad with oil and vinegar

Ντοματοσαλάτα
doh-mah-toh-sah-LAH-tah
Tomato salad

Ὀρεκτικά
oh-reh-ktee-KAH
Hors d'oeuvre

Ντολμάδες
dohl-MAH-thehs
Stuffed grapeleaves

Κεφτέδες
keh-FTEH-thehs
Meat balls

Ντομάτες γεμιστές
doh-MAH-tehs yeh-mee-STEHS
Stuffed tomatoes

Τυρόπηττα
tee-ROH-pee-tah
Tyropitta

Μπριτζόλες (ἀρνίσιες, μοσχαρίσιες, χοιρινές)
bree-DZOH-lehs (ahr-NEE-syehs, moh-skhah-REE-syehs, khee-ree-NEHS).
Chops (lamb, veal, pork)

Ψητὸ ἀρνί (κοτόπουλο, γαλοπούλα)
psee-TOH ahr-NEE (koh-TOH-poo-loh-POO-lah)
Roast lamb (chicken, turkey)

Ροσμπίφ
rohz-BEEF
Roastbeef

Μπιφτέκι στὴ σκάρα
beef-TEH-kee stee-SKAH-rah
Broiled steak

Ἀρνὶ τῆς σούβλας
ahr-NEE tees-SOO-vlahs
Barbecued lamb

Σουβλάκια
soo-VLAH-kyah
Shish-kebab

Κοκορέτσι
koh-koh-REH-tsee
Kokoresti

Στιφάδο
stee-FAH-thoh
Onion stew

Κρέας μὲ χόρτα (ἀρνί, μοσχάρι)
KREH-ahs meh KHOHR-tah (ahr-NEE, mohs-KHAH-ree)
Stew (lamb, veal)

Κρέας κοκκινιστό
KREH-ahs koh-kee-nee-STOH
Braised beef

Χορταρικά:
khohr-tah-ree-KAH:
Vegetables:

σπανάκι
spah-NAH-kee
spinach

(καρμπο) λάχανο
(kahr-boh-)LAH-khah-noh
cabbage

μελιτζάνες
meh-leen-DZAH-nehs
eggplants

φασολάκια
fah-soh-LAH-kyah
stringbeans

πιπεριές
pee-peh-RYEHS
peppers

μπιζέλια
bee-ZEH-lyah
peas

κουνουπίδι
koo-noo-PEE-thee
cauliflower

καρότα
kah-ROH-tah
carrots

κολοκυθάκια
koh-loh-kee-THAH-kyah
squash

ἀγγινάρες
ahn-gee-NAH-rehs
artichokes

σέλινο
SEH-lee-noh
celery

ντομάτες
doh-MAH-tehs
tomatoes

Γιαούρτι
yah-OOR-tee
Yogurt

Τυρί
tee-REE
Cheese

Τυριά:
tee-RYAH:
Cheeses:

φέτα
FEH-tah
feta

κεφαλοτύρι
keh-fah-loh-TEE-ree
kephalotyri

κασέρι
kah-SEH-ree
caseri

μανούρι
mah-NOO-ree
manouri

Ψάρια καὶ θαλασσινά:
psah-RYAH keh thah-lah-see-NAH:
Fish and seafood:

συναγρίδα	**μπαρμπούνι**	**γαρίδα**
see-nah-GHREE-*th*ah	bahr-BOO-nee	ghah-REE-*th*ah
gurnet	(red) mullet	shrimp

καλαμάρι	**ἀστακός**
kah-lah-MAH-ree	ah-stah-KOHS
squid	lobster

Φροῦτα:	**μῆλο**	**ἀχλάδι**
FROO-tah:	MEE-loh	ahkh-LAH-*th*ee
Fruits:	apple	pear

πορτοκάλι	**ρό(ϊ)δι**	**ροδάκινο**
pohr-toh-KAH-lee	ROH-(ee-)*th*ee	roh-*TH*AH-kee-noh
orange	pomegranate	peach

κορόμηλο	**δαμάσκηνο**	**βερύκοκο**
koh-ROH-m(ee)-loh	*th*ah-MAH-skee-noh	veh-REE-koh-koh
plum	prune	apricot

σταφύλι	**καρπούζι**	**πεπόνι**	**μπανάνα**
stah-FEE-lee	kahr-POO-zee	peh-POH-nee	bah-NAH-nah
grapes	watermelon	melon	banana

ἀνανάς	**φράπα**	**μανταρίνι**	**σῦκα**
ah-nah-NAHS	FRAH-pah	mahn-dah-REE-nee	SEE-kah
pineapple	grapefruit	tangerine	figs

κεράσια	**φράουλες**	**ἀμύγδαλα**	**καρύδια**
keh-RAH-syah	FRAH-oo-lehs	ah-MEEGH-*th*ah-lah	kah-REE-*th*yah
cherries	strawberries	almonds	walnuts

Ποτά:	**κρασί**	**μπύρα**	**οῦζο**
poh-TAH:	krah-SEE	BEE-rah	·OO-zoh
Drinks:	wine	beer	ouzo

κονιάκ	**λικέρ**	**μεταλλικὸ νερό**
koh-NYAHK	lee-KEHR	meh-tah-lee-KOH neh-ROH
brandy	liqueur, cordial	mineral water

Γλυκίσματα:	**πάστες**	**ρυζόγαλο**	**παγωτό**
ghlee-KEEZ-mah-tah:	PAH-stehs	ree-ZOH-ghah-loh	pah-ghoh-TOH
Desserts:	pastries	rice pudding	ice cream

THE SIDEWALK CAFÉ

Γκαρσόν! ˝Εναν καφέ, παρακαλῶ!
hr-SOHN! EH-nahn-gah-FEH, pah-rah-kah-LOH!
Waiter! Coffee, please!

Πῶς προτιμᾶτε τὸν καφέ σας;
OHS proh-tee-MAH-teh tohn-gah-FEH-sahs?
ow do you like your coffee?

Μέτριο.
MEH-tree-oh.
With little sugar.

Μιὰ λεμονάδα γιὰ τὴν κυρία, παρακαλῶ.
yah leh-moh-NAH-*th*ah yah-teen-gee-REE-ah, pah-rah-kah-LOH.
lemonade for the lady please.

Τὰ παιδιὰ θὰ πάρουν παγωτό.
h-peh-*TH*YAH thah-PAH-roon pah-ghoh-TOH.
he children will have ice-cream.

Τί γλυκὰ ἔχετε; ˝Εχομε μερικὰ πολὺ καλὰ ἀνατολίτικα γλυ-
κά, μπακλαβά, κανταΐφι, ρεβανί.
EE ghlee-KAH EH-kheh-teh? EH-khoh-meh meh-ree-KAH poh-LEE-
kah-LAH ah-nah-toh-LEE-tee-kah ghlee-KAH, bah-klah-VA H,
kahn-dah-EE-fee, reh-vah-NEE.
What kind of pastries do you have? We have some very good
oriental pastries, baklava, kataifi, revani.

Τί χυμοὺς φρούτων ἔχετε; ˝Εχομε πορτοκάλι, τομάτα, καὶ
σταφύλι.
EE khee-moos FROO-tohn EH-kheh-teh? EH-khoh-meh pohr-toh-KAH-
lee, toh-MAH-tah, keh stah-FEE-lee.
What fruit juices do you have? We have orange, tomato,
and grape juice.

Τὸ λογαριασμό, παρακαλῶ.
h-loh-ghah-ryah-ZMOH, pah-rah-kah-LOH.
he check, please.

Περιλαμβάνεται τὸ φιλοδώρημα (or πουρμπουὰρ) τῆς ὑπη-
ρεσίας;
h-ree-lahm-VAH-neh-teh toh-fee-loh-*TH*OH-ree-mah (or poor-boo-
AHR) tees-ee-pee-reh-SEE-ahs?
the service included?

Ὄχι, [δὲν περιλαμβάνεται].
OH-khee, [THEHN peh-ree-lahm-VAH-neh-teh].
No, it is not.

SIGHTSEEING

Θὰ μείνω ἐδῶ τρεῖς ἡμέρες.
thah-MEE-noh eh-THOH TREES-ee-MEH-rehs.
I will stay here three days.

Θὰ ἤθελα νὰ ἰδῶ τὴν Ἀκρόπολη.
thah-EE-theh-lah nah-ee-THOH teen-ah-KROH-poh-lee.
I would like to see the Acropolis.

Θὰ ἤθελα νὰ ἰδῶ μερικοὺς ἱστορικοὺς τόπους.
thah-EE-theh-lah nah-ee-THOH meh-ree-KOOS ee-stoh-ree-KOOS TO poos.
I would like to see some historical sites.

Μποροῦμε νὰ κάνωμε ἕναν περίπατο στὰ ἐρείπια αὐτά;
boh-ROO-meh nah-KAH-noh-meh EH-nahm-peh-REE-pah-toh stah REE-pee-ah-ahf-TAH?
Can we take a tour of these ruins?

Θὰ ἤθελα νὰ ἰδῶ μερικὲς παλιὲς ἐκκλησίες.
thah-EE-theh-lah nah-ee-THOH meh-ree-KEHS pah-LYEHS eh-klee-S ehs.
I would like to see some old churches.

Εἶναι τόσα πολλὰ τὰ μνημεῖα ποὺ ἔχει κανεὶς νὰ ἐπισκεφθῆ
EE-neh TOH-sah pah-LAH tah-mnee-MEE-ah poo-EH-khee kah-N nah-eh-pee-skeh-FTHEE.
There are so many monuments to visit.

Θέλω νὰ ἰδῶ τὰ πιὸ σπουδαῖα πράγματα.
THEH-loh nah-ee-THOH tah-PYOH-spoo-THEH-ah-PRAHGH-mah
I want to see the most important things.

Θὰ ἤθελα νὰ καθίσωμε περισσότερο ἐδῶ.
thah-EE-theh-lah nah-kah-THEE-soh-meh peh-ree-SOH-teh-roh THOH.
I would like to spend more time here.

πάρχουν ὠργανωμένα τούρ;
PAHR-khoon ohr-ghah-noh-MEH-nah-TOOR?
e there any organized tours?

λπίζω νὰ μὴ στοιχίζουν ἀκριβά.
-PEE-zoh nah-mee-stee-KHEE-zoon ah-kree-VAH.
hope they are not very expensive.

μίζω εἶδα ἀρκετά.
n-MEE-zoh EE-*th*ah ahr-keh-TAH.
think I've seen enough.

κ ἤθελα νὰ ἐπιστρέψω στὸ ξενοδοχεῖο μου.
h-EE-theh-lah nah-eh-pee-STREH-psoh stoh-kseh-noh-*th*oh-KHEE-oh-
moo.
would like to return to my hotel.

SNAPSHOTS FOR REMEMBRANCE

ῦ ἐπιτρέπετε νὰ σᾶς φωτογραφίσω;
o-eh-pee-TREH-peh-teh nah-sahs-foh-toh-ghrah-FEE-soh?
ould you mind letting me take your picture?

ξακολουθῆστε τὴ δουλειά σας. Μὴ κοιτάζετε τὴ μηχανή.
-ksah-koh-loo-THEE-steh tee-*th*oo-LYAH-sahs. MEE-kee-TAH-zeh-teh
tee-mee-khah-NEE.
st continue your work. Don't look at the camera.

ρίστε ἀπὸ ἐδῶ, παρακαλῶ.
-REE-steh ah-POH- (eh-)*T*HOH, pah-rah-kah-LOH.
rn this way, please.

ς εὐχαριστῶ πολύ.
s-ehf-khah-ree-STOH poh-LEE.
ank you very much.

κ ἤθελα ἕνα φίλμ, ἀριθμὸς 8.
h-EE-theh-lah EH-nah FEELM, ah-reeth-MOHS oh-KTOH.
would like a roll of number eight film.

῎Εχετε ἔγχρωμο φίλμ;
EH-kheh-teh EHGH-khroh-moh FEELM?

Do you have color film?

Περάσετε τὸ φίλμ στὴ μηχανή, σᾶς παρακαλῶ.
peh-RAH-steh toh-FEELM stee-mee-khah-NEE, sahs-pah-rah-kah-LOH.

Will you load the camera, please.

Νομίζετε ὅτι πρέπει νὰ χρησιμοποιήσω φίλτρο;
noh-MEE-zeh-teh O H-tee P R E H-pee nah-khree-see-moh-pee-EE-soh
FEEL-troh?

Do you think I should use a filter?

Παρακαλῶ, ἐμφανίσετε αὐτὸ τὸ φίλμ.
pah-rah-kah-LOH, ehm-fah-NEE-seh-teh ahf-TOH-toh-FEELM.

Please, develop this roll.

Παρακαλῶ, κάμετε μία φωτογραφία ἀπὸ κάθε ἀρνητικό.
pah-rah-kah-LOH, kah-MEH-teh MEE-ah-foh-toh-ghrah-FEE-ah ah-POH-
KAH-theh-ahr-nee-tee-KOH.

Please, make one print of each negative.

Πότε θὰ εἶναι ἕτοιμο;
POH-teh thah-EE-neh EH-tee-moh?

When will it be ready?

῎Εχετε κινηματογραφικὸ φίλμ τῶν 16 χιλιοστομέτρων;
EH-kheh-teh 'kee-nee-mah-toh-ghrah-fee-KOH-FEELM tohn-theh-kah-EH-
ksee khee-lee-oh-stoh-MEH-trohn?

Do you have a 16 mm. movie film?

SHOPPING

Ποῦ εἶναι τὰ κεντρικὰ καταστήματα;
POO EE-neh tah-kehn-dree-KAH kah-tah-STEE-mah-tah?

Where are the main department stores?

Εἶναι πολὺ μακρυὰ νὰ πάω μὲ τὰ πόδια;
EE-neh poh-LEE-mah-KRYAH nah-PAH-oh meh-tah-POH-thyah?

Is is too far to walk?

Μὲ ποιὸ λεωφορεῖο μπορῶ νὰ πάω;
neh-PYOH-leh-oh-foh-REE-oh boh-ROH nah-PAH-oh?

What bus will take me there?

Μπορῶ νὰ ρίξω μιὰ ματιὰ στὰ εἴδη τοῦ καταστήματος;
oh-ROH nah-REE-ksoh MYAH-mah-TYAH stah-EE-*thee* too-kah-tah-
    STEE-mah-tohs?

May I look at your merchandise?

Ἔχετε ὡραῖα πράγματα.
EH-kheh-teh oh-REH-ah PRAHGH-mah-tah.

You have some nice things for sale.

Θὰ ἤθελα νὰ δῶ ἕνα φόρεμα (παλτό, κοστούμι, φούστα, μπλούζα, γάντια, καπέλλο).
hah-EE-theh-lah nah-*THOH* EH-nah FOH-reh-mah (pahl-TOH, koh
    STOO-mee, FOO-stah, BLOO-zah, GAHN-dyah, kah-PEH-loh).

would like to see a dress (coat, suit, skirt, blouse, gloves, hat).

Στὴν Ἀμερικὴ φορῶ ἀριθμὸ 14 φορέματα.
teen-ah-meh-ree-KEE foh-ROH ah-reeth-MOH *theh*-kah-TEH-seh-rah
    foh-REH-mah-tah.

n America I wear size 14.

Αὐτὸ εἶναι πολὺ μικρὸ (μεγάλο).
hf-TOH EE-neh po-LEE mee-KROH (meh-GHAH-loh).

This is too small (large).

Αὐτὸ εἶναι πολὺ στενὸ (φαρδύ).
hf-TOH EE-neh poh-LEE steh-NOH (fahr-*THEE*).

This is too tight (loose).

Θὰ ἤθελα κάτι σ' ἕνα χρῶμα πιὸ ἀνοιχτὸ (σκοῦρο).
hah EE-theh-lah KAH-tee SEH-nah KHROH-mah PYOH ah-neekh-
    TOH (SKOO-roh).

would like something of a lighter (darker) color.

Ἀπὸ τί ὕφασμα εἶναι;
h-POH-TEE-EE-fahz-mah EE-neh?

What material is it made of?

Ἔχετε κάτι καλύτερο;
EH-kheh-teh KAH-tee kah-LEE-teh-roh?
Have you something better?

Πόσο ἔχει;
POH-soh EH-khee?
How much is it?

Αὐτὸ μ' ἀρέσει πολὺ ἀλλὰ εἶναι πολὺ ἀκριβό.
ahf-TOH mah-REH-see poh-LEE ah-LAH EE-neh poh-LEE-ah-kree-VOH.
I like this very much, but it is too expensive.

Θὰ σᾶς τὸ ἀφήσω γιὰ 60 δραχμές.
thah-sahs-toh-ah-FEE-soh yah-eh-KSEEN-dah-thrahkh-MEHS.
I will let you have it for 60 drachmas.

Ὡραῖα. Τυλίξτε το σᾶς παρακαλῶ.
oh-REH-ah. tee-LEEKS-teh-toh sahs-pah-rah-kah-LOH.
That is fine. Please wrap it up.

Παρακαλῶ στεῖλτε το στὸ ξενοδοχεῖο μου.
pah-rah-kah-LOH STEEL-teh-toh stoh-kseh-noh-thoh-KHEE-oh-moo.
Please send it to my hotel.

Θὰ τὸ πάρω μαζί μου.
thah-toh-PAH-roh mah-ZEE-moo.
I will take it with me.

Παρακαλῶ μοῦ δίνετε μιὰ ἀπόδειξη.
pah-rah-kah-LOH moo-THEE-neh-teh MYAH-ah-POH-thee-ksee.
Please let me have a receipt.

Πόσο ἔχει αὐτό, τὸ μέτρο;
POH-soh EH-khee ahf-TOH-toh-MEH-troh?
How much is the meter?

Εἶναι τὸ ὕφασμα αὐτὸ ἀπὸ τὸ ἐξωτερικό;
EE-neh toh-EE-fah-zmah-ahf-TOH ah-POH-toh-eh-ksoh-teh-ree-KOH?
Is this an imported fabric?

Ὄχι, εἶναι ἐντόπιο κουκουλάρικο.
OH-khee, EE-neh ehn-DOH-pyoh koo-koo-LAH-ree-koh.
No, this is raw silk made here.

ἶναι πολὺ καλὸ γιὰ καλοκαιρινὸ κοστούμι.
E-neh poh-LEE-kah-LOH yah-kah-loh-keh-ree-NOH--koh-STOO-mee.
is very good for a summer suit.

οῦ εἶναι τὸ τμῆμα δερμάτινων εἰδῶν;
)O EE-neh toh-TMEE-mah *th*ehr-MAH-tee-nohn ee-*THOHN*?
here is the leather goods counter?

τὸ πρῶτο πάτωμα.
ἱh-PROH-toh-PAH-toh-mah.
n the first floor.[1]

έλω νὰ ἀγοράσω ἕνα ζευγάρι παπούτσια.
HEH-loh n (ah-)ah-ghoh-RAH-soh EH-nah-zehv-GHAH-ree pah-POO-
tsyah.

want to buy a pair of shoes.

χρῶμα προτιμᾶτε: μαῦρο, καφέ, ἄσπρο;
EE-KHROH-mah proh-tee-MAH-teh: MAH-vroh, kah-FEH, AHS-proh?
hich color do you prefer: black, brown, or white?

ρειάζομαι ἕνα ζευγάρι καφὲ παπούτσια.
ree-AH-zoh-meh EH-nah-zehv-GHAH-ree kah-FEH-pah-POO-tsyah.
want a pair of brown shoes.

θοῦμαι πὼς αὐτὰ δὲν σᾶς κάνουν· εἶναι πολὺ στενὰ καὶ πολὺ
κοντὰ ἐπίσης.
a-VOO-meh pohs ahf-TAH *th*ehn sahs-KAH-noon; EE-neh poh-LEE
steh-NAH keh poh-LEE kohn-DAH eh-PEE-sees.

am afraid these would not fit you; they are too tight and also
too short.

κ ἤθελα νὰ ἀγοράσω μερικὰ δῶρα καὶ ἐνθύμια.
ah-EE-theh-lah n (ah) -ah-ghoh-RAH-soh meh-ree-KAH *TH*OH-rah keh
ehn-THEE-mee-ah.

would like to buy presents and souvenirs.

Ͻτὰ θὰ τὰ βρῆτε σὲ εἰδικὰ καταστήματα.
ἱ-TAH thah-tah-VREE-teh seh-ee-*th*ee-KAH-kah-tah-STEE-mah-tah.

ɦese are sold in special stores.

---

uropeans call "first floor" what Americans call "second floor" because
ἱe ground floor is not being counted as a story.

Τί ἔχετε γιά ἕνα κοριτσάκι ἕξι χρόνων;
T E E   E H-kheh-teh   yah-E H-nah-koh-ree-T S A H-kee   E H-ksee-khroh-
    NOHN?
What do you have for a six-year old girl?

Αὐτὸ τὸ κεντημένο φόρεμα εἶναι πολὺ ὅμορφο.
ahf-TOH-toh-kehn-dee-MEH-noh-FOH-reh-mah   EE-neh   poh-LEE-OH-
    mohr-foh.
This embroidered dress is very beautiful.

Θά (ἡ)θέλατε νά ἰδῆτε αὐτὲς τὶς φοῦστες ἀπὸ ὕφασμα τοῦ
    ἀργαλειοῦ;
thah- (ee) -THEH-lah-teh   nah-ee-THEE-teh   ahf-TEHS-tees-FOO-stehs   ah-
    POH-EE-fah-zmah   too-ahr-ghah-LYOO?
Would you like to see those skirts made of handwoven material?

Θά ἤθελα νά ἰδῶ μερικά ἀσημένια κοσμήματα.
thah-EE-theh-lah   nah-ee-THOH   meh-ree-KAH   ah-see-MEH-nyah   koh-
    ZMEE-mah-tah.
I would like to see some silver jewelry.

Ποῦ τά φτιάχνουν; Εἶναι τόσο πρωτότυπα.
POO   tah-FTYAHKH-noon?   EE-neh   TOH-soh   proh-TOH-tee-pah?
Where are they made? They are so original.

Τά φέρνομε ἀπὸ τά Γιάννινα.
tah-FEHR-noh-meh   ah-p(oh)-tah-YAH-nee--nah.
We bring them from Jannina.

Πόσο ἔχει αὐτή ἡ καρφίτσα; "Εχετε σκουλαρίκια μὲ τὸ ἴδιο
    σχέδιο;
POH-soh   EH-khee   ahf-TEE-ee-kahr-FEE-tsah?   EH-kheh-teh   skoo-lah-
    REE-kyah   meh-toh-EE-thyoh-SKHEH-thee-oh?
How much is this pin? Do you have earrings with the same
    design?

Μάλιστα, πολλά ἀπὸ τά κοσμήματα αὐτά γίνονται σὲ σύνολα.
MAH-lee-stah,   poh-LAH   ah-POH-tah-koh-ZMEE-mah-tah-ah-TAH   YEE-
    nohn-deh   seh-SEE-noh-lah.
Yes, many of these jewels come in sets.

Ἔχομε ἐπίσης μιὰ μεγάλη συλλογὴ ἀπὸ εἴδη κεραμικῆς.
EH-khoh-meh eh-PEE-sees MYAH-meh-GHAH-lee-see-loh-YEE ah-POH-EE-thee-keh-rah-mee-KEES.
We have a large collection of ceramics, too.

Αὐτὰ τὰ πιάτα καὶ τὰ ἀγγεῖα μ' ἐνδιαφέρουν πολύ.
ahf-TAH-tah-PYAH-tah keh tah-ahn-GEE-ah mehn-thee-ah-FEH-roon poh-LEE.
Those plates and vases are very interesting.

Τὰ σχέδιά τους εἶναι ἀντιγραμμένα ἀπὸ ἀρχαῖα πιάτα καὶ ἀγγεῖα.
tah-SKHEH-thee-AH-toos EE-neh ahn-dee-ghrah-MAH-nah ah-POH-ahr-KHEH-ah-PYAH-tah keh ahn-GEE-ah.
Their designs are copied from ancient plates and vases.

LAUNDRY AND DRY-CLEANING

Παρακαλῶ, αὐτὸ εἶναι γιὰ καθάρισμα.
pah-rah-kah-LOH, ahf-TOH EE-neh yah-kah-THAH-ree-zmah.
Please have this dry-cleaned.

Πόσον καιρὸ θὰ πάρη;
POH-sohn-geh-ROH thah-PAH-ree?
How long will it take?

Θὰ ἤθελα νὰ σιδερώσετε αὐτὸ τὸ κοστούμι.
thah-EE-theh-lah nah-see-theh-ROH-seh-teh ahf-TOH toh-koh-STOO-mee.
I would like this suit pressed.

Μπορῶ νὰ τὸ ἔχω σήμερα τὸ ἀπόγευμα;
boh-ROH nah-toh-EH-khoh SEE-meh-rah toh-ah-POH-yehv-mah?
Can I get it back this afternoon?

Αὐτὰ τὰ πουκάμισα εἶναι γιὰ πλύσιμο.
ahf-TAH-tah-poo-KAH-mee-sah EE-neh yah-PLEE-see-moh.
These shirts need laundering.

Παρακαλῶ, νὰ μὴ βάλετε κόλλα.
pah-rah-kah-LOH, nah-MEE-VAH-leh-teh KOH-lah.
Please do not starch them.

Θὰ τὰ ἔχετε ἕτοιμα μεθαύριο;
thah-tah-EH-kheh-teh EH-tee-mah meh-THAHV-ree-oh?
Will you have them ready the day after tomorrow?

Παρακαλῶ, νὰ μοῦ πλύνετε αὐτὸ τὸ φόρεμα.
pah-rah-kah-LOH, nah-moo-PLEE-neh-teh ahf-TOH-toh-FOH-reh-mah.
Please wash this dress.

Παρακαλῶ, νὰ σιδερώσετε αὐτὸ τὸ παντελόνι.
pah-rah-kah-LOH, nah-see-theh-ROH-seh-teh ahf-T O H-toh-pahn-deh
        LOH-nee.
Please press the trousers.

Πότε μπορεῖτε νὰ τὸ ἔχετε ἕτοιμο;
POH-teh boh-REE-teh nah-toh-EH-kheh-teh EH-tee-moh?
When can you have it ready?

Πρέπει νὰ τὸ ἔχω αὔριο.
PREH-pee nah-toh-EH-khoh AHV-ree-oh.
I must have it tomorrow.

Μπορεῖτε νὰ ράψετε ἕνα κουμπὶ στὸ πουκάμισο αὐτό;
boh-REE-teh nah-RAH-pseh-teh EH-nah-koo-BEE stoh-poo-KAH-mee
        soh-ahf-TOH?
Can you sew a button on this shirt?

Αὐτὸ εἶναι σχισμένο. Μπορεῖτε νὰ τὸ μπαλώσετε;
ahf-TOH   EE-neh skhee-ZMEH-noh. boh-REE-teh nah-toh-bah-LOH
        seh-teh?
This is torn. Can you mend it?

HAIRDRESSERS AND BARBERS

Μπορεῖτε νὰ μοῦ (ὑπο)δείξετε (or συστήσετε) ἕνα καλὸ
        κουρεῖο;
boh-REE-teh nah-moo-(ee-poh-)THEE-kseh-teh (or see-STEE-seh-teh) EH
        nah-kah-LOH-koo-REE-oh?
Could you direct me to a good hairdresser?

Θέλω ἕνα «σαμπού» καὶ μία «μίζ-αν-πλί».
THEH-loh EH-nah "sahm-BOO" keh MEE-ah "'meez-ahn-PLEE".
I would like to have my hair washed and set.

Θέλετε μία «περμανάντ»;
THEH-leh-teh MEE-ah "pehr-mah-NAHND"?

Do you want a permanent wave?

Πόσο κοστίζει;
POH-soh koh-STEE-zee?

What is the charge?

100 δραχμές.
eh-kah-TOH *th*rahkh-MEHS.

100 drachmas.

Ὄχι σήμερα. Ἀλλὰ θὰ ἤθελα νὰ κάνω «μανικιούρ».
OH-khee SEE-meh-rah. ah-LAH thah-EE-theh-lah nah-KAH-noh "mah-nee-KYOOR".

Not today. But I will have a manicure.

Θὰ ἤθελα νὰ μοῦ κόψετε τὰ μαλλιά, παρακαλῶ.
thah-EE-theh-lah nah-moo-KOH-pseh-teh tah-mah-LYAH, pah-rah-kah-LOH.

I would like a haircut, please.

Κόψτε τα πιὸ κοντά, παρακαλῶ.
KOHPS-teh-tah PYOH-kohn-DAH, pah-rah-kah-LOH.

Cut it shorter, please.

Θέλω ξύρισμα.
THEH-loh KSEE-ree-zmah.

I want to have a shave.

✭ THEATERS AND NIGHT CLUBS

Θέλω δύο εἰσιτήρια γιὰ τὴν παράσταση «Οἰδίπους Τύραννος».
THEH-loh *TH*EE-oh-ee-see-TEE-ree-ah yah-teem-bah-RAH-stah-see "ee-*TH*EE-poos TEE-rah-nohs".

I would like two tickets for the performance of "Oedipus Rex".

Ἔχετε θέσεις γιὰ ἀπόψε;
EH-kheh-teh THEH-sees y(ah)-ah-POH-pseh?

Have you any seats for tonight?

Μπορεῖτε νὰ μοῦ δείξετε τὸ σχεδιάγραμμα τοῦ θεάτρου τῆς Ἐπιδαύρου;
boh-REE-teh nah-moo-*TH*EE-kseh-teh toh-skheh-*th*ee-AH-ghrah-mah too-theh-AH-troo tees-eh-pee-*TH*AH-vroo?

Can you show me a seating plan of the Epidaurus theater?

Θέλω ἀριθμημένες θέσεις.
THEH-lah ah-reeth-mee-MEH-nehs THEH-sees.
I want numbered seats.

Τί ὥρα ἀρχίζει ἡ παράσταση;
TEE OH-rah-ahr-KHEE-zee ee-pah-RAH-stah-see?
At what time does the performance start?

Θὰ ἤθελα νὰ πάω σ' ἕνα νυχτερινὸ κέντρο κοντὰ στὴ θάλασσα
thah-EE-theh-lah nah-PAH-oh SEH-nah-neekh-teh-ree-NOH-KEHN-droh
kohn-DAH-stee-THAH-lah-sah.
I would like to go to a nightclub by the seaside.

Ποιά κέντρα μοῦ συστήνετε;
PYAH KEHN-drah moo-see-STEE-neh-teh?
Which places do you recommend?

Κοστίζουν πολὺ ἀκριβά;
koh-STEE-zoon poh-LEE ah-kree-VAH?
Are they very expensive?

Ἔχουν πρόγραμμα ποικιλιῶν;
EH-khoon PROH-ghrah-mah pee-kee-lee-OHN?
Do they have a floor show?

Τί ὥρα ἀρχίζει τὸ πρόγραμμα;
TEE OH-rah ahr-KHEE-zee toh-PROH-ghrah-mah?
What time does the floor show start?

EXCHANGING MONEY

Ποιά εἶναι ἡ τιμὴ συναλλάγματος τοῦ δολλαρίου σήμερα στὴ ἐλεύθερη ἀγορά;
PYAH EE-neh ee-tee-MEE-see-nah-LAHGH-mah-tohs too-thoh-lah-REE-oo SEE-meh-rah steen-eh-LEHF-theh-ree-ah-ghoh-RAH?
What is today's free market rate on the dollar?

Πληρώνομε μόνον τὴ νόμιμη τιμή.
plee-ROH-noh-meh MOH-nohn tee-NOH-mee-mee-tee-MEE.
We pay only the legal rate.

Θέλω νὰ ἐξαργυρώσω μία ταξιδιωτικὴ ἐπιταγή.
HEH-loh nah-eh-ksahr-yee-ROH-soh MEE-ah-tah-ksee-*thee*-oh-tee-KEE-
eh-pee-tah-YEE.

would like to cash a traveler's check.

Ποιὰ εἶναι ἡ τιμὴ τοῦ συναλλάγματος;
YAH EE-neh ee-tee-MEE-too-see-nah-LAHGH-mah-tohs?

What is the rate of exchange?

Μοῦ δίνετε 100 δραχμὲς ψιλά;
oo-*THEE*-neh-teh eh-kah-TOH *thr*ahkh-MEHS psee-LAH?

May I have 100 drachmas in small change?

Ποῦ μπορῶ νὰ πάρω μία τραπεζιτικὴ ἐπιταγή;
OO boh-ROH nah-PAH-roh MEE-ah-trah-peh-zee-tee-KEE-eh-pee-tah-
YEE?

Where can I buy a bank draft?

Στὴ διπλανὴ θυρίδα.
ee-*thee*-plah-NEE-*thee*-REE-*th*ah.

t the next window.

Παρακαλῶ, χαλάστε μου αὐτὸ τὸ χαρτονόμισμα.
h-rah-kah-LOH, khah-LAH-steh-moo ahf-TOH-toh-khahr-toh-NOH-
mee-zmah.

lease, change this note for me.

COMMUNICATIONS

Mail

Ποῦ εἶναι τὸ πλησιέστερο ταχυδρομεῖο;
OO EE-neh toh-plee-see-EH-steh-roh-tah-khee-*thr*oh-MEE-oh?

Where is the nearest post office?

Μέχρι ποιὰ ὥρα εἶναι ἀνοιχτό;
EH-khree-PYAH-OH-rah EE-neh ah-neekh-TOH?

ntil what time is it open?

Κλείνει στὶς πέντε.
_LEE-nee-stees-PEHN-deh.

closes at five o' clock.

Σὲ ποιὰ θυρίδα νὰ πάω γιὰ γραμματόσημα;
sch-PYAH-thee-REE-*th*ah nah-PAH-oh yah-ghrah-mah-TOH-see-mah?
To which window do I go for stamps?

Πόσο εἶναι γιὰ νὰ στείλω ἕνα γράμμα ἀεροπορικῶς;
POH-soh EE-neh yah-nah-STEE-loh EH-nah-GHRAH-mah ah-eh-ro
poh-ree-KOHS?
What is the rate for airmail?

Πόσα γραμματόσημα χρειάζομαι γι' αὐτὸ τὸ γράμμα;
POH-sah-ghrah-mah-TOH-see-mah khree-AH-zoh-meh yahf-T O H-to
GHRAH-mah?
How much postage do I need for this letter?

Θέλω νὰ στείλω αὐτὸ τὸ γράμμα συστημένο.
THEH-loh nah-STEE-loh ahf-TOH-toh-GHRAH-mah see-stee-MEH-n
I would like to have this letter registered.

Θέλω νὰ στείλω αὐτὸ τὸ γράμμα ἐπεῖγον.
THEH-loh nah-STEE-loh ahf-TOH-toh-GHRAH-mah eh-PEE-ghohn
I would like to send this letter special delivery.

Θέλω νὰ στείλω αὐτὸ τὸ δέμα μὲ τὸ κανονικὸ ταχυδρομεῖο.
THEH-loh nah-STEE-loh ahf-TOH-toh-*TH*EH-mah meh-toh-kah-n
nee-KOH-tah-khee-*th*roh-MEE-oh.
I want to send this package by regular mail.

Τί περιέχει;	Βιβλία καὶ ἔντυπα.
TEE peh-ree-EH-khee?	vee-VLEE-ah keh EHN-dee-pah.
What does is contain?	Books and printed matter.

Ποῦ εἶναι τὸ ταχυδρομικὸ κουτί (or γραμματοκιβώτιο);
POO EE-neh toh-tah-khee-*th*roh-mee-KOH koo-TEE (or ghrah-mah-t
kee-VOH-tee-oh)?
Where is the mail box?

Παρακαλῶ, στέλνετε τὴν ἀλληλογραφία μου στὴ νέα μου
εὔθυνση.
pah-rah-kah-LOH, S T E H L-neh-teh teen-ah-lee-loh-ghrah-FEE-ah-n
stee-NEH-ah-moo-*th*ee-EHF-theen-see.
Please, forward my mail to my new address.

TELEGRAMS AND CABLES

Θέλω νά στείλω ἕνα τηλεγράφημα στὴ Νέα Ὑόρκη.
THEH-loh nah-STEE-loh EH-nah-tee-leh-GHRAH-fee-mah stee-NEH-ah-
ee-OHR-kee.

I would like to send a telegram to New York.

Παρακαλῶ, δῶστε μου ἕνα ἔντυπο τηλεγραφήματος γιά τό
ἐξωτερικό.
pah-rah-kah-LOH, THOH-steh-moo EH-nah EHN-dee-poh tee-leh-ghrah-
FEE-mah-tohs yah toh-eh-ksoh-teh-ree-KOH.

Please give me a blank for a foreign telegram.

Πόσο κοστίζουν οἱ δεκαπέντε λέξεις;
POH-soh koh-STEE-zoon ee-theh-kah-PEHN-deh-LEH-ksees?

How much do fifteen words cost?

Θά τό στείλετε «ἡμέρας» ἢ «νυκτός» (or νυχτερινό);
thah-toh-STEE-leh-teh "ee-MEH-rahs" ee "nee-KTOHS" (or neekh-teh-
ree-NOH)?

Are you sending it day rate or night rate?

Πότε θά φτάση ἐκεῖ;
POH-teh thah-FTAH-see eh-KEE?

When will it get there?

TELEPHONING

Ἔχετε κέρματα γιά τό τηλέφωνο;
EH-kheh-teh KEHR-mah-tah yah-toh-tee-LEH-foh-noh?

Do you have tokens for the telephone?

Δῶστε μου τέσσερα.
THOH-steh-moo TEH-seh-rah.

Give me four.

Ποῦ εἶναι ὁ τηλεφωνικὸς θάλαμος;
POO EE-neh oh-tee-leh-foh-nee-KOHS-THAH-lah-mohs?

Where is the telephone booth?

Ποῦ εἶναι ὁ τηλεφωνικὸς κατάλογος;
POO EE-neh oh-tee-leh-foh-nee-KOHS-kah-TAH-loh-ghohs?

Where is the telephone directory?

Ἐμπρός. Εἶναι τοῦ κυρίου Πετρίδη;
ehm-BROHS. EE-neh too-kee-REE-oo-peh-TREE-*thee*?
Hello. Is this Mr. Petrides' residence?

Ἐδῶ ὁ κύριος Γεωργιάδης.
eh-*THOH* oh-KEE-ree-ohs-yeh-ohr-yee-AH-*thees*.
This is Mr. Georgiadis calling.

Κέντρον, πῆρα λάθος τὸν ἀριθμό.
KEHN-drohn, PEE-rah LAH-thohs tohn-ah-reeth-MOH.
Operator, I have dialed the wrong number.

Εἶναι ὁ κ. Παπαδόπουλος ἐκεῖ;
EE-neh oh-KEE-ree-ohs pah-pah-*THOH*-poo-lohs eh-KEE?
Is Mr. Papadopoulos in?

Ὄχι, δὲν εἶναι ἐδῶ αὐτὴ τὴ στιγμή.
OH-khee, *TH*EHN-EE-neh eh-*THOH* ahf-TEE-tee-steegh-MEE.
No, he is not in right now.

Πότε, νομίζετε, θὰ ἐπιστρέψη;
POH-teh, noh-MEE-zeh-teh, thah-eh-pee-STREH-psee?
When do you expect him?

Μπορεῖτε νὰ τοῦ δώσετε ἕνα σημείωμα;
boh-REE-teh nah-too-*THOH*-seh-teh EH-nah-see-MEE-oh-mah?
Would you give him a message?

Μπορῶ νὰ ἔχω τὸν κ. Χρηστίδη;
boh-ROH nah-nah-EH-khoh tohn-GEE-ree-oh-khree-STEE-*thee*?
May I speak to Mr. Christides?

Μία στιγμή, παρακαλῶ, νὰ σᾶς συνδέσω.
MEE-ah-steegh-MEE, pah-rah-kah-LOH, nah-sahs-seen-*TH*EH-soh.
Just a moment please, I'll put him on.

Συγγνώμη, ὅλες οἱ γραμμὲς εἶναι πιασμένες.
see-GNOH-mee, OH-lehs-ee-ghrah-MEHS EE-neh pyah-ZMEH-nehs.
I am sorry; all the lines are busy.

Θέλω νὰ κάνω ἕνα ὑπεραστικὸ τηλεφώνημα.

THEH-loh-nah-KAH-noh EH-nah-ee-peh-rah-stee-KOH-tee-leh-PHOH-nee-mah.

I want to make a long distance call.

Θέλω νὰ τηλεφωνήσω στὴν Πάτρα στὶς πέντε.

THEH-loh-nah-tee-leh-foh-NEE-soh steem-PAH-trah stees-PEHN-deh.

I would like to call Patras at 5:00.

Πόσο στοιχίζει ἕνα τηλεφώνημα στὴ Νέα Ὑόρκη;

POH-soh stee-K H E E-zee EH-nah-tee-leh-FOH-nee-mah stee-NEH-ah-ee-OHR-kee?

How much is it a call to New York?

Εἰδοποιῆστε με, ὅταν περάσουν τὰ τρία λεπτά.

ee-thoh-pee-EE-steh-meh, OH-tahn-peh-RAH-sooh tah-T R E E-ah-leh-PTAH.

Signal me when the three minutes are up.

TOURIST INFORMATION

Ποῦ εἶναι τὸ πλησιέστερο τουριστικὸ πρακτορεῖο (Γραφεῖο Τουρισμοῦ);

POO EE-neh toh-plee-see-EH-steh-roh too-ree-stee-KOH-prah-ktoh-REE-oh (ghrah-FEE-oh-too-ree-ZMOO)?

Where is the nearest tourist agency (office)?

Πότε εἶναι ἡ ἐπόμενη ἐκδρομὴ γιὰ τὴν Πεντέλη;

POH-teh EE-neh ee-eh-POH-meh-nee-ehk-throh-MEE yah-teen-behn-DEH-lee?

When is the next tour for Penteli?

Ποιὸ νησὶ μοῦ συστήνετε νὰ ἐπισκεφτῶ;

PYOH nee-SEE moo-see-STEE-neh-teh nah-eh-pee-skeh-FTOH?

What island do you recommend I visit?

Πῶς μπορεῖ νὰ πάη κανεὶς ἐκεῖ;

POHS boh-REE nah-PAH-ee kah-NEES eh-KEE?

How can one go there?

Εἶναι τὸ χωριὸ αὐτὸ γραφικό;

EE-neh toh-khoh-RYOH-ahf-TOH ghrah-fee-KOH?

Is that village picturesque?

Μάλιστα, πάρα πολύ.

MAH-lees-tah, PAH-rah-poh-LEE.

Yes, very much so.

Εἶναι δύσκολο νὰ πάῃ κανένας ἐκεῖ;
EE-neh *THEE*-skoh-loh nah-PAH-ee kah-NEH-nahs eh-KEE?

Is it difficult to reach?

"Οχι, ὑπάρχει τακτικὴ συγκοινωνία μὲ τὸ λεωφορεῖο.
OH-khee,ee-PAHR-khee tah-ktee-KEE-seen-gee-noh-NEE-ah meh-toh-leh-
oh-foh-REE-oh.

No, there is a regular bus service.

Μπορεῖ κανεὶς νὰ βρῇ ἕνα καλὸ καὶ φτηνὸ ξενοδοχεῖο ἐκεῖ;
boh-REE kah-NEES nah-VREE EH-nah-kah-LOH-keh-ftee-NOH-kseh-noh-
thoh-KHEE-oh eh-KEE?

Can one find a good inexpensive hotel there?

CONDUCTING BUSINESS

Θέλω νὰ κάνω αἴτηση γιὰ μία βίζα.
THEH-loh-nah-KAH-noh EH-tee-see yah-MEE-ah-VEE-zah.

I wish to apply for a visa.

Πότε θὰ εἶναι ἕτοιμη ἡ βίζα μου;
POH-teh thah-EE-neh EH-tee-mee ee-VEE-zah-moo?

When will my visa be ready.

Ὁρίστε τὸ δελτίο ταυτότητος (τὸ διαβατήριό μου).
oh-REE-steh toh-*thehl*-TEE-oh-tahf-TOH-tee-tohs (toh-*thee*-ah-vah-TEE-
ree-OH-moo).

Here is my identification card (passport).

Γιὰ πόσον καιρὸ ἰσχύει τὸ δελτίο μου;
yah-POH-sohn-geh-ROH ees-KHEE-ee toh-*thehl*-TEE-oh-moo?

For how long a period is my card valid?

Ἐὰν μετακομίσω ἀπὸ ἐδῶ, τί πρέπει νὰ κάνω;
eh-AHN meh-tah-koh-MEE-soh ah-POH- (eh-)THOH. TEE PREH-pee
nah-KAH-noh?

If I move from here, what must I do?

Δὲν ἔχω ποτὲ χρεωκοπήσει.
THEHN-EH-khoh poh-TEH khreh-oh-koh-PEE-see.

I have never gone bankrupt.

Δὲν ἔχω ποινικὸ μητρῶο.
THEHN-EH-khoh pee-nee-KOH mee-TROH-oh.
I have no criminal record.

Θὰ ἤθελα νὰ ἔλθω σὲ ἐπαφὴ μὲ μιὰ ἑταιρία ὑφαντουργίας.
thah-EE-theh-lah nah-EHL-thoh seh-eh-pah-FEE meh-MYAH-eh-teh-REE-ah-ee-fahn-door-YEE-ahs.
I would like to contact a textile firm.

Ἀντιπροσωπεύω μία ἀμερικανικὴ ἑταιρία.
ahn-dee-proh-soh-PEH-voh MEE-ah-ah-meh-ree-kah-nee-KEE-eh-teh-REE-ah.
I represent an American firm.

Πόσους ὑπαλλήλους (or ἐργάτες) ἔχετε;
POH-soos ee-pah-LEE-loos (or ehr-GHAH-tehs) EH-kheh-teh?
How many employees (or workers) do you have?

Μπορῶ νὰ ἐπιθεωρήσω τὸ ἐργοστάσιό σας;
boh-ROH nah eh-pee-theh-oh-REE-soh toh-ehr-ghoh-STAH-see-OH-sahs?
May I inspect your plant?

Ποιὸ εἶναι τὸ κεφάλαιό σας; (or Τί κεφάλαια ἔχετε;)
PYOH EE-neh toh-keh-FAH-leh-OH-sahs? (or TEE keh-FAH-leh-ah EH-kheh-teh?)
What is your capital?

Θὰ ἤθελα τραπεζιτικὰς ἐγγυήσεις.
thah-EE-theh-lah trah-peh-zee-tee-KAHS-ehn-gee-EE-sees.
I would like bank references.

Θὰ πληρώσω γιὰ τὰ ἐμπορεύματα σὲ δολλάρια.
thah plee-ROH-soh yah-tah-ehm-boh-REHV-mah-tah seh-thoh-LAH-ree-ah.
I will pay for the goods in dollars.

Πότε μπορεῖτε νὰ ἀποστείλετε τὰ ἐμπορεύματα;
POH-teh boh-REE-teh nah-ah-poh-STEE-leh-teh tah-ehm-boh-REHV-mah-tah?
When can you ship the merchandise?

Εἶμαι περιοδεύων παραγγελιοδόχος.
EE-meh peh-ree-oh-*THEH*-vohn pah-rahn-geh-lee-oh-*THOH*-khohs.
I am a traveling salesman.

Μπορῶ νὰ σᾶς δείξω αὐτὰ τὰ δείγματα;
boh-REE nah-sahs-*THEE*-ksoh ahf-TAH-tah-*THEEGH*-mah-tah?
May I show you these samples?

Ἦλθα νὰ ἐξετάσω τὴν ἀγορά.
EEL-thah nah-eh-kseh-TAH-soh teen-ah-ghoh-RAH.
I am here to survey the market.

**Χρειάζομαι ἕναν ἐντόπιο ἐμπορικὸ πράκτορα γιὰ τὸ προϊὸν
        μου.**
khree-AH-zoh-meh EH-nahn-ehn-DOH-pee-oh ehm-boh-ree-KOH-PRAH-
        ktoh-rah yah-toh-proh-ee-OHN-moo.
I need a local distributor for my product.

GOING TO CHURCH

Θὰ ἤθελα νὰ πάω στὴν ἐκκλησία.
thah-EE-theh-lah nah-PAH-oh steen-eh-klee-SEE-ah.
I would like to go to church.

Ποῦ εἶναι ἡ Μητρόπολη;
POO EE-neh ee-mee-TROH-poh-lee?
Where is the cathedral?

Ποῦ εἶναι ἡ πλησιέστερη (Ἑλληνικὴ Ὀρθόδοξη) ἐκκλησία;
POO EE-neh ee-plee-see-EH-steh-ree (eh-lee-nee-KEE ohr-THOH-*thoh*-
        ksee) eh-klee-SEE-ah?
Where is the nearest church?

Ποῦ εἶναι ἡ Προτεστάντικη (or Διαμαρτυρόμενη) Ἐκκλησία;
POO EE-neh ee-proh-teh-stahn-dee-KEE (*or* thee-ah-mahr-tee-ROH-meh-
        nee) eh-klee-SEE-ah?
Where is the Protestant church?

Ποῦ εἶναι ἡ Καθολικὴ Ἐκκλησία;
POO EE-neh ee-kah-thoh-lee-KEE eh-klee-SEE-ah?
Where is the Catholic church?

Ποῦ εἶναι ἡ Συναγωγή;
POO EE-neh ee-see-nah-ghoh-YEE?
Where is the synagogue?

Τί ὥρα ἀρχίζει ἡ λειτουργία (ὁ ἑσπερινός);
TEE-OH-rah ahr-KHEE-zee ee-lee-toor-YEE-ah (oh-eh-speh-ree-NOHS)?
At what time does the service (the vesper) begin?

Σὲ ποιὰ ἐκκλησία γίνεται ἡ λειτουργία στὰ ἀγγλικά;
seh PYAH eh-klee-SEE-ah YEEneh-teh ee-lee-toor-YEE-ah stah-ahn-glee-KAH?
What church holds the Mass in English?

Μποροῦμε νὰ παρακολουθήσωμε τὴ λειτουργία;
boh-ROO-meh nah-pah-rah-koh-loo-THEE-soh-meh tee-lee-toor-YEE-ah?
May we attend this service?

Θὰ ἤθελα νὰ δῶ ενα ἱερέα (πάστορα, ραββῖνο).
thah-EE-theh-lah nah-THOH EH-nah ee-eh-REH-ah (PAH-stoh-rah, rah-VEE-noh).
I would like to see a priest (minister, rabbi).

TAKE CARE OF YOURSELF

Δὲν αἰσθάνομαι καλά.
THEHN-eh-STHAH-noh-meh kah-LAH.
I don't feel well.

Μοῦ πονεῖ τὸ στομάχι.
moo-poh-NEE toh-stoh-MAH-khee.
I have an upset stomach.

Χρειάζομαι ἕνα γιατρὸ (ὀδοντογιατρό, ὀφθαλμίατρο) ποὺ νὰ
   μιλᾶ ἀγγλικά.
khree-AH-zoh-meh EH-nah yah-TROH (oh-thohn-doh-yah-TROH, ohf-
   thahl-MEE-ah-troh) poo-nah-mee-LAH ahn-glee-KAH.
I need a doctor (dentist, oculist) who speaks English.

Στραμπούληξα (Ἔσπασα) τὸ πόδι μου.
strahm-BOO-lee-ksah (EH-spah-sah) toh-POH-thee-moo.
I have sprained (broken) my ankle.

Ἔχω πυρετό.
EH-khoh pee-reh-TOH.
I have a fever.

Εἶμαι κρυωμένος. (or Ἔχω ἕνα ἄσχημο κρυολόγημα).
EE-meh kree-oh-MEH-nohs. (or EH-khoh EH-nah-AH-skhee-moh-kree-oh-
　　　LOH-yee-mah.)
I have a bad cold.

Ἔχω πονοκέφαλο. (or Μοῦ πονεῖ τὸ κεφάλι.)
EH-khoh poh-noh-KEH-fah-loh, (or moo-poh-NEE toh-keh-FAH-lee.)
I have a headache.

Ποῦ πονᾶτε;
POO poh-NAH-teh?
Where does it hurt?

Μοῦ πονεῖ ἡ πλάτη (ὁ λαιμός, τὸ κεφάλι).
moo-poh-NEE ee-PLAH-tee (oh-leh-MOHS, toh-keh-FAH-lee).
My back (throat, head) hurts.

Πρέπει νὰ μείνω στὸ κρεβάτι;
PREH-pee nah-MEE-noh stoh-kreh-VAH-tee?
Will I have to stay in bed?

Μοῦ πονεῖ τὸ δόντι. (or Ἔχω πονόδοντο.)
moo-poh-NEE toh-THOHN-dee. (or EH-khoh poh-NOH-thohn-doh.)
I have a toothache.

Πρέπει νὰ σφραγισθῆ τὸ δόντι;
PREH-pee nah-sfrah-yee-sthee toh-THOHN-dee?
Must the tooth be filled?

Ποιά εἶναι ἡ ἀμοιβή σας, γιατρέ;
PYAH EE-neh ee-ah-mee-VEE-sahs, yah-TREH?
What is your fee, doctor?

Ποῦ εἶναι τὸ πλησιέστερο φαρμακεῖο;
POO EE-neh toh-plee-see-EH-steh-roh-fahr-mah-KEE-oh?
Where is the nearest drugstore?

Μπορεῖτε νὰ ἐκτελέσετε αὐτὴ τὶ συνταγή;
boh-REE-teh nah-eh-kteh-LEH-seh-teh ahf-TEE-tee-seen-dah-YEE?
Can you fill this prescription?

Πότε θὰ εἶναι ἕτοιμο [τὸ φάρμακο];
POH-teh thah-EE-neh EH-tee-moh (toh-FAHR-mah-koh)?
When will it be ready?

Θὰ ἐπιστρέψω νὰ τὸ πάρω.
thah-eh-pee-STREH-psoh nah-toh-PAH-roh.
I will come back to pick it up.

Χρειάζομαι ἀσπιρίνη (ἰώδιο, βορικὸ ὀξύ).
khree-AH-zoh-meh ah-spee-REE-nee (ee-OH-thee-oh, voh-ree-KOH oh-KSEE).
I need aspirin (iodine, boric acid).

Δῶστε μου λίγο βαμβάκι καὶ ἕνα ἐπίδεσμο.
THOH-steh-moo LEE-ghoh vahm-VAH-kee keh EH-nah-eh-PEE-thehzmoh.
Give me some cotton and a bandage.

῞Εσπασα τὰ γυαλιά μου.
EH-spah-sah tah-yah-LYAH-moo.
I have broken my glasses.

Μπορεῖτε νὰ βάλετε καινούργιο γυαλί;
boh-REE-teh nah-VAH-leh-teh keh-NOOR-yoh-yah-LEE?
Can you put in a new lens.

SPORTS

Swimming

Μπορῶ νὰ ἐνοικιάσω ἕνα κουστούμι τοῦ μπάνιου (or μπανιερό);
boh-ROH nah-eh-nee-kee-AH-soh EH-nah-koo-STOO-mee-too-BAH-nyoo (or bah-nyeh-ROH)?
Can I rent a suit?

Περιλαμβάνεται ἡ πετσέτα στὸ εἰσιτήριο;
peh-ree-lahm-VAH-neh-teh ee-peh-TSEH-tah stoh-ee-see-TEE-ree-oh?
Is the towel included in the price of admission?

Θὰ ἤθελα νὰ ἐνοικιάσω μία καμπίνα.
thah-EE-theh-lah nah-eh-nee-kee-AH-soh MEE-ah-kahm-BEE-nah.
I would like to rent a cabin.

Πόσο κοστίζει;
POH-soh koh-STEE-zee?
What is the charge?

Ἔχετε λάδι τοῦ ἡλίου;
EH-kheh-teh LAH-*thee*-too-ee-LEE-oo?
Do you sell suntan oil?

Fishing

Θὰ ἤθελα νὰ ἐνοικιάσω μία βάρκα.
thah-EE-theh-lah nah-eh-nee-kee-AH-soh MEE-ah-VAHR-kah.
I would like to rent a boat.

Πόσο παίρνετε τὴν ὥρα;
POH-soh PEHR-neh-teh teen-OH-rah?
How much do you charge for one hour?

Προτιμῶ βάρκα μὲ πανί.
proh-tee-MOH VAHR-kah-meh-pah-NEE.
I prefer the sailboat.

Χρειάζομαι ἕνα καλάμι μὲ μῦλο, λίγο σπάγγο (or ἁρμίδι) καὶ ἀγκίστρια.
khree-AH-zoh-meh EH-nah-kah-mee-meh-MEE-loh, LEE-ghoh-SPAHN-goh (or ahr-MEE-*thee*) keh ahn-GEE-stryah.
I need a rod and reel, some line and hooks.

Τί εἶδος δόλωμα χρειάζεται γιὰ τὴ συναγρίδα;
TEE EE-*thohs* *T*HOH-loh-mah khree-AH-zeh-teh yah-tee-see-nahgh-REE-*th*ah?
What kind of bait for gurnet?

Ποῦ μποροῦμε νὰ ψαρέψωμε μπαρμπούνια;
POO boh-ROO-meh nah-psah-REH-psoh-meh bahr-BOO-nya?
Where can we fish for red mullets?

Hunting

Χρειάζομαι ἕνα κυνηγετικὸ τουφέκι.
khree-AH-zoh-meh EH-nah-kee-nee-yee-tee-KOH-too-FEH-kee.
I need a gun for hunting.

Ποῦ μπορῶ νὰ ἀγοράσω φυσίγγια;
POO boh-ROH n(ah)-ah-ghoh-RAH-soh fee-SEEN-gce-ah?
Where can I buy ammunition?

Ποιὸ εἶναι τὸ καλύτερο μέρος γιὰ τὸ κυνήγι τῆς πέρδικας;
PYOH EE-neh toh-kah-LEE-teh-roh MEH-rohs yah-toh-kee-NEE-yee-
tees-PEHR-thee-kahs?
What is the best place for hunting partridge?

Ἡ ἐποχὴ τοῦ κυνηγιοῦ εἶναι ἀπὸ τὸ Δεκέμβριο ὡς τὸ Μάρτιο.
ee-eh-poh-KHEE too-kee-nee-YOO EE-neh ah-POH- toh-theh-KEHM-
vree-oh ohs-toh-MAHR-tee-oh.
The hunting season is from December to March.

Tennis and Soccer

Πόσο στοιχίζει γιὰ νὰ χρησιμοποιήσωμε τὸ γήπεδο;
POH-soh stee-KHEE-zee yah-nah-khree-see-moh-pee-EE-soh-meh toh-YEE-
peh-thoh?
What is the charge for using the courts?

Μπορῶ νὰ ἔχω μία ρακέτα καὶ ἕνα κουτὶ μπάλλες;
boh-ROH nah-EH-khoh MEE-ah-rah-KEH-tah keh EH-nah-koo-TEE-
BAH-lehs?
Can I have a racket and a can of balls?

Ποῦ εἶναι τὰ ἀποδυτήρια;
POO EE-neh tah-ah-poh-thee-TEE-ree-ah?
Where is the locker room?

Δύο θέσεις, παρακαλῶ.
THEE-oh THEH-sees, pah-rah-kah-LOH.
Two seats, please.

Ποιὰ ὁμάδα εἶναι πρωταθλήτρια;
PYAH oh-MAH-*thah* EE-neh proh-tah-THLEE-tree-ah?

Which team is leading?

Μπορεῖτε νὰ μοῦ πῆτε τὴ βαθμολογία;
boh-REE-teh nah-moo-PEE-teh tee-vahth-moh-loh-YEE-ah?

Can you tell me the score?

REFERENCE
GRAMMAR

In the following pages we have attempted to present the essentials of modern Greek grammar very concisely and to point out the basic grammatical differences between Demotic (Δημοτική) and Puristic (Καθαρεύουσα).

The development and existence of Demotic, the standard spoken and literary language, and of Puristic, the language of the official documents and news reports, can be best understood if we present a cursory view of the history of the Greek language since Christ's time.

In the first century B.C. the *Koine* (Common Greek) was the language spoken in the Hellenized regions of the Near and Middle East and used in the New Testament. However, some scholars condemned the Koine as vulgar and incorrect and advocated the return to the use of Attic Greek in writing. From that time on to the fall of Constantinople (1453), with the exception of a few manifestations of the spoken language in written documents, Atticistic Greek had been used as written Greek. During the four centuries of the occupation of Greece by the Turks, both Atticistic and modern Greek had been used.

At the beginning of the nineteenth century a Greek scholar, Adamantios Korais, who lived in Paris, suggested a compromise between the nearly un-intelligible Atticistic Greek and the vernacular by recommending the use of a purified vernacular which would gradually come closer to Attic Greek.

This puristic Greek, which was adopted as the official language after the liberation of Greece, became more and more archaic during the period of 1830-1880 and was used almost exclusively as the literary language on the mainland of Greece.

After 1880 the Demotic started replacing the Puristic in poetry. In 1892 the last collection of poems written in Puristic appeared. In 1888 the first important prose work in Demotic (John Psycharis' *To Taxidi*) was published. Since then the Demotic, incorporating most of the abstract lexicon of the Puristic and accepting some inflectional irregularities, has become the standard spoken and literary language. Nevertheless, the Puristic is still used in all official documents, most news reports, editorials, scientific treatises, university lectures and sermons.

1. THE ARTICLE

1.0. The Definite Article in Greek is inflected for number, gender and case. In modern Greek there are two numbers (singular and plural), three grammatical genders (masculine, feminine and neuter) and actually[1] three cases (nominative [the case of the subject], genitive [primarily the case of possession], accusative [the object case]).

1.1. The article agrees in number, gender, and case with the noun it modifies.

1.2. Declension of the Definite Article.

	Singular		
	Masculine	*Feminine*	*Neuter*
Nominative	ὁ	ἡ	τό
Genitive	τοῦ	τῆς	τοῦ
Accusative	τόν[2]	τήν[2]	τό

	Plural		
Nominative	οἱ	οἱ (αἱ)	τά
Genitive	τῶν	τῶν	τῶν
Accusative	τούς	τίς (τάς)	τά

The forms in parentheses are those of the Puristic. They are given only when they differ from those of the Demotic.

1.3. The definite article is used much more often in Greek than in English. The most important of its special uses are:

1. Before nouns used in an abstract or a general sense:
   Μοῦ ἀρέσει παρὰ πολὺ ἡ εἰλικρίνεια.
   I like sincerity very much.

   Τὸ φιλότιμο εἶναι τὸ κυριώτερο χαρακτηριστικὸ τοῦ ῞Ελληνα.
   Self-pride is the Greek's foremost characteristic.

   Τοὺς ἀρέσει ὁ καφές.
   They like coffee.

2. Before proper names:
   ῾Ο Γιάννης θὰ ἔλθη αὔριο.
   John will come tomorrow.

---

1 In classical Greek there were five cases, but today the dative (the case of the indirect object) is almost never used. It has been replaced by the accusative preceded by a preposition or by the genitive (as in the case of personal pronouns).
2 The ν of the accusative is dropped in spoken Greek before nouns beginning with a continuant consonant (φ, θ, χ, σ, ζ, ρ, λ, μ, ν) and assimilated to π, τ, κ into mb, nd, ng respectively.

Ὁ κύριος Καρύδης δὲν εἶναι ἐδῶ.
Mr. Carydis is not here.

3. Before the names of places and geographical divisions:

Ἡ Ἀθήνα εἶναι ἡ πρωτεύουσα τῆς Ἑλλάδος.
Athens is the capital of Greece.

4. Before the names of avenues, streets and squares:

Ἡ κυρία Παπαδοπούλου μένει στὴν ὁδὸν Ἑρμοῦ.
Mrs. Papadopoulos lives on Mercury Street.

5. Before titles or names of professions followed by a person's name:

Ὁ καθηγητὴς κ. Μπουφίδης δὲν ἦλθε νὰ μᾶς ἰδῇ.
Professor Boufidis did not come to see us.

6. In a series of nouns, before each of these nouns:

Στεῖλτε μου τὰ βιβλία, τὰ περιοδικὰ καὶ τοὺς δίσκους ποὺ
ἀγόρασα προχθές.
Send me the books, magazines and records I bought the day before
yesterday.

7. Before designations of time such as the year, the week, and the
hour, as well as before the names of the seasons and the days of
the week, except when they follow some form of the verb εἶμαι
and are unmodified:

Τὸ τραῖνο φεύγει στὶς δέκα.
The train leaves at ten o'clock.

Ὁ Πέτρος θὰ φύγῃ τὴ Δευτέρα.
Peter will leave on Monday.

8. Before expressions of measure and weight, instead of the indefinite article used in English:

Πόσο ἔχει τὸ τυρὶ αὐτό; Δέκα (δραχμὲς) ἡ ὀκά.
How much is this cheese? Ten (drachmas) an oka*

---

* A measure of weight about 2¾ pounds used in Greece, the Balkans and the
countries of the Near and Middle East.

9. Before nouns designating parts of the body, personal articles of clothing:

Τὰ χέρια τῆς ᾽Αννούλας εἶναι πάντοτε καθαρά.
Little Ann's hands are always clean.

10. Before nouns modified by a possessive adjective which follows the noun:

᾽Ο φίλος μου ὁ Παῦλος δὲ(ν) θὰ ἔλθη ἀπόψε.
My friend Paul will not come tonight.

11. Before nouns modified by a demonstrative adjective. In this case the definite article is placed between the demonstrative adjective and the noun:

Αὐτὸ τὸ κορίτσι εἶναι πολὺ καλό.
This girl is very good.

12. Before a noun indicating a class of objects or persons:

Τὰ κάρβουνα εἶναι ἀκριβὰ ἐφέτος.
Coal is expensive this year.

Οἱ στρατιῶτες εἶναι πειθαρχικοί.
Soldiers are obedient.

1.4. The indefinite article in Greek is identical with the numeral for one ἕνας (for the masculine), μία or μιά (for the feminine), and ἕνα (for the neuter).

It is declined as follows:

Nominative	ἕνας	μία or μιά	ἕνα
Genitive	ἑνός	μίας or μιᾶς	ἑνός
Accusative	ἕνα(ν)	μία(ν) or μιά	ἕνα

The final ν of the accusative forms is used before a vowel and the consonants π, τ and κ. In the latter case it is assimilated with the following consonant and it is pronounced respectively mb, nd and ng.

1.5. The indefinite article is not used in Greek as often as in English because it expresses to a certain extent the idea of the numeral for *one*, since it has exactly the same form as the numeral. The indefinite article is omitted:

1. Before predicate nouns modified or unmodified by adjectives:

Εἶναι δικηγόρος.
He is a lawyer.

Εἶναι ἔξυπνη κοπέλλα.
She is a smart girl.

2. Very often before nouns which function as the object of a verb:

Ὁ Νῖκος εἶχε γράμμα ἀπὸ τὴ μητέρα του.
Nick has received a letter from his mother.

3. In exclamations, with nouns preceded by τί:

Τί ὄμορφη γυναίκα!
What a beautiful woman!

Τί καλὸ παιδί!
What a good boy!

4. Before a noun preceded by σάν "like":

Ὁ Κώστας φαίνεται σὰν γίγαντας μπροστὰ στὸν Πέτρο.
Gus looks like a giant next to Peter.

5. In proverbs:

Σκυλὶ ποὺ γαυγίζει δὲν δαγκώνει.
A dog that barks does not bite.

2. THE NOUN

2.0. The gender in Greek is grammatical; that is, it does not depend on the sex of the noun * but on its ending. There are three genders: masculine, feminine, and neuter.

2.1. Ancient Greek and Puristic (Katharevousa) has three declensions.

The first declension includes masculine nouns in -ας (as ταμί-ας cashier, teller, treasurer) and in -ης (as ναύτ-ης sailor) feminine nouns in -α (as χώρ-α land, country) and in -η (as ζών-η zone, belt).

The second declension comprises masculine nouns in -ος (as ἄνθρωπος man), feminine in -ος (as νῆσ-ος island) and neuter in -ον (as μῆλ-ον apple).

The third declension includes masculine, feminine and neuter nouns which have one more syllable in the genitive than they do in the no-

---

* Nouns designating male beings are normally masculine and female feminine. Names of winds, months, rivers are masculine and those of trees feminine.

minative (as ὁ κόραξ, τοῦ κόρακ-ος crow; ἡ ἐφημερίς, τῆς ἐφημε-ρίδ-ος newspaper; ἡ πόλις, τῆς πόλεως city; τὸ μάθημα, τοῦ μαθή-ματ-ος lesson).

In the Demotic the third declension merges with the first declension as far as its masculine and feminine* nouns are concerned.

The other declensions present a number of differences in endings from those of their counterparts in the Katharevousa.

2.2. The First Declension

Nouns of the first declension are declined in Katharevousa as follows:

SINGULAR

	MASCULINE			FEMININE	
Nom.:	ὁ	ταμί-ας	ναύτ-ης	ἡ	χώρ-α	ζών-η
Gen.:	τοῦ	ταμί-ου	ναύτ-ου	τῆς	χώρ-ας	ζών-ης
(Dat.:	τῷ	ταμί-ᾳ	ναύτ-ῃ	τῇ	χώρ-ᾳ	ζών-ῃ)
Acc.:	τὸν	ταμί-αν	ναύτ-ην	τὴν	χώρ-αν	ζών-ην
Voc.:	ὦ	ταμί-α	ναῦτ-α	ὦ	χώρ-α	ζών-η

PLURAL

	MASCULINE			FEMININE	
Nom.:	οἱ	ταμί-αι	ναῦτ-αι	αἱ	χῶρ-αι	ζών-αι
Gen.:	τῶν	ταμι-ῶν	ναυτ-ῶν	τῶν	χωρ-ῶν	ζων-ῶν
(Dat.:	τοῖς	ταμί-αις	ναύτ-αις	ταῖς	χώρ-αις	ζών-αις)
Acc.:	τοὺς	ταμί-ας	ναύτ-ας	τὰς	χώρ-ας	ζών-ας
Voc.:	ὦ	ταμί-αι	ναῦτ-αι	ὦ	χῶρ-αι	ζών-αι

The dative is scarcely used even in Puristic. It has been replaced by the genitive or the accusative preceded by a preposition, usually εἰς. The same nouns in the Demotic are declined as follows:

SINGULAR

	MASCULINE			FEMININE	
Nom.:	ὁ	ταμί-ας	ναύτ-ης	ἡ	χώρ-α	ζών-η
Gen.:	τοῦ	ταμί-α	ναύτ-η	τῆς	χώρ-ας	ζών-ης
Acc.:	τὸν	ταμί-α	ναύτ-η	τὴ(ν)	χώρ-α	ζών-η
Voc.:	ὦ	ταμί-α	ναύτ-η	ὦ	χώρ-α	ζών-η

PLURAL

	MASCULINE			FEMININE	
Nom.:	οἱ	ταμί-ες	ναύτ-ες	οἱ	χῶρ-ες	ζῶν-ες
Gen.:	τῶν	ταμι-ῶν	ναυτ-ῶν	τῶν	χωρ-ῶν	ζων-ῶν
Acc.:	τοὺς	ταμί-ες	ναύτ-ες	τὶς	χῶρ-ες	ζῶν-ες
Voc.:	ὦ	ταμί-ες	ναύτ-ες	ὦ	χῶρ-ες	ζῶν-ες

---

* The feminine nouns retain some of the third declension endings in the com-mon Demotic used today, as ἡ πόλη, τῆς πόλης or πόλεως, τὴν πόλη, οἱ πόλεις, τῶν πόλεων, τὶς πόλεις.

2.3. The Second Declension

Nouns of the second declension are declined in Katharevousa as follows:

SINGULAR

	MASCULINE		FEMININE	NEUTER	
Nom.:	ὁ	ἄνθρωπ-ος	ἡ νῆσ-ος	τό	μῆλ-ον
Gen.:	τοῦ	ἀνθρώπ-ου	τῆς νήσ-ου	τοῦ	μήλ-ου
(Dat.:	τῷ	ἀνθρώπ-ῳ	τῇ νήσ-ῳ	τῷ	μήλ-ῳ)
Acc.:	τόν	ἄνθρωπ-ον	τήν νῆσ-ον	τό	μῆλ-ον
Voc.:	ὦ	ἄνθρωπ-ε	ὦ νῆσ-ε	ὦ	μῆλ-ον

PLURAL

Nom.:	οἱ	ἄνθρωπ-οι	αἱ νῆσ-οι	τά	μῆλ-α
Gen.:	τῶν	ἀνθρώπ-ων	τῶν νήσ-ων	τῶν	μήλ-ων
(Dat.:	τοῖς	ἀνθρώπ-οις	ταῖς νήσ-οις	τοῖς	μήλ-οις)
Acc.:	τούς	ἀνθρώπ-ους	τάς νήσ-ους	τά	μῆλ-α
Voc.:	ὦ	ἄνθρωπ-οι	ὦ νῆσ-οι	ὦ	μῆλ-α

The declension of the nouns of the second declension in the Demotic is almost the same as in the Puristic. The only actually used feminine noun of the second declension is ἡ ὁδός (street), as it appears on the street signs. There is another category of neuter nouns in the Demotic that belongs to the second declension, that of nouns in -ι (as νησί island, παιδί child).

SINGULAR

Nom.:	ὁ	ἄνθρωπ-ος	τό νησ-ί	τό	μῆλ-ο
Gen.:	τοῦ	ἀνθρώπ-ου	τοῦ νησ-ιοῦ	τοῦ	μήλ-ου
Acc.:	τόν	ἄνθρωπ-ο	τό νησ-ί	τό	μῆλ-ο

PLURAL

Nom.:	οἱ	ἄνθρωπ-οι	τά νησ-ιά	τά	μῆλ-α
Gen.:	τῶν	ἀνθρώπ-ων	τῶν νησ-ιῶν	τῶν	μήλ-ων
Acc.:	τούς	ἀνθρώπ-ους	τά νησ-ιά	τά	μῆλ-α

2.4. The Third Declension

Nouns of the third declension are declined in Katharevousa as follows:

SINGULAR

	MASCULINE		FEMININE	NEUTER	
Nom.:	ὁ	κόραξ	ἡ ἐφημερίς	τό	μάθημα
Gen.:	τοῦ	κόρακ-ος	τῆς ἐφημερίδ-ος	τοῦ	μαθήματ-ος
(Dat.:	τῷ	κόρακ-ι	τῇ ἐφημερίδ-ι	τῷ	μαθήματ-ι)
Acc.:	τόν	κόρακ-α	τήν ἐφημερίδ-α	τό	μάθημα
Voc.:	ὦ	κόραξ	ὦ ἐφημερίς	ὦ	μάθημα

PLURAL

Nom.:	οἱ	κόρακ-ες	αἱ	ἐφημερίδ-ες	τὰ	μαθήματ-α
Gen.:	τῶν	κοράκ-ων	τῶν	ἐφημερίδ-ων	τῶν	μαθημάτ-ων
(Dat.:	τοῖς	κόραξι	ταῖς	ἐφημερί-σι	τοῖς	μαθήμα-σι)
Acc.:	τοὺς	κόρακ-ας	τὰς	ἐφημερίδ-ας	τὰ	μαθήματ-α
Voc.:	ὦ	κόρακ-ες	ὦ	ἐφημερίδ-ες	ὦ	μαθήματ-α

2.5. The masculine and feminine nouns of the third declension merged with the nouns of the first declension. The neuters of the third declension that are still used have retained in the Demotic the same endings that they have in the Katharevousa. They could not merge with the nouns of the first declension because the first declension does not have any neuter nouns. Other types of neuter nouns of the third declension that are used in the Demotic are: τὸ δάσος (the forest), τοῦ δάσους (which is derived from the uncontracted form τοῦ δάσεσ-ος [the σ between two vowels drops and the vowels ε and ο are contracted to ου]), τὸ κρέας (the meat) τοῦ κρέατ-ος. They are declined in both the Demotic and the Katharevousa as follows:

	SINGULAR				PLURAL		
Nom.:	τὸ	δάσος	τὸ	κρέας	τὰ	δάση	τὰ	κρέατ-α
Gen.:	τοῦ	δάσους	τοῦ	κρέατ-ος	τῶν	δασῶν	τῶν	κρεάτ-ων
Acc.:	τὸ	δάσος	τὸ	κρέας	τὰ	δάση	τὰ	κρέατ-α
Voc.:	ὦ	δάσος	ὦ	κρέας	ὦ	δάση	ὦ	κρέατ-α

2.6 Imparisyllabic Nouns

These nouns are used only in the Demotic. They are characterized by one more syllable in the plural than they have in the singular. Most of the nouns of this group are of foreign origin. Their stems are characterized by the vowel sounds of Greek with the exception of o which is the characteristic of the second declension.

Typical examples of masculine and feminine nouns of this group are: ὁ σαράφης (the money-exchanger), ὁ κεφτές (the meat ball), ὁ ψαράς (the fisher or the fish-monger), ἡ γιαγιά (the grand-mother), ὁ παππούς (the grandfather), ἡ ἀλεπού (the fox).

Declension of the imparisyllabics

SINGULAR

Nom.:	ὁ	σαράφης	κεφτές	ψαράς
Gen.:	τοῦ	σαράφη	κεφτέ	ψαρᾶ
Acc.:	τὸν	σαράφη	κεφτέ	ψαρά

Nom.:	ὁ	παππούς	ἡ	γιαγιά	ἀλεπού
Gen.:	τοῦ	παππού	τῆς	γιαγιᾶς	ἀλεπούς
Acc.:	τὸν	παππού	τὴν	γιαγιά	ἀλεπού

PLURAL.

| Nom.: | οἱ | σαράφηδες | | κεφτέδες | ψαράδες |
| Acc.: | τοὺς | σαράφηδες | | κεφτέδες | ψαράδες |

| Nom.: | | παππούδες | οἱ | γιαγιάδες | ἀλεπούδες |
| Acc.: | τοὺς | παππούδες | τὶς | γιαγιάδες | ἀλεπούδες |

The genitive plural in colioquial Greek is very seldom used in general. In the imparisyllabic class of nouns, it is never actually used, except in the case "of fishermen" τῶν ψαράδων.

3. THE ADJECTIVE

3.1. Adjectives, as in English, precede the noun they modify (e.g. ὁ καλός ἄνθρωπος, the good man; ἡ καλή γυναίκα, the good woman; τὸ καλὸ παιδί, the good child; καλά παιδιά, good children). As you see from thé examples, they agree in gender, case, and number with the noun they modify.

3.2. In classical Greek and Katharevousa, the regular adjectives are declined according to three basic schemes of declension:

1. The so-called second declension, in which the masculine and neuter are declined according to the second declension and the feminine according to the first declension:

SINGULAR

Nom.:	ὁ	καλός	ἡ	καλή	τὸ	καλόν
Gen.:	τοῦ	καλοῦ	τῆς	καλῆς	τοῦ	καλοῦ
Acc.:	τὸν	καλόν	τὴν	καλήν	τὸ	καλόν
Voc.:	ὦ	καλέ	ὦ	καλή	ὦ	καλόν

PLURAL

Nom.:	οἱ	καλοί	αἱ	καλαί	τὰ	καλά
Gen.:	τῶν	καλῶν	τῶν	καλῶν	τῶν	καλῶν
Acc.:	τοὺς	καλούς	τὰς	καλάς	τὰ	καλά
Voc.:	ὦ	καλοί	ὦ	καλαί	ὦ	καλά

This declension has not been greatly changed in Demotic. The only changes in the singular are found in the accusative masculine and feminine, where the ν is usually dropped and the nominative, accusative and vocative of the neuter, where the ν is also dropped. In the plural the changes are limited only to the feminine, where the nominative is οἱ καλές, the accusative τίς καλές and the vocative (ὦ) καλές.

2. The so-called third declension, in which the masculine and neuter are declined according to the third declension of nouns and the feminine according to the first declension:

SINGULAR

Nom.:	ὁ βαθύς	ἡ βαθεῖα	τὸ βαθύ	
Gen.:	τοῦ βαθέος	τῆς βαθείας	τοῦ βαθέος	
Acc.:	τὸν βαθύν	τὴν βαθεῖαν	τὸ βαθύ	
Voc.:	ὦ βαθύ	ὦ βαθεῖα	ὦ βαθύ	

PLURAL

Nom.:	οἱ βαθεῖς	αἱ βαθεῖαι	τὰ βαθέα
Gen.:	τῶν βαθέων	τῶν βαθειῶν	τῶν βαθέων
Acc.:	τοὺς βαθεῖς	τὰς βαθείας	τὰ βαθέα

The vocative in the plural is always identical with the nominative. The adjective βαθύς (deep) is declined in Demotic as follows:

SINGULAR

Nom.:	ὁ βαθύς	ἡ βαθιά	τὸ βαθύ
Gen.:	τοῦ βαθιοῦ	τῆς βαθιᾶς	τοῦ βαθιοῦ
Acc.:	τὸ(ν) βαθύ	τὴ(ν) βαθιά	τὸ βαθύ

PLURAL

Nom.:	οἱ βαθιοί	οἱ βαθιές	τὰ βαθιά
Gen.:	τῶν βαθιῶν	τῶν βαθιῶν	τῶν βαθιῶν
Acc.:	τοὺς βαθιούς	τὶς βαθιές	τὰ βαθιά

In spoken Greek the Puristic forms of the masculine plural are used sometimes instead of those of the Demotic.

3. An additional scheme of the third declension, in which the masculine and feminine have the same endings and all three genders are declined according to the third declension:

SINGULAR

Nom.:	ὁ ἡ συνήθης		τὸ σύνηθες
Gen.:	τοῦ τῆς συνήθους		τοῦ συνήθους
Acc.:	τὸν τὴν συνήθη		τὸ σύνηθες
Voc.:	ὦ ὦ σύνηθες		ὦ σύνηθες

PLURAL

Nom.:	οἱ αἱ συνήθεις		τὰ συνήθη
Gen.:	τῶν τῶν συνήθων		τῶν συνήθων
Acc:	τοὺς τὰς συνήθεις		τὰ συνήθη

In Demotic, the adjectives like συνήθης (usual) change declension and become adjectives of the so-called second declension and are declined as the adjectives belonging to that declension. For example: ὁ ἡ συνήθης, τὸ σύνηθες becomes ὁ συνηθισμένος, ἡ συνηθισμένη, τὸ συνηθισμένο.

3.3. In colloquial Greek, there are some adjectives which are declined differently from the three schemes given above. A typical adjective of this group is ὁ ζηλιάρης (jealous). This adjective in all its three genders is used very often as a noun. It is declined as an imparisyllabic in the masculine, as a first declension noun in -a in the feminine and as a second-declension noun in -o in the neuter.

SINGULAR

Nom.:	ὁ	ζηλιάρης	ἡ	ζηλιάρα	τὸ ζηλιάρικο
Gen.:	τοῦ	ζηλιάρη	τῆς	ζηλιάρας	τοῦ ζηλιάρικου
Acc.:	τὸ(ν)	ζηλιάρη	τὴ(ν)	ζηλιάρα	τὸ ζηλιάρικο

PLURAL

Nom.:	οἱ	ζηλιάρηδες	οἱ	ζηλιάρες	τὰ ζηλιάρικα
Gen.:	τῶν	ζηλιάρηδων	τῶν	ζηλιάρων	τῶν ζηλιάρικων
Acc.:	τοὺς	ζηλιάρηδες	τὶς	ζηλιάρες	τὰ ζηλιάρικα

3.4. Irregular Adjectives

There are two irregular adjectives which are used very often. Their frequent use seems to have helped them retain their irregularities. They are ὁ πολύς (much), which in the plural is οἱ πολλοί (many) which is used also in literary English as *hoi polloi* with its classical pronunciation, and ὁ μέγας (great, large) which in Demotic became a regular second-declension adjective ὁ μεγάλος, ἡ μεγάλη, τὸ μεγάλο.

SINGULAR

Nom.:	ὁ	πολύς	ἡ	πολλή	τὸ	πολύ
Gen.:	τοῦ	πολλοῦ	τῆς	πολλῆς	τοῦ	πολλοῦ
Acc.:	τὸν	πολύ(ν)	τὴν	πολλή(ν)	τὸ	πολύ
Voc.:	ὦ	πολύ	ὦ	πολλή	ὦ	πολύ

Nom.:	ὁ	μέγας	τὸ	μέγα
Gen.:	τοῦ	μεγάλου	τοῦ	μεγάλου
Acc.:	τὸν	μέγαν	τὸ	μέγα
Voc.:	ὦ	μέγα	ὦ	μέγα

The plural of both adjectives is regular and is declined as the rest of the so-called second declension adjectives: οἱ πολλοί, αἱ πολλαί or οἱ πολλές, τὰ πολλά; οἱ μεγάλοι, αἱ μεγάλαι or οἱ μεγάλες, τὰ μεγάλα. The singular of the feminine of μέγας, ἡ μεγάλη is also declined regularly according to the first declension.

3.5. Comparison of Adjectives

The comparative and superlative are formed by the suffixes -τερος and -τατος respectively; e.g., βαθύς (deep), βαθύτερος (deeper), βαθύτατος (deepest).

In Demotic the comparative is usually formed by placing the particle πιό in front of the positive form of the adjective; e.g., πιὸ βαθύς, πιὸ βαθιά, πιὸ βαθύ. The superlative is formed by placing the definite article in front of the comparative: ὁ πιὸ βαθύς or ὁ βαθύτερος, ἡ πιὸ βαθιά or ἡ βαθύτερη, τὸ πιὸ βαθύ or τὸ βαθύτερο.

The forms in -τέρος are also used in Demotic. But there are some adjectives which form their comparative only by means of the particle πιό. They are: unchangeable adjectives as γκρί (gray) and μπλέ (blue); adjectives that are primarily used as nouns as ὁ ζηλιάρης (jealous), ὁ κατεργάρης (sly), ὁ τεμπέλης (lazy); certain of the longer adjectives as ὁ περίεργος (curious), ὁ ἀσυγύριστος (untidy); a few of the shorter adjectives as ὁ κρύος (cold); most of the adjectives denoting color as ὁ ἄσπρος (white), ὁ μαῦρος (black), ὁ πράσινος (green).

Four adjectives have irregular comparative forms:

καλός (good)	καλύτερος or καλλίτερος (better)
κακός (bad)	χειρότερος (worse)
μεγάλος (big or large)	μεγαλύτερος (large or bigger)
πολύς (much)	περισσότερος (more)

3.51. The comparison of superiority is expressed by the comparative of the adjective followed either by ἀπό with the accusative or by παρά with the nominative. The latter is used less frequently.

> Ἡ Κατίνα εἶναι πιὸ ψηλή ἀπὸ τὴν Ἑλένη.
> Kate is taller than Helen.

Ἡ Μαρία εἶναι πιὸ ἔξυπνη ἀπὸ τὴν Ἀγνή.
Mary is smarter than Agnes.

Αὐτὴ εἶναι ψηλότερη παρὰ ἡ ἄλλη.
She is taller than the other.

3.52. The comparison of inferiority is expressed by (ὁ) λιγώτε-
ρο(ν) (less) plus the adjective plus ἀπό with accusative or very sel-
om plus παρά with nominative.

Ὁ Κώστας εἶναι λιγότερο ἐπιμελὴς ἀπὸ τὸν Γιῶργο.
Gus is less diligent than George.

In Katharevousa the comparative is followed by the genitive.

Ὁ Χρῆστος εἶναι μεγαλύτερος τοῦ Γεωργίου.
Chris is older than George.

3.53. The comparison of equality is expressed by:

) τόσο ... ὅσο:

Εἶναι τόσο καλὸ ὅσο καὶ τὸ ἄλλο.
It is as good as the other.

) σὰν (καὶ):

Εἶναι (τόσο) καλὸ σὰν (καὶ) τὸ ἄλλο.
It is as good as the other.

The latter is preferred in negative sentences.

4. THE NUMERAL

4.1. The cardinal numbers from 1 to 199 are not declined with
e exception of ἕνα, τρία and τέσσερα which are declined both
one and in compounds. The declension of ἕνας, μία, ἕνα is given
the indefinite article. The forms of τρία and τέσσερα are:

om. Acc.:	τρεῖς	τρεῖς	τρία	τέσσερε(ι)ς	τέσσερε(ι)ς	τέσσερα
en.:	τριῶν	τριῶν	τριῶν	τεσσάρων	τεσσάρων	τεσσάρων

4.2. The numbers above two hundred are declinable as plural
djectives: διακόσιοι, διακόσιες, διακόσια. From two thousand
wards the noun χιλιάδες (fem. plur.) is used for thousands.

4.3. The ordinal adjectives are declined like adjectives of the so-
lled second declension: πρῶτος, πρώτη, πρῶτο(ν) (first).

4.4. Table of Cardinal and Ordinal Numbers.

ARABIC NUMBERS	GREEK	CARDINAL NUMERALS	ORDINAL NUMERALS
1	α′	ἕνας, μία - μιά, ἕνα	πρῶτος
2	β′	δύο - δυό	δεύτερος
3	γ′	τρεῖς, τρία	τρίτος
4	δ′	τέσσερε(ι)ς, τέσσερα	τέταρτος
5	ε′	πέντε	πέμπτος
6	ς′	ἕξι	ἕκτος
7	ζ′	ἑπτά - ἐφτά	ἕβδομος
8	η′	ὀκτώ - ὀχτώ	ὄγδοος
9	θ′	ἐννέα - ἐννιά	ἔνατος
10	ι′	δέκα	δέκατος
11	ια′	ἕνδεκα - ἕντεκα	ἑνδέκατος
12	ιβ′	δώδεκα	δωδέκατος
13	ιγ′	δεκατρεῖς, δεκατρία	δέκατος τρίτος
14	ιδ′	δεκατέσσερε(ι)ς, δεκατέσσερα	δέκατος τέταρτος
15	ιε′	δεκαπέντε	δέκατος πέμπτος
16	ις′	δεκαέξι - δεκάξι	δέκατος ἕκτος
17	ιζ′	δεκαεπτά	δέκατος ἕβδομος
18	ιη′	δεκαοκτώ	δέκατος ὄγδοος
19	ιθ′	δεκαεννέα	δέκατος ἔνατος
20	κ′	εἴκοσι	εἰκοστός
21	κα′	εἴκοσι ἕνας (μία, ἕνα)	εἰκοστὸς πρῶτος
22	κβ′	εἴκοσι δύο	εἰκοστὸς δεύτερος
30	λ′	τριάντα	τριακοστός
40	μ′	σαράντα	τεσσαρακοστός
50	ν′	πενήντα	πεντηκοστός
60	ξ′	ἑξήντα	ἑξηκοστός
70	ο′	ἑβδομήντα	ἑβδομηκοστός
80	π′	ὀγδόντα	ὀγδοηκοστός
90	η′	ἐνενήντα	ἐνενηκοστός
100	ρ′	ἑκατό(ν)	ἑκατοστός
101	ρα′	ἑκατὸν ἕνας (μία, ἕνα)	ἑκατοστὸς πρῶτος
102	ρβ′	ἑκατὸ δύο	ἑκατοστὸς δεύτερος
200	σ′	διακόσιοι, -ες, -α	διακοσιοστός
300	τ′	τριακόσιοι, -ες, -α	τριακοσιοστός
400	υ′	τετρακόσιοι, -ες, -α	τετρακοσιοστός
500	φ′	πεντακόσιοι, -ες, -α	πεντακοσιοστός
600	χ′	ἑξακόσιοι, -ες, -α	ἑξακοσιοστός

700	ψ´	ἑπτακόσιοι, -ες, -α	ἑπτακοσιοστός
800	ω´	ὀκτακόσιοι, -ες, -α	ὀκτακοσιοστός
900	λ´	ἐννιακόσιοι, -ες, -α	ἐννιακοσιοστός
1000	´α	χίλι-οι, -ες, -α	χιλιοστός
2000	´β	δύο χιλιάδες	δισχιλιοστός
10,000*	´ι	δέκα χιλιάδες	δεκακισχιλιοστός
100,000	´ρ	ἑκατὸ χιλιάδες	ἑκατοντάκισχιλιοστός
1,000,000		ἕνα ἑκατομμύριο	ἑκατομμυριοστός
1,000,000,000		ἕνα δισεκατομμύριο	δισεκατομμυριοστός

A hint about the spelling of the numbers from one to ten: If they start with a vowel in Greek, they take the rough breathing when their counterpart in English begins with s; e.g. ἕξι six, ἑπτά seven; otherwise they take the smooth breathing. The only exception to this rule is ἕνας, ἕνα.

5. THE PRONOUN

5.1. Subject Pronouns

1. The personal pronouns used as subjects of verbs are:

SINGULAR		PLURAL	
ἐγώ	I	ἐμεῖς (ἡμεῖς)	we
ἐσύ (σύ)	you	ἐσεῖς (σεῖς)	you
αὐτός	he	αὐτοί	they (masc.)
αὐτή	she	αὐτές (αὐταί)	they (fem.)
αὐτό	it	αὐτά	they (neut.)

The forms in parenthesis are the ones used in Puristic. They are given only when they differ from those of the Demotic.

2. Σύ (the pronoun of the second person singular) is used only in addressing a single preson with whom the speaker is on intimate terms, for example, between members of a family, children, close friends, peasants, workers, and adults speaking to children, or addressing animals. Σύ is also used in prayers, in addressing God and saints, and in exalted, poetic language.

---

* In Greek the comma is used (instead of a period as in English) as a decimal point; the period is used (instead of the comma as in English) to separate the thousands. For example, the number 12,345.67 will be written in Greek as 12.345,67.

Σεῖς (the pronoun of the second person plural) is used by mere acquaintances, in polite conversation, by children in addressing adults, by subordinates in addressing their superiors.

3. The personal subject pronouns are generally omitted, except in case of ambiguity or emphasis:

> Αὐτὴ δὲν (ἐ)πῆγε νὰ ἰδῆ τὴ μητέρα της.
> She did not go to see her mother.

> Ἐνῶ αὐτὸς γράφει, αὐτὴ διαβάζει.
> While he writes, she reads.

> Ἐγὼ γράφω καὶ σεῖς μιλᾶτε.
> I write and you talk.

5.2. The object pronouns are:

Simple forms:

1st person	2nd person		3rd person	
		SINGULAR		
		m.	f.	n.
Gen.: μοῦ	σοῦ	τοῦ	τῆς	τοῦ
Acc.: μέ	σέ	τόν	τήν	τό
		PLURAL		
Gen.: μᾶς	σᾶς	τούς or τῶν		
Acc.: μᾶς	σᾶς	τούς	τίς	τά

Emphatic forms:

		SINGULAR		
Gen.:		αὐτου (νοῦ)	αὐτη (νῆ)ς	αὐτου (νοῦ)
Acc.: (ἐ) μένα	(ἐ) σένα	αὐτόν	αὐτήν	αὐτό
		PLURAL		
Gen.:		αὐτῶν or αὐτονῶν		
Acc.: (ἐ) μᾶς	(ἐ) σᾶς	αὐτούς	αὐτές	αὐτά

The object pronouns are placed before the verb. Only in the case of an imperative they follow the verb: Μοῦ τὸ ἔδωσε (He gave it to me); Δός μου το (Give it to me).

The indirect object must precede the direct object when a verb governs two object pronouns: Τῆς τὸ ἐπλήρωσε (He paid it to her). The negative precedes the object pronouns: Δὲν τῆς τὸ ἐπλήρωσε (He did not pay it to her).

For emphasis and to avoid ambiguity, the emphatic forms of the object pronouns, preceded by a preposition, are sometimes used. The emphatic object pronouns are placed after the verbal form: (Αὐτός) τὰ ἔδωσε τὰ χρήματα σ' αὐτούς (He gave the money to them).

Note that the direct object in the above sentence is repeated; the first time it is expressed as a pronoun (τά) and the second time as a noun (τὰ χρήματα). The indirect object may also be expressed twice for emphasis: (Αὐτοὶ) μοῦ τὰ ἔδωσαν σὲ μένα (They gave it to me); (Ἐγὼ) τοῦ τὰ ἔδωσα τοῦ Νίκου (I gave it to Nick).

5.3. Possessive Pronouns

The possessive pronouns are identical in form with the genitive of the personal pronouns. The only difference between the two is that the possessive pronouns are not accented because they are enclitic words following the nouns they modify: ὁ πατέρας μας (our father). When the noun is accented on the third from the last syllable (the antepenult) the accent of the enclitic possessive pronoun goes to the last syllable of the preceding noun: ὁ προϊστάμενός μας (our manager).

The forms of the possessives are:

μου	my	μας	our
σου	your (familiar)	σας	your
του	his	τους	their
της	her	or	
του	its	των	

These forms are actually pronominal adjectives. They cannot be used by themselves without modifying a noun. When they are used as pronouns equivalent to the English *mine, yours*, etc., they are preceded by the substantivized adjective (ἱ)δικός (for the masculine), (ἱ)δική (for the feminine), (ἱ)δικό (for the neuter). This adjective is declined as a regular adjective of the so-called second declension.

Its forms are used as follows:

(ὁ) δικός μου   (ἡ) δική μου   (τὸ) δικό μου
mine (my own)

(ὁ) δικός σου   (ἡ) δική σου   (τὸ) δικό σου
yours (fam.) (your own)

(ὁ) δικός του   (ἡ) δική του   (τὸ) δικό του
his or its (his own)

(ὁ) δικός της   (ἡ) δική της   (τὸ) δικό ιης
hers (her own)

(ὁ) δικός μας   (ἡ) δική μας   (τὸ) δικό μας
ours (our own)

(ὁ) δικός σας   (ἡ) δική σας   (τὸ) δικό σας
yours (your own)

(ὁ) δικός τους   (ἡ) δική τους   (τὸ) δικό τους
theirs (their own)

5.4. Interrogative Pronouns

The interrogative pronouns are:

1. Ποιός, ποιά, ποιό (who, which, which one) which is declined as a regular adjective of the so-called second declension. Its Puristic forms are: ποῖος, ποία, ποῖον.

2. Τί (what) which is indeclinable. In Puristic, however, it is declined; its masculine and feminine form is τίς (who), which is declined as follows:

	SINGULAR		PLURAL	
Nom.:	τίς	τί	τινές	τινά
Gen.:	τινός	τινός	τινῶν	τινῶν
(Dat.:	τινί	τινί	τισί	τισί
Acc.:	τινά	τί	τινάς	τινά

3. Πόσος, πόση, πόσο (how much), πόσοι, πόσες, πόσα (how many) which is also declined as a regular second declension adjective. Its Puristic forms are: πόσος, πόση, πόσον, πόσοι, πόσαι, πόσα. Both ποῖος and πόσος can also be used as pronominal adjectives.

5.5. Demonstrative Pronouns

he demonstrative pronouns are:

. Αὐτός, αὐτή, αὐτό (this or that) which is also used as a third
erson personal pronoun.

. Τοῦτος, τούτη, τοῦτο (this right here).

. Ἐκεῖνος, ἐκείνη, ἐκεῖνο (that).

There are three degrees of *deixis* (that is, pointing out):
a) indicating something or someone near the speaker;
b) indicating something or someone near the listener;
c) indicating something or someone far from both the speaker
   and the listener.

Many languages use only two types of deixis, combining the second
ther with the first or with the third. The Greek αὐτός represents
) and b) and ἐκεῖνος, c). English *this* represents a) and *that* b) and
. Thus αὐτός could mean either this or that. *That* could be rendered
ther by αὐτός or by ἐκεῖνος depending on what it refers to.

ther demonstrative pronouns are:

Τέτοιος, τέτοια, τέτοιο (such).

Ἴδιος, ἴδια, ἴδιο (same).

There is no difference in form between the demonstrative pronouns
d the demonstrative adjectives. All these pronouns are declined as
gular adjectives of the so-called second declension.

In Puristic, in addition to αὐτός and ἐκεῖνος, there is οὗτος which
declined as follows:

	SINGULAR		
Nom.:	οὗτος	αὕτη	τοῦτο
Gen.:	τούτου	ταύτης	τούτου
(Dat.:	τούτῳ	ταύτῃ	τούτῳ)
Acc.:	τοῦτον	ταύτην	τοῦτο

PLURAL

Nom.:	οὗτοι	αὗται	ταῦτα
Gen.:	τούτων	τούτων	τούτων
(Dat.:	τούτοις	ταύταις	τούτοις)
Acc.:	τούτους	ταύτας	ταῦτα

Other pronouns in Puristic are: τοιοῦτος, τοιαύτη, τοιοῦτον (such and τοσοῦτος, τοσαύτη, τοσοῦτον (so much). Both are declined as adjectives in -ος, -η, -ον.

The only difference between the demonstrative pronouns and the demonstrative adjectives is that the pronouns stand by themselves, but the demonstrative adjectives precede the nouns which they limit and modify. Examples: Pronoun: Αὐτὰ εἶναι τὰ βιβλία της (These are her books). Adjective: Αὐτὰ τὰ βιβλία εἶναι τῆς κυρίας Μαρίας Παπαδοπούλου (These books belong to Mrs. Mary Papadopoulos). Note that the definite article precedes the noun in Greek even when the latter is modified by a demonstrative pronoun.

5.6. Indefinite Pronouns

The indefinite pronouns are:

1. Those that are declined as the numeral for one ἕνας, μία, ἕνα:

   καθένας (or καθείς), καθεμία, καθένα (each one)
   κανένας (or κανείς), κα(μ)μία, κανένα (no one, none, nobody)

2. Those that are declined as adjectives of the second declension:

   ἄλλος, ἄλλη, ἄλλο (other, another)
   κάποιος, κάποια, κάποιο (someone)
   ὅλος, ὅλη, ὅλο (all, every)

3. Those that are declined as adjectives of the second declension the plural:

   μερικοί, μερικές, μερικά (a few, some pl.)

4. Those that are invariable:

   κάθε (each)
   τίποτε or τίποτα (nothing)

5. Those that are differentiated only by the definite article that precedes them:

ὁ δεῖνα, ἡ δεῖνα, τὸ δεῖνα (one such and such)
ὁ τάδε, ἡ τάδε, τὸ τάδε (one such and such)

The indefinite adjectives have identical forms with the indefinite pronouns.

5.7. Relative Pronouns

The most common of the relative pronouns in Demotic is the invariable πού (who, whom, which, that) which stands for all the forms that are expressed in Puristic by ὁ ὁποῖος, ἡ ὁποία, τὸ ὁποῖον which is declined as a regular adjective of the second declension.

Other relative pronouns which are used also as adjectives and are close to the indefinite pronouns in meaning are:

1. ὅποιος, ὅποια, ὅποιο (whoever); e.g., "Οποιος θέλει ἄς ἔλθη. (Whoever wants to come, let him come.).

2. ὅ,τι (that which); e.g., "Ο,τι θέλει ἄς γίνη. (That which is to take place, let it take place.); Κάμε ὅ,τι σοῦ εἶπα. (Do what I told you.); (The last sentence can also be expressed by: Κάμε ἐκεῖνο πού σοῦ εἶπα.) "Ο,τι πρᾶγμα κι' ἄν εἶναι, φέρε το. (Whatever [thing] is, bring it.)

3. ὅσος, ὅση, ὅσο (as much); ὅσοι, ὅσες, ὅσα (as many).

4. τόσος, τόση, τόσο (so much); τόσοι, τόσες, τόσα (so many).

In archaic Puristic there is also the relative pronoun ὅστις (who) which is declined as follows:

SINGULAR

Nom.:	ὅστις	ἥτις	ὅ,τι
Gen.:	οὗτινος	ἧστινος	οὗτινος
(Dat.:	ᾧτινι	ᾗτινι	ᾧτινι)
Acc.:	ὅντινα	ἥντινα	ὅ,τι

PLURAL

Nom.:	οἵτινες	αἵτινες	ἅτινα
Gen.:	ὧντινων	ὧντινων	ὧντινων
(Dat.:	οἷστισι	αἷστισι	οἷστισι)
Acc.:	οὕστινας	ἅστινας	ἅτινα

In Puristic there are also the compound pronouns ὁποιοσδήποτε (whoever), ὁσοσδήποτε (howsoever great), ὁστισδήποτε (whoever).

6. THE PREPOSITION

6.1. The use of the preposition is one of the most difficult things to master in learning a foreign language because prepositional usage is largely idiomatic. You should form the habit of observing and learning, through repetition and practice, the prepositional usages which differ from English, as you encounter them.

6.2. In classical Greek and to a certain extent in Puristic, the prepositions govern various cases; that is, they are followed by definite cases. They may be grouped according to the cases they require:

a. Prepositions that require the genitive: ἄνευ · (without), ἀντί (instead), πρό (before) as in πρὸ μεσημβρίας (before noon) which is still used and is abbreviated as π.μ. which is the equivalent of English a.m.

b. Prepositions that require the dative: ἐν (in, into), σύν (with). They are very seldom used even in Puristic. They are mostly used in classical and biblical proverbial expressions which are used in modern Greek as quotations.

c. Prepositions that require the accusative: ἀνά (over), εἰς (to, in).

d. Prepositions that take either the genitive or the accusative: διά (with gen., through; with acc., because of), κατά (with gen., against; with acc., during), μετά (with gen., with; with acc., after), περί (with gen., over, about; with acc., around), ὑπέρ (with gen., for; with acc., above), ὑπό (with gen., by; with acc., under).

e. Prepositions that take either the genitive or the dative or the accusative: ἐπί (with gen., on; with dat., because of; with acc., against, during), παρά (with gen., from; with dat., by; with acc., beside), πρός (with gen., by; with dat. or acc., to).

6.3. In modern Greek most of those complicated uses have been eliminated and if some of them still occur, their occurrence is limited to a number of stereotyped expressions. In Demotic there are only seven simple prepositions which take the accusative:* ἀπό (from), γιά (for), μέ (with), μετά (after), χωρίς (without), ὡς (as far as), εἰς or σέ (to, in, on,at). The preposition εἰς is usually combined with the definite article and appears as στό(ν) (masc., sing.), στή(ν) (fem., s.), στό (neut. s.); στούς (masc. pl.), στίς (fem. pl.), στά (neut. pl.).

6.4. The simple prepositions are often preceded by adverbs with which they form many new compound prepositions: ἀνάμεσα or ἀναμεταξὺ σέ (between), ἀπάνω σὲ (on or upon), ἀπέναντι ἀπὸ (across), κάτω ἀπό (underneath), ἀποπάνω ἀπό (over, above), γύρω σέ (around), δίπλα or πλαï σέ (beside), ἔξω ἀπό (out of) κοντά or σιμά σέ (near), μαζὶ μέ (together with), μακριὰ ἀπό (far from), μέσα σέ (inside), μπροστὰ σέ (in front of), πισὼ ἀπό (behind), πρωτύτερα or πρὶν ἀπό (before), ὕστερα ἀπό (after).

*There is also the preposition μεταξύ (between, among) which takes the genitive and is used in standard spoken Greek. However, with plural pronouns it takes also the accusative as μεταξύ μας (between or among us).

7. THE ADVERB

7.1. The ending of most adverbs in Puristic is -ως. Many of these adverbs are used in spoken Greek. The regular ending of the same adverb in Demotic is -α. For example: καλῶς, καλά (well), but ἀμέσως (immediately) in both Demotic and Puristic. There are a few adverbs which have different meanings in their two forms as ἀκριβῶς (exactly), ἀκριβά (expensively).

7.2. The comparative of the adverbs is formed as that of the adjectives. For example: καλά (well), καλύτερα or πιὸ καλά (better). The superlative is ἄριστα or κάλλιστα (best).

7.3. The most important adverbs are:

a. *Place*: ποῦ* (where [interrogative]), ὅπου (where), ἐδῶ (here), ἐκεῖ (there), ἐπάνω (up), κάτω (down), μέσα (inside), ἔξω (outside), μπροστά (in front), πίσω (behind), παντοῦ (every-

where), πλησίον, κοντά or σιμά (near), μακριά (far), πλάϊ or
δίπλα (next).

b. *Manner*: πῶς* (how), ἔξαφνα (suddenly).

c. *Time*: πότε (when), τώρα (now), τότε (then), σήμερα
(today), χθές (yesterday), προχθές (day before yesterday), παρα-
προχθές (two days before yesterday), αὔριο(ν) tomorrow, μεθαύ-
ριο(ν) (day after tomorrow), ἀμέσως (immediately), ὄχι ἀκόμη
(not yet), πόσον καιρό (how long), πόσην ὥρα (how long), πόσες
φορές (how many times), πολλὲς φορές (many times), συχνά
(often), σπανίως (seldom), πάλι(ν) (again).

d. *Others*: ναί (yes), μάλιστα (yes [emphatic or formal]), ὄχι
(no), καθόλου (not at all).

8. THE CONJUNCTION

8.1. Coordinating conjunctions join sentences, clauses, phrases, and
words of equal rank. The most common ones are: καί (and), ἀλλά
(but), μά (but [emphatic colloquial]), ἤ (or), ἤ...ἤ (either...or)
μήτε...μήτε or οὔτε...οὔτε (neither...nor).

8.2. Subordinating conjunctions introduce dependent clauses. The
most common ones are: ὅταν (when), ἀφοῦ (when, since), ἐνῶ
(while), πώς or ὅτι (that), ἐπειδή, γιατί or διότι (because), ἐάν
ἄν, σάν or ἅμα (if), πρὶν (νά) or προτοῦ (νά) (before), ὕστερα
ποὺ (after), μόλις (just), καθὼς or ὅπως (as), ὥστε (so that), γιὰ
νά or νά (in order to).

9. THE INTERJECTION

9.1. Some of the most common interjections in Greek are:

ἄ! ah! oh!	εἴθε! God grant!	οὔφ! oh!
ἄϊ! ah!	εὖγε! bravo!	ὄχ! oh! ow!
ἀλ(λο)ίμονο! alas!	μακάρι! God grant!	πούφ! pf!
ἄλτ! stop!	μάρς! march!	σοὐτ! or στ! (hu)sh!
ἄου! ouch!	μπράβο! bravo!	φτού! ugh!
ἄχ! ah! oh!	μπά! pshaw! so what!	ὤ! say!
ἔ! say! hey!	ὄ! oh!	ὤχ! ow!

*Ποῦ and πῶς are differentiated by a different accent from πού (who
which, that), the relative pronoun, and πώς (that), the conjunction.

9.2.Exclamative phrases are used as interjections:

(Τί) Κρίμα!	What a pity!	Θεέ μου!	My God!
Χριστὸς καὶ Παναγιά!	Christ and Virgin (may help us)!		
Κακομοίρη (μου)	(My) poor man!		
Τὸν καημένο!	The poor man!	"Ελα (δά)!	Come (now)!
'Ορίστε!	Here is!	Ζήτω!	Long live! Hurrah!
'Εμπρός!	Forward! Come in!	'Εν τάξει!	O.K.!
"Εξω!	Out!	Περαστικά!	Speedy recovery!
Τί ὅμορφη!	How beautiful!	Σὲ καλό σου!	How could you!
Μάτια μου!	My dearest! (Lit., my eyes!)		
Δὲν πειράζει!	Never mind!	Λοιπόν!	Then! So!
Γρήγορα!	Hurry up!	Σιγά-σιγά!	Take it easy!
Προσοχή!	Attention! Look out!	Καρδιά!	Courage!

10. THE VERB

10.1. In English the form of the verb changes according to the subject. We say: *I am, you are, he is*, etc. In most cases, however, the English verb changes only in the third person singular in the present. For example, we say: *I think, you think, we think, they think*, but *he thinks* or *she thinks*. Since five of the six possible forms are identical, we are not especially conscious of the problem of verb endings. On the other hand, the Greek verb has a large number of endings which differ according to subject, tense, and mood. The best way to learn the verb forms properly is in the context in which they are used.

Memorizing the endings without learning the sentence patterns of speech in which they occur may help you recognize them but not actually use them.

10.12. In the verbal system of modern Greek both the tense and the aspect are important. The concept of the aspect is expressed by two different stems: the stem of the present and the stem of the aorist; from these two stems are formed all the tenses and moods.

10.13. Modern Greek has eight tenses:

1. The *present* (ὁ ἐνεστώς) which expresses something that is going on, or a state of existence. Examples: παίζω (I play, I do

play, I am playing); πεινῶ (I am hungry); προοδεύω (I make progress).

2. The *imperfect* (ὁ παρατατικός) that expresses an action which went on for sometime in the past or has been repeated or was customary. Example: ἔπαιζα (I was playing, I used to play); (ἐ)πεινοῦσα (I was hungry [during an indefinite period of time]); (ἐ)προόδευα (I kept making progress).

3. The *durative future* (ὁ ἐξακολουθητικὸς μέλλων) which expresses an action that will be going on. Example: θὰ παίζω (I will be playing); θὰ πεινῶ (I will be hungry [for an indefinite time]); θὰ προοδεύω (I will be or keep progressing).

4. The *punctual future* (ὁ στιγμιαῖος μέλλων) that expresses an action that will take place in the future and will be completed. Example: θὰ παίξω (I will play); θὰ πεινάσω (I will be hungry [during a certain period of time]); θὰ προοδεύσω (I will make certain progress).

5. The *aorist or simple past* (ὁ ἀοριστός) which expresses a completed action or a single act in past time. Example: ἔπαιξα (I played); (ἐ)πείνασα (I was hungry [during a certain period]); (ἐ)προόδευσα (I made progress).

6. The *perfect or present perfect* (ὁ παρακείμενος) that represents an action as having taken place and having been completed. Example: ἔχω παίξει (I have played); ἔχω πεινάσει (I have been hungry); ἔχω προοδεύσει (I have made progress).

7. The *pluperfect or past perfect* (ὁ ὑπερσυντέλικος) which expresses an action that had taken place. Example: εἶχα παίξει (I had played): εἶχα πεινάσει (I had been hungry); εἶχα προοδεύσει (I had made progress).

8. The *future perfect* (ὁ τετελεσμένος μέλλων) that expresses an action that will have taken place. Example: θὰ ἔχω παίξει (I will have played); θὰ ἔχω πεινάσει (I will have been hungry): θὰ ἔχω προοδεύσει (I will have made progress). This tense is very seldom used.

10.131. The indicative of the simple past tenses (imperfect and aorist) take a prefix called augment (αὔξηση).

There are two kinds of augment, the syllabic (ἡ συλλαβική) and the temporal (ἡ χρονική).

The syllabic augment is an ε- prefixed to verbs which begin with a consonant. Example: παίζω (I play), ἔπαιζα (I was playing), ἔπαιξα (I played).

The initial ρ is usually doubled after the augment, especially in Puristic. Example: ῥέει (it flows), ἔῤῥεε (it flowed).

The temporal augment is a lengthening or change of the initial vowel (as α changes to η, ε to η, ο to ω, οι to ῳ, αι to η, αυ to ηυ, and ευ to ηυ).

In Demotic the temporal augment is not used and the syllabic is dropped when it is not accented, as μάθαμε (we learned) instead of ἐμάθαμε.

10.14. Modern Greek has only three moods: the *indicative* (ὁριστική), the *subjunctive* (ὑποτακτική) which is used in addition to its other uses in cases in which the infinitive is used in English because modern Greek has no infinitive, and the *imperative* (προστακτική). Modern Greek also has two *conditionals* (the simple and the perfect) *. From the stem of the present are formed three tenses: The present, the imperfect, and the durative future; and from the stem of the aorist are formed the aorist and the punctual future. The perfect tenses are formed by the present, imperfect and future of the auxiliary ἔχω (have) and a stereotyped form derived from the aoristic stem.

10.15. The semantic difference between the *present* (or *imperfective*) and *aorist* (or *perfective*) aspects can be briefly stated thus: in the forms formed from the present stem the interest is generally in the duration of the action described by the verb, and in those formed from the aorist stem, in the completion of the action described by the verb.

10.2. A few of the most frequently used verbs have only three tenses: present, imperfect and future. Two of these verbs are the auxiliaries ἔχω (to have) and εἶμαι (to be):

PRESENT

Indicative		Subjunctive	
ἔχ-ω	εἶμαι	νὰ ἔχ-ω	νὰ εἶμαι
ἔχ-εις	εἶσαι	νὰ ἔχ-ης	etc.
ἔχ-ει	εἶναι	νὰ ἔχ-η	

---

* The *simple conditional* is formed by the particle θά plus the imperfect and the *perfect conditional* by θά plus the pluperfect.

ἔχ-ομε	εἴμαστε (εἴμεθα)	νὰ ἔχ-ωμε or ἔχουμε
ἔχ-ετε	εἶστε (εἶσθε)	νὰ ἔχ-ετε
ἔχ-ουν	εἶναι	νὰ ἔχ-ουν

The forms in parenthesis indicate the Puristic forms when they differ from those of the Demotic.

Note that the pronouns ἐγώ for *I*, αὐτός for *he*, etc. do not have to be expressed, because the endings themselves indicate the subject. Thus, by means of the ending -ω we know that ἔχω means *I have* and ἔχουν the ending of which is -ουν means *they have*.

Note also that there are two forms which express the so-called second person: a singular form in -εις and a plural form in -ετε. Concerning the use of these two forms, see 5.1.2.

The real present imperative of ἔχω (ἔχε *sing.*, ἔχετε *plur.*) is very seldom used. Instead of it, the subjunctive of both verbs may be used with the sense of the imperative: Νὰ εἶσθε ἕτοιμοι! Be ready!

IMPERFECT

εἶχ-α (εἶχ-ον) I had	ἤμουν (ἤμην) I was
εἶχ-ες	ἤσουν (ἦσο)
εἶχ-ε	ἦταν (ἦτο)
εἶχ-αμε (εἶχ-ομεν)	ἤμαστε (ἤμεθα)
εἶχ-ατε	ἤσαστε (ἦσθε)
εἶχ-αν (εἶχ-ον)	ἦταν (ἦσαν)

The forms in parenthesis indicate the puristic forms when they differ from those of the Demotic. However, some of the forms of the Puristic, especially the form ἦσαν, are used more frequently than others. There are in Demotic some additional forms for the imperfect of *to be*: ἤμουνα, ἤσουνα, ἦτανε, ἤμασταν or ἤμασθε, ἤσασταν or ἤσασθε, ἦτανε or ἦσανε. All those forms which are spelled by some writers with ει (εἴμουνα) are given only for the purpose of being recognized when encountered. Their use, nevertheless, is not recommended.

FUTURE

θὰ ἔχω I shall have	θὰ εἶμαι I shall be
θὰ ἔχης	θὰ εἶσαι
θὰ ἔχη	θὰ εἶναι
θὰ ἔχωμε or ἔχουμε	θὰ εἴμαστε
θὰ ἔχετε	θὰ εἶστε
θὰ ἔχουν	θὰ εἶναι

10.3. The best presentation of the verb can be done in a tabular form. The endings are separated from the stem of the tense by a hyphen.

There are two main categories of regular verbs in Greek: The un-contracted which are accented on the next to the last syllable and the contracted which are accented on the last syllable and take a circumflex (because of that, they are called περισπώμενα in Greek).

Concerning the formation of the aorist of a number of verbs — the stem of which ends in a certain way, here are a few rules:

1. Verbs ending in -αινω form the aorist in -ανα or in -ηνα (πεθαίνω [I die], πέθανα [I died]).

2. Verbs ending in -ωνω form the aorist in -ωσα (σκοτώνω [I kill], σκότωσα) and the passive aorist in -θηκα (σκοτώθηκα).

3. Verbs ending in -ιζω form the aorist in -ισα (φωτίζω [I light], φώτισα) and the passive aorist in -σθηκα (φωτίσθηκα).

4. Verbs ending in -αζω form the aorist in -αξα (φωνάζω [I shout], φώναξα).

5. Verbs the stem of which end in π, μπ, φ, β and ευ form the aorist in -ψα (in the Demotic) (κόβω [I cut], ἔκοψα; μαζεύω [I gather], μάζεψα*).

6. Verbs the stem of which end in θ, δ, σ form the aorist in -σα (πλάθω [I mold], ἔπλασα).

7. Verbs in the stem of which end in κ, γγ (γκ), χ, γ form the aorist in -ξα (τρέχω [I run], ἔτρεξα).

In Puristic the aorist of this verb is ἐμάζευσα.

Present - stem λυν-   Aorist - stem λυσ-

ACTIVE VOICE

Present - stem λυν-

Present	Indicative Imperfect	Durative Future	Subjunctive Present	Imperative Present
λύν-ω	ἔλυν-α	θὰ λύνω	νὰ λύν-ω	
λύν-εις	ἔλυν-ες	θὰ λύνῃς	νὰ λύν-ῃς	λύν-ε
λύν-ει	ἔλυν-ε	θὰ λύνῃ	νὰ λύν-ῃ	
λύν-ομε	(ἐ) λύν-αμε	θὰ λύνωμε	νὰ λύν-ωμε	
λύν-ετε	(ἐ) λύν-ατε	θὰ λύνετε	νὰ λύν-ετε	λύν-ετε
λύν-ουν	ἔλυν-αν	θὰ λύνουν	νὰ λύν-ουν	

Aorist - stem λυσ-

Aorist	Punctual Future	Aorist (Subjunctive)	Aorist (Imperative)
ἔλυσ-α	θὰ λύσω	νὰ λύσ-ω	
ἔλυσ-ες	θὰ λύσῃς	νὰ λύσ-ῃς	λῦσ-ε
ἔλυσ-ε	θὰ λύσῃ	νὰ λύσ-ῃ	
(ἐ) λύσ-αμε	θὰ λύσωμε	νὰ λύσ-ωμε	
(ἐ) λύσ-ατε	θὰ λύσετε	νὰ λύσ-ετε	λῦσ-(ε)τε
ἔλυσ-αν	θὰ λύσουν	νὰ λύσ-ουν	

Perfect	Pluperfect	Future Perfect	Perfect	Perfect
ἔχω λύσει	εἶχα λύσει	θὰ ἔχω λύσει	νὰ ἔχω λύσει	

Present - stem **λυν-**   Aorist - stem **λυ-θ-**

PASSIVE VOICE

Present	Indicative Imperfect	Durative Future	Subjunctive Present	Imperative Present
λύν-ομαι	λυν-όμουν	θα λύνωμαι	να λύνωμαι	
λύν-εσαι	λυν-όσουν	θα λύνεσαι	να λύνεσαι	
λύν-εται	λυν-όταν	θα λύνεται	να λύνεται	
λυν-όμαστε	λυν-όμασταν	θα λυνόμαστε	να λυνόμαστε	
λύν-εστε	λυν-όσαστε	θα λύνεστε	να λύνεστε	
λύν-ονται	λύν-ονταν	θα λύνωνται	να λύνωνται	

	Aorist	Punctual Future	Aorist	Aorist
	λύθηκα	θα λυθώ	να λυθώ	
	λύθηκες	θα λυθής	να λυθής	λύσου
	λύθηκε	θα λυθή	να λυθή	
	λυθήκαμε	θα λυθούμε	να.λυθούμε	
	λυθήκατε	θα λυθήτε	να λυθήτε	λυθήτε
	λύθηκαν	θα λυθούν	να λυθούν	

Perfect	Pluperfect	Future Perfect	Perfect	Perfect
έχω λυθή	είχα λυθή	θα έχω λυθή	να έχω λυθή	

ACTIVE VOICE

Present - stem ἀγαπ-   **Aorist - stem ἀγαπησ-**

Present stem

Indicative

Present:
ἀγαπ-ῶ
ἀγαπ-ᾶς
ἀγαπ-ᾷ
ἀγαπ-οῦμε
ἀγαπ-ᾶτε
ἀγαπ-οῦν

Imperfect:
ἀγαπ-οῦσα
ἀγαπ-οῦσες
ἀγαπ-οῦσε
ἀγαπ-ούσαμε
ἀγαπ-ούσατε
ἀγαπ-οῦσαν

Durative Future:
θὰ ἀγαπῶ
θὰ ἀγαπᾶς
θὰ ἀγαπᾷ
θὰ ἀγαποῦμε
θὰ ἀγαπᾶτε
θὰ ἀγαποῦν

Subjunctive Present:
νὰ ἀγαπῶ
νὰ ἀγαπᾶς
νὰ ἀγαπᾷ
νὰ ἀγαποῦμε
νὰ ἀγαπᾶτε
νὰ ἀγαποῦν

Imperative Present:
ἀγάπα
ἀγαπᾶτε

Aorist stem

Indicative

Aorist:
ἀγάπησ-α
ἀγάπησ-ες
ἀγάπησ-ε
ἀγαπήσ-αμε
ἀγαπήσ-ατε
ἀγάπησ-αν

Punctual Future:
θὰ ἀγαπήσω
θὰ ἀγαπήσῃς
θὰ ἀγαπήσῃ
θὰ ἀγαπήσωμε
θὰ ἀγαπήσετε
θὰ ἀγαπήσουν

Subjunctive Aorist:
νὰ ἀγαπήσω
νὰ ἀγαπήσῃς
νὰ ἀγαπήσῃ
νὰ ἀγαπήσωμε
νὰ ἀγαπήσετε
νὰ ἀγαπήσουν

Imperative Aorist:
ἀγάπησε
ἀγαπῆστε

Perfect:
ἔχω ἀγαπήσει

Pluperfect:
εἶχα ἀγαπήσει

Future Perfect:
θὰ ἔχω ἀγαπήσει

Perfect (Subjunctive):
νὰ ἔχω ἀγαπήσει

Present · stem **ἀγαπ-**   Aorist · stem **ἀγαπηθ-**

PASSIVE VOICE

Indicative Present	Imperfect	Durative Future	Subjunctive Present	Imperative
ἀγαπιέμαι	ἀγαπιόμουν	θὰ ἀγαπιέμαι	νὰ ἀγαπιέμαι	
ἀγαπιέσαι	ἀγαπιόσουν	θὰ ἀγαπιέσαι	νὰ ἀγαπιέσαι	
ἀγαπιέται	ἀγαπιόταν	θὰ ἀγαπιέται	νὰ ἀγαπιέται	
ἀγαπιούμαστε	ἀγαπιόμαστε	θὰ ἀγαπιούμαστε	νὰ ἀγαπιούμαστε	
ἀγαπιέστε	ἀγαπιόσαστε	θὰ ἀγαπιέστε	νὰ ἀγαπιέστε	
ἀγαπιοῦνται	ἀγαπιόνταν	θὰ ἀγαπιοῦνται	νὰ ἀγαπιοῦνται	

Aorist	Punctual Future	Aorist (Subjunctive)	Aorist (Imperative)
ἀγαπήθηκα	θὰ ἀγαπηθῶ	νὰ ἀγαπηθῶ	
ἀγαπήθηκες	θὰ ἀγαπηθῇς	νὰ ἀγαπηθῇς	
ἀγαπήθηκε	θὰ ἀγαπηθῇ	νὰ ἀγαπηθῇ	
ἀγαπηθήκαμε	θὰ ἀγαπηθοῦμε	νὰ ἀγαπηθοῦμε	
ἀγαπηθήκατε	θὰ ἀγαπηθῆτε	νὰ ἀγαπηθῆτε	
ἀγαπήθηκαν	θὰ ἀγαπηθοῦν	νὰ ἀγαπηθοῦν	

Perfect	Pluperfect	Future Perfect	Perfect	Perfect
Ἔχω ἀγαπηθῆ	εἶχα ἀγαπηθῆ	θὰ ἔχω ἀγαπηθῆ	νὰ ἔχω ἀγαπηθῆ	

	Present - stem λυ-	Aorist - stem λυσ-

ACTIVE VOICE (KATHAREVOUSA)

Present	Indicative Imperfect	Durative Future	Subjunctive Present	Imperative Present
λύ-ω	ἔλυ-ον	θὰ λύ-ω	νὰ λύ-ω	
λύ-εις	ἔλυ-ες	θὰ λύ-ῃς	νὰ λύ-ῃς	λύ-ε
λύ-ει	ἔλυ-ε	θὰ λύ-ῃ	νὰ λύ-ῃ	
λύ-ομεν	ἐλύ-ομεν	θὰ λύ-ωμεν	νὰ λύ-ωμεν	
λύ-ετε	ἐλύ-ετε	θὰ λύ-ητε	νὰ λύ-ητε	λύ-ετε
λύ-ουν	ἔλυ-ον	θὰ λύ-ουν	νὰ λύ-ουν	

	Aorist	Punctual Future	Aorist	Aorist
	ἔλυ-σ-α	θὰ λύ-σ-ω	νὰ λύ-σ-ω	
	ἔλυ-σ-ας	θὰ λύ-σ-ῃς	νὰ λύ-σ-ῃς	λύ-σ-ον
	ἔλυ-σ-ε	θὰ λύ-σ-ῃ	νὰ λύ-σ-ῃ	
	ἐλύ-σ-αμεν	θὰ λύ-σ-ωμεν	νὰ λύ-σ-ωμεν	
	ἐλύ-σ-ατε	θὰ λύ-σ-ητε	νὰ λύ-σ-ητε	λύ-σ-ατε
	ἔλυ-σ-αν	θὰ λύ-σ-ουν	νὰ λύ-σ-ουν	

Perfect	Pluperfect	Future Perfect	Perfect	
ἔχω λύσει	εἶχον λύσει	θὰ ἔχω λύσει	νὰ ἔχω λύσει	

PASSIVE VOICE (KATHAREVOUSA)

Present - stem λυ-   Aorist - stem λυ-θ-

Present	Indicative Imperfect	Durative Future	Subjunctive Present	Imperative Present
λύ-ομαι	ἐλυ-όμην	θὰ λύ-ωμαι	νὰ λύ-ωμαι	
λύ-εσαι	ἐλύ-εσο	θὰ λύ-ησαι	νὰ λύ-ησαι	λύ-ου
λύ-εται	ἐλύ-ετο	θὰ λύ-ηται	νὰ λύ-ηται	
λυ-όμεθα	ἐλυ-όμεθα	θὰ λυ-ώμεθα	νὰ λυ-ώμεθα	
λύ-εσθε	ἐλύ-εσθε	θὰ λύ-ησθε	νὰ λύ-ησθε	λύ-εσθε
λύ-ονται	ἐλύ-οντο	θὰ λύ-ωνται	νὰ λύ-ωνται	

	Aorist	Punctual Future	Aorist	Aorist
	ἐλύ-θην	θὰ λυ-θῶ	νὰ λυ-θῶ	
	ἐλύ-θης	θὰ λυ-θῇς	νὰ λυ-θῇς	λύ-θητι
	ἐλύ-θη	θὰ λυ-θῇ	νὰ λυ-θῇ	
	ἐλύ-θημεν	θὰ λυ-θῶμεν	νὰ λυ-θῶμεν	
	ἐλύ-θητε	θὰ λυ-θῆτε	νὰ λυ-θῆτε	λυ-θῆτε
	ἐλύ-θησαν	θὰ λυ-θοῦν	νὰ λυ-θοῦν	

Perfect	Pluperfect	Future Perfect	Perfect
ἔχω λυθῆ	εἶχον λυθῆ	θὰ ἔχω λυθῆ	νὰ ἔχω λυθῆ

LIST OF IRREGULAR VERBS

This list includes the most common verbs of spoken Demotic.

PRESENT	AORIST	PASSIVE AORIST	PAST PASSIVE PARTICIPLE
ἀνεβαίνω (I go up; climb)	ἀνέβηκα		ἀνεβασμένος
ἀρέσω (I am liked)	ἄρεσα		
αὐξάνω (I increase)	αὔξησα	αὐξήθηκα	αὐξημένος
ἀφήνω (I leave; let)	ἄφησα		ἀφημένος
βάζω (I put)	ἔβαλα	βάλθηκα	βαλμένος
βγάζω (I take out)	ἔβγαλα	(βγάλθηκα)	βγαλμένος
βγαίνω (I come out, I go out)	βγῆκα		βγαλμένος
βλέπω (I see)	εἶδα		
βρέχω (I wet)	ἔβρεξα	βράχηκα	βρε(γ)μένος
βρίσκω (I find)	βρῆκα	βρέθηκα	
γίνομαι (I become)	ἔγινα	γίνηκα	γινωμένος
γδέρνω (I flay, I skin)	ἔγδαρα	γδάρθηκα	γδαρμένος
γέρνω (I lean)	ἔγειρα		γερμένος
δέρνω (I beat)	ἔδειρα	δάρθηκα	δαρμένος
διαβαίνω (I pass [through])	διάβηκα		
διαμαρτύρομαι (I protest)		διαμαρτυρήθηκα	διαμαρτυρημ
διδάσκω (I teach)	δίδαξα	διδάχθηκα	διδαγμένος
δίνω or δίδω (I give)	ἔδωσα	δόθηκα	δο(σ)μένος
ἐγκατασταίνω (or ἐγκαθιστῶ) (I establish)	ἐγκατέστησα	ἐγκαταστάθηκα	ἐγκαταστημ
ἔρχομαι (I come)	ἦλθα		

εὑρίσκω (I find)	ηὗρα	εὑρέθην	
εὔχομαι (I wish)		εὐχήθηκα	
θέλω (I want)	θέλησα		
θέτω (I set)	ἔθεσα	ἐτέθην	-θεμένος
κάθομαι (I sit down)	κάθισα (or κάθησα)		καθισμένος
καίω (I burn)	ἔκαυσα (or ἔκαψα)	κάηκα	καμένος
κάνω (I do; make)	ἔκανα (or ἔκαμα)		καμωμένος
καταλαβαίνω (I understand)	κατάλαβα		
κατεβαίνω (I go down)	κατέβηκα		κατεβασμένος
κλαίω (I weep; cry)	ἔκλαυσα (or ἔκλαψα)	κλαύθηκα	κλαμένος
λαβαίνω (or λαμβάνω) (I take; receive)	ἔλαβα		
λέ(γ)ω (I say)	εἶπα		εἰπωμένος
μαθαίνω (or μανθάνω) (I learn)	ἔμαθα	(μαθεύτηκε)	μαθημένος
μένω (I stay)	ἔμεινα		
μπαίνω (I go in; get in)	μπῆκα		
ντρέπομαι (I am ashamed)		ντράπηκα	
παθαίνω (I suffer)	ἔπαθα		
πεθαίνω (I die)	πέθανα		πεθαμένος
πετυχαίνω (I succeed)	πέτυχα		πετυχημένος
πέφτω (I fall) (or πίπτω)	ἔπεσα		πεσμένος

πηγαίνω (I go) (or πάω)	(ἐ) πῆγα		
πίνω (I drink)	ἤπια		πιωμένος
πλέω (I wash)	ἔπλυνα	πλύθηκα	πλυμένος
σέβομαι (I respect)		σεβάσθηκα	
σέρνω (or σύρω) (I drag)	ἔσυρα	σύρθηκα	συρμένος
σπέρνω (I sow) (or σπείρω)	ἔσπειρα	σπάρθηκα	σπαρμένος
στέκομαι (I stand [up])		στάθηκα	
στέλνω (or στέλλω) (I send)	ἔστειλα	στάλθηκα	σταλμένος
στρέφω (I turn)	ἔστρεψα	στράφηκα	στραμμένος

σωπαίνω
   (or σιωπῶ)
(I keep silence)
	σώπασα
	   (or σιώπησα)		

τρώ(γ)ω (I eat)	ἔφαγα	φαγώθηκα	φαγωμένος
τυχαίνω (or τυγχάνω) (I chance)	ἔτυχα		(ἀπο-τυχημένος)
ὑπόσχομαι (I promise)		ὑποσχέθηκα	ὑποσχεμένος
φαίνομαι (I seem)		φάνηκα	
φεύγω (I flee, I run away)	ἔφυγα		
χαίρομαι (I am glad)		χάρηκα	
χορταίνω (I am satiated)	χόρτασα		χορτασμένος
ψέλνω (or ψάλλω) (I chant)	ἔψαλα	ψάλθηκα	ψαλμένος

GREEK-ENGLISH
DICTIONARY

A

ἀγάπη f. love

ἀγαπημένος, -η, -ο beloved, favorite

ἀγαπητός, -ή, -ό dear

ἀγαπῶ to love, to like, to be fond of

ἀγγελία f. announcement

ἄγγελος m. angel

ἀγγίζω to touch

ἀγελάδα f. cow

ἅγιος, -α, -ο holy, saint

ἀγκαλιάζω to embrace

ἀγκώνας m. elbow

ἄγνοια f. ignorance

ἀγνός, -ή, -ό pure

ἀγορά f. market, purchase

ἀγοράζω to buy, to purchase

ἀγόρι n. boy

ἀγώνας m. fight, struggle, contest

ἀδιάβροχο raincoat

ἄδεια f. permission, vacation

ἄδειος, -α, -ο empty

ἀδελφός m. brother

ἀδελφή f. sister

ἀδιάσπαστος, -η, -ο unbroken, unbreakable

ἄδικος, -η, -ο unjust, unfair

ἄδικο, ἔχω to be wrong

ἀδυναμία f. weakness

ἀδύνατος, -η, -ο weak, thin

ἀδύνατο, εἶναι it is impossible

ἀέρας m. air

ἀεροδρόμιο n. airfield, airport

ἀεροπλάνο n. airplane

ἀεροπόρος m. airman, pilot

ἀεροπορικῶς by air, via airmail

ἀηδία f. disgust

ἀθλητής m. sportsman, athlete

ἀθλητισμός m. sport

αἷμα n. blood

αἰσθάνομαι to feel

αἴσθημα n. feeling, emotion

αἴτηση* f. application, request

αἰτία f. cause, reason

αἰώνας m. century

αἰώνιος, -α, -ο eternal

In the Greek-English dictionary the following points should be noted: In the case of nouns, gender is always indicated by m. (masculine), f. (feminine) or n. (neuter). Nouns of the third declension in -ις, -εως, as πρᾶξις (act), πράξεως are given only in their Demotic form, as πράξη* (marked by an asterisk), unless the Puristic is the only one used. Adjectives, pronouns and participles are given in all three genders: καλός m., καλή f., καλό n. (good) as καλός, -ή, -ό. In the case of verbs, the first person singular of the present indicative is given in Greek. This is the basic verbal form since there is no infinitive as such in modern Greek. The corresponding English translation is given in the infinitive. In case of doublets, the first is either the Demotic form or the most frequently used spelling variant in contemporary books.

121

ἀκάθαρτος, -η, -ο dirty

ἀκούω to hear, to listen

ἀκολουθῶ to follow

ἀκόμη still

ἀκριβός, -ή, -ό expensive

ἀκριβῶς exactly

ἀκρογιαλιά f. beach, seaside

ἀλάτι (ἅλας) n. salt

ἀλατίζω to season

ἀλήθεια f. truth

ἀληθινός, -ή, -ό real, true

ἀλλά but

ἀλλαγή f. change

ἀλλάζω, ἀλλάσσω to change

ἀλληλογραφία
   f. correspondence

ἀλλιῶς otherwise

ἄλλος, -η, -ο other

ἀλμυρός, -ή, -ό salty

ἄλογο n. horse

ἀλοιφή f. ointment

'Αμερικανίδα f. American

'Αμερική f. America

'Αμερικανός m. American

ἄμεσος, -η, -ο immediate,
   direct

ἀμέσως immediately,
   at once, right away

ἄμμος m. sand

ἀμπέλι n. vineyard

ἄμυνα f. defense

ἀμφιβάλλω to doubt

ἀμφιβολία f. doubt

ἄν if

ἀναβάλλω to postpone

ἀναβολή f. postponement

ἀναγγέλλω to announce

ἀναγκαῖος, -α, -ο necessary

ἀνάγκη f. need

ἀναγνωρίζω to recognize

ἀνακαλύπτω to discover,
   to find out

ἀνακάλυψη* f. discovery

ἀνακατεύω to mix, to stir

ἀναλαμβάνω to assume

ἀνάμεσα between, among

ἀνάμνηση* f. remembrance,
   recollection

ἀναμφιβόλως undoubtedly

ἀναπαύομαι to rest

ἀνάπαυση* f. rest

ἀναπνέω to breathe

ἀναπτήρας m. lighter

ἀνάπτυξη* f. development,
   growth

ἀναπτύσσω, ἀναπτύσσομαι
   to develop, to grow

ἀναστατώνω to upset

ἀνατολή f. east, sunrise

ἀναχώρηση* f. departure

ἀναχωρῶ to depart, to leave

ἀναψυκτικά n. pl. refreshments

ἄνδρας m. man, husband

ἀνεβαίνω to go up, to ascend

ἄνεμος m. wind

ἀνεξαρτησία f. independence

ἄνεση* f. comfort

ἄνετος, -η, -ο comfortable

ἀνησυχία f. worry, anxiety

ἀνησυχῶ to worry, to disturb

ἀνθίζω to bloom

ἀνθισμένος, -η, -ο blooming

ἄνθος n. flower

ἀνθρώπινος, -η, -ο human

ἄνθρωπος m. man

ἀνθρωπότης f. humanity

ἀνθυγεινός, -ή, -ό unhealthy

ἀνίσχυρος, -η, -ο powerless

ἀνεψιός m. nephew

ἀνεψιά f. niece

ἀνοίγω to open

ἀνοικτός, -ή, -ό open

ἄνοιξη* spring

ἀνταμώνω to meet, to join

ἀντίγραφο n. copy

ἀντιγράφω to copy

ἀντίδραση* f. reaction

ἀντιδρῶ to react

ἀντίθεση* f. contrast,
  opposition

ἀντίθετος, -η, -ο contrary,
  opposed

ἀντικαθιστῶ to replace

ἀντικατάσταση* f. replacement

ἀντικείμενο n. object

ἀντιλαμβάνομαι to understand,
  to perceive

ἀντίληψη* f. conception,
  perception

ἀντιπρόσωπος m.' representative

ἀνώτερος, -η, -ο superior

ἀξία f. value

ἀξίζω to deserve,
  to be worthy

ἄξιος,-α, -ο worthy

ἀπαίτηση* f. demand

ἀπαιτῶ to demand

ἁπαλός, -ή, -ό soft, smooth

ἀπάντηση* f. answer

ἀπαντῶ to answer, to meet

ἀπαραίτητος, -η, -ο
  indispensable, necessary

ἀπασχολημένος, -η, -ο busy

ἀπάτη f. deceit

ἀπατῶ to deceive

ἀπεικονίζω to represent,
  to portray

ἀπειλή f. threat

ἀπειλῶ to threaten

ἀπελευθερώνω to liberate

ἀπελευθέρωση* f. liberation

ἀπέναντι opposite to

ἁπλός, -ή, -ό simple

ἁπλότης f. simplicity

ἁπλώνω to spread, to lay

ἀπό from

ἀπόγευμα n. afternoon

ἀποδεικνύω to prove

ἀπόδειξη* f. proof, receipt

ἀποθηκεύω to store

ἀποθήκη f. store-room

ἀποκατάσταση* recovery
  f. reestablishment,

ἀποκοιμοῦμαι to fall asleep

ἀπολαμβάνω to enjoy

ἀπόλαυση* f. enjoyment

ἀπόλυτα or ἀπολύτως
  absolutely

ἀποσκευές f. pl. baggage

ἀπόσταση* f. distance

ἀποτελοῦμαι to consist

ἀποτελῶ to constitute

ἀπουσία f. absence

ἀπουσιάζω to be absent

ἀπόφαση* f. decision, resolution

ἀποφασίζω to decide,
  to resolve

ἀπόψε tonight

ἄποψη* view

Ἀπρίλιος m. April

ἀργά late, slowly

ἀργός, -ή, -ό slow

ἀργότερα later

ἄρθρο n. article

ἀριθμός m. number

ἀριστερά to the left

ἀριστερός, -ή, -ό left
ἄριστος, -η, -ο excellent
ἀρκετά enough, sufficiently
ἀρκετός, -ή, -ό sufficient
ἄρνηση* f. refusal
ἀρνί n. sheep, lamb
ἀρνοῦμαι to refuse, to deny
ἁρπάζω to grab, to catch
ἄρρωστος, -η, -ο sick
ἀρρώστια f. sickness, disease
ἀρχαῖος, -α, -ο ancient
ἀρχή f. beginning
ἀρχηγός m. leader, chief
ἀρχίζω to begin, to start
ἀρχικός, -ή, -ό initial, original
ἄρωμα n. perfume, fragrance
ἀσήμι n. silver
ἀσημικά n. pl. silverware
ἀσθένεια f. illness, disease
ἀσθενής ill, weak
ἄσκηση* f. exercise, practice
ἀσπρόρουχα n. pl. linen,
ἀστακός m. lobster
ἀστειεύομαι to joke
ἀστεῖο n. joke
ἀστεῖος, -α, -ο funny
ἀστέρι (ἄστρο) n. star
ἀστραπή f. lightning
ἀστυνομία f. police
ἀστυνόμος m. police officer,
  sheriff
ἀστυνομικό τμῆμα n. police
  station
ἀσφάλεια f. security, insurance
ἀσφαλής, -ής, -ές secure
ἀσφαλισμένος, -η, -ο insured
ἀσφαλῶς surely
ἄσχημος, -η, -ο ugly, bad

ἀτμός m. steam
ἄτομο n. individual
αὐγή f. dawn
αὐγό n. egg
Αὔγουστος m. August
αὐξάνω to increase, to grow
αὔξηση* f. increase, growth
αὔριο tomorrow
αὐτί n. ear
αὐτός, -ή, -ό this
αὐτοκίνητο n. automobile, car
αὐτόματος, -η, -ο automatic
ἀφήνω to leave, to let
ἄφθονος, -η, -ο abundant,
  copious
ἀχθοφόρος m. porter
ἀχλάδι n. pear
ἄχρηστος, -η, -ο useless
ἄψητος, -η, -ο raw, uncooked

B

βαγόνι n. railroad car, wagon
βάζω to put, to put on
βάθος n. depth
βαθύς, -ιά, -ύ deep
βαθμός m. degree, grade
βαλίτσα f. suitcase
βαμπάκι n. cotton
βάρκα f. boat
βάρος n. weight
βαρύς, -ιά, -ύ heavy
βασίλειο n. kingdom
βασιλεύω to reign
βασιλεύς, βασιλιάς m. king
βασίλισσα f. queen
βαφή f. dye
βάφω to paint, to dye
βάψιμο n. painting, dyeing
βγάζω to take off

βέβαια, βεβαίως certainly, surely, of course
βέβαιος, -α, -ο certain, sure
βεβαιώνω to assure
βελόνα f. needle
βελόνι n. needle
βελοῦδο n. velvet
βελτιώνω to improve
βενζίνη f. gasoline
βήχας m. cough
βήχω to cough
βιάζομαι to hurry, to be in a hurry
βιάζω to force
βιαστικός, -ή, -ό in a hurry
βιβλίο n. book
βιβλιοθήκη f. book case, library
βιομηχανία f. industry
βλέπω to see
βόδι, βώδι n. ox
βοήθεια f. help, assistance
βοηθός m. helper, assistant
βοηθητικός, -ή, -ό auxiliary
βορράς (βοριάς) m. north (wind)
βοσκός m. shepherd
βουνό n. mountain
βούρτσα f. brush
βουρτσίζω to brush
βούτυρο n. butter
βραβείο n. prize, award
βράδυ n. evening
βραδυνός, -ή, -ό evening (adj.)
βράζω to boil
βραστός, -ή, -ό boiled
βράχος m. rock
βρεγμένος, -η, -ο wet
βρέχω to wet, to soak

βρέχει it rains
βρίσκομαι to be, to be located
βρίσκω to find
βροντή f. thunder
βροχή f. rain

Γ

γάιδαρος m. donkey, ass
γάλα n. milk
γαλανός, -ή, -ό blue, blond
γάμος m. marriage
γαμπρός m. bridegroom, son-in-law, brother-in-law
γάντι n. glove
γαρίφαλο, γαρύφαλλο n. carnation
γάτα f. cat
γεγονός n. event
γείτονας m. neighbor
γειτονιά f. neighborhood
γέλιο n. laughter
γελῶ to laugh
γεμάτος, -η, -ο full, filled
γεμίζω to fill
γενικά, γενικῶς generally
γενικός, -ή, -ό general
γενέθλια n. pl. birthday
γέννηση* f. birth
γεῦμα n. meal, midday meal
γεύομαι to taste
γεύση* f. taste
γέφυρα f. bridge
γεωργός m. farmer
γῆ f. earth
γιά for
γιαγιά f. grandmother
γιακάς m. collar
γιαλί n. glass
γιατί why, because, for

γιατρός m. physician, doctor
γίνομαι to become
γιός, γυιός m. son
γκαράζ n. garage
γκρεμίζω to demolish,
 to throw down
γκρί(ζος), (-α), (-ο) gray
γλιστρῶ to slip
γλύκισμα n. pastry, cake
γλυκό n. jam
γλυκός, -ιά, -ό sweet
γλῶσσα f. tongue
γνώμη f. opinion
γνωρίζω to know, to inform
γνώρισμα n. trait
γνώση* f. knowledge
γνώσεις f. pl. knowledge
γνωστός m. acquaintance
γνωστή f. acquaintance
γνωστός, -ή, -ό known
γόνατο n. knee
γονιός m. parent
γονεῖς m. pl. parents
γούνα f. fur
γραβάτα f. necktie
γραμματεύς m. secretary
γραμματόσημο n. stamp
γραμμή f. line
γραφεῖο n. desk, office
γράφω to write
γρήγορα quickly
γυμνάσιο n. high school
γυμναστήριο n. gymnasium
γυναίκα f. woman
γυρεύω to look for, to seek
γυρίζω to turn
γύρος, γῦρος m. tour, round,
 turn

γύρω round, around
γωνία, γωνιά f. corner, angle

Δ

δάγκαμα, δάγκωμα n. bite
δαγκάνω, δαγκώνω to bite
δάκρυ n. tear
δακυλογράφος m. f. typist
δακτυλογραφῶ to type
δάκτυλος m. finger
δανείζομαι to borrow
δανείζω to lend
δασκάλα f. teacher
δάσκαλος m. teacher
δαχτυλίδι n. ring
δάχτυλο n. finger, toe
δείκτης m. pointer, hand
 (watch)
δεῖπνο n. supper, dinner
δείχνω to show
δέκα ten
δέκατος, -η, -ο tenth
Δεκέμβριος m. December
δέμα n. package
δέντρο n. tree
δεξιός, -ά, -ό right
δένω to bind, to tie
δέρμα n. skin, leather
δεσποινίς f. miss, young lady
Δεσπότης m. Bishop
Δευτέρα f. Monday
δευτερόλεπτο n. second (time)
δεύτερος, -η, -ο second
δέχομαι to accept
δηλώνω to declare, to state
δήλωση* f. declaration,
 statement
δήμαρχος m. mayor
δημιούργημα n. creation

μιουργός m. creator
μιουργῶ to create
μοκρατία f. democracy, republic
αβάζω to read
αβαίνω to pass
αβατήριο n. passport
αβεβαίωνω to assure
αίρεση* f. division, separation
αιρῶ to divide, to separate
ακοπές f. pl. vacation
ακοπή f. interruption
ακόπτω to interrupt
ακόσια two hundred
ακρίνω to distinguish
άκριση* f. distinction, discrimination
αλέγω to choose, to select
άλεξη* f. lecture, talk
αλύω to dissolve
αμάντι n. diamond
αμαρτυρία f. protest
αμαρτύρομαι to protest
αμέρισμα n. apartment
αμονή f. residence, stay
χμορφώνω to form, to mold
άρκεια f. duration
αρκῶ to last
αρκῶς continually
ασκεδάζω to amuse (oneself), to have a good time
ασκέδαση* f. amusement, entertainment
ασκεδαστικός, -ή, -ό amusing, entertaining
ασχίζω to cut through, to tear
χταγή f. order
χτάζω to order

διατηρῶ to maintain, to preserve
διαφέρω to differ
διαφορά f. difference
διαφορετικός, -ή, -ό different
διαλέγω to pick up, to select
διδάσκω to teach
διαλέγομαι to converse
δίδυμος, -η, -ο twin
διεθνής, -ής, -ές international
διεύθυνση* f. address, management
διευθυντής, -τρια director, manager, principal
διευθύνω to direct, to manage
διήγημα n. short story
δικαιολογία f. excuse, justification
δικαιολογημένος, -η, -ο justified, excused
δικαιολογῶ to justify, to excuse
δίκαιος, -η, -ο just, fair
δικαιοσύνη f. justice
δικαστής m. judge
δίκη f. trial, lawsuit
δίκαιο, έχω to be right
δίνω to give
διοίκηση* f. administration
διότι because
δίπλα beside, near by
διπλός, -ή, -ό double
δίπλωμα n. diploma
διπλώνω to fold
δίσκος m. tray, record, disk
διστάζω to hesitate
δισταγμός m. hesitation
διστακτικός, -ή, -ό hesitating

δοκιμάζω to try, to test
δοκιμή f. trial, test
δολλάριο n. dollar
δόντι n. tooth
δόξα f. glory
δοξάζω to glorify
δουλεύω to work
δοῦλος m. slave
δράμα n. drama, play
δραματικός, -ή, -ό dramatic
δραστήριος, -α, -ο active,
  efficient
δρομολόγιο n. itinerary
δρόμος m. street, road
δροσερός, -ή, -ό cool
δροσιά f. coolness
δροσιστικός, -ή, -ό refreshing
δύναμη* f. strength, power,
  might
δυναμικός, -ή, -ό dynamic
δυνατόν, εἶναι it is possible
δυνατός, -ή, -ό strong, mighty
δύο two
δυσάρεστος, -η, -ο unpleasant
δύση* f. west, sunset
δυσκολία f difficulty, hardship
δύσκολος, -η, -ο difficult, hard
δυστύχημα n. accident
δυστυχής, -ής, -ές unfortunate
δυστυχία f. misfortune
δυστυχῶς unfortunately
δώδεκα twelve
δωδέκατος, -η, -ο twelfth
δωμάτιο n. room
δωρίζω to offer a present
δῶρο n. present, gift

E

ἑβδομάδα f. week

ἑβδομήντα seventy
ἕβδομος, -η, -ο seventh
Ἑβραῖος, -α Jew, Hebrew
ἐγγονός m. grandson
ἐγγονή f. granddaughter
ἐγγράφω to register, to enroll
ἐγκατάσταση* f. establishment
  installation
ἐγκρίνω to approve
ἔγκριση* f. approval
ἐγώ I
ἐδῶ here
ἐθνικός, -ή, -ό national
ἐθνικότης f. nationality
ἔθνος n. nation
εἰδικός, -ή, -ό special, specific
εἰδοποίηση* f. notice, advice
εἰδοποιῶ to notify, to inform
εἶδος n. kind, soft
εἰλικρινά sincerely
εἰλικρίνεια f. sincerity
εἰλικρινής, -ής, -ές sincere
εἰκόνα f. picture, icon
εἴκοσι twenty
εἰκοστός, -ή, -ό twentieth
εἰρήνη f. peace
εἰρωνεύομαι to speak ironically
εἰρωνία f. irony
εἰσάγω to import, to introduce
εἰσαγωγή f. import,
  introduction
εἰσιτήριο n. ticket
εἰσόδημα n. revenue, income
εἴσοδος f. entrance, entry
ἑκατό one hundred
ἑκατό, τοῖς per cent
ἑκατοστός, -ή, -ό hundredth
ἑκατομύριο n. million

εκδήλωση* f. manifestation, expression

έκδοση* publication, edition, issue

εκδρομή picnic, excursion

εκεί there

εκείνος, -η, -ο that

έκθεση* f. exhibition, display composition

εκκλησία f. church

εκλέγω to elect, to choose

εκλογή f. election

έκπληξη* f. surprise

εκπλήττω to surprise

έκταση* area

εκτίμηση* f appreciation, esteem

εκτιμώ to appreciate, to estimate

έκτος, -η, -ο sixth

εκφράζω to express

έκφραση* f. expression

ελατήριο n. spring, motive

ελαφρός, -ή, -ό light

Ελβετία f. Switzerland

ελέγχω to control, to check up

ελιά f. olive

ελκυστικός, -ή, -ό attractive

ελκύω to attract

Ελλάδα, Ελλάς f. Greece

Έλληνας m. Greek

Ελληνίδα f. Greek

ελληνικός, -ή, -ό Greek

ελληνολάτρης admirer (lit., worshiper) of Greece

ελπίδα f. hope

ελπίζω to hope

εμείς we

έμμεσος, -η, -ο indirect

εμπειρία f. experience

εμπιστεύομαι to trust

εμπνέω to inspire

εμποδίζω to prevent, to hinder

εμπόδιο n. obstacle

εμπόρευμα n. merchandise

εμπορικός, -ή, -ό commercial

εμπόριο n. commerce, trade

έμπορος n. merchant, trader

εμφανίζομαι to appear

εμφανίζω to present

εμφάνιση* f. appearance

ένας m. one   μία f. one

ένα n. one

ένδεκα eleven

ενδιαφέρον n. interest

ενδιαφέρων, -ουσα, -ον interesting

ενενήντα ninety

ενέργεια f. action, energy

ενεργητικός, -ή, -ό active

ενεργώ to act

ενθαρρύνω to encourage

ενθουσιάζομαι to become enthusiastic

ενθουσιάζω to inspire enthusiasm

ενθουσιασμός n. enthusiasm

ενθουσιώδης, -ης, -ες enthusiastic

ενθύμιο n. souvenir

έννατος, -η, -ο ninth

εννέα nine

έννοια f. meaning

εννοώ ·to mean, to understand

ενοικιάζω to rent

ενοίκιο n. rent

ενότης f. unity

ἐνόχληση* f. annoyance,
nuisance
ἐνοχλητικός, -ή, -ό annoying,
troublesome
ἐνοχλῶ to annoy, to bother
ἔνοχος m. f. guilty
ἔνστικτο n. instinct
ἐν τάξει all right, O.K.
ἔνταση* f. intensity, tension
ἔντομο n. insect
ἐντύπωση* f. impression
ἐνῶ while, whereas
ἐνωμένος, -η, -ο united
ἐνώνω to unite, to join
ἕνωση* f. union, junction
ἐξάγω to export, to extract
ἐξαγωγή f. export, exportation
extraction
ἐξάδελφος, -η m., f. cousin
ἐξαίρεση* f. exception
ἐξαιρετικός, -ή, -ό exceptional.
excellent
ἐξαιρῶ to except, to exempt
ἐξακολουθῶ to continue
ἐξακόσια six hundred
ἐξαπατῶ to cheat, to deceive
ἐξαργυρώνω to cash
ἐξαρτῶμαι to depend on
ἐξασφαλίζω to secure
ἐξαφανίζομαι to disappear,
to vanish
ἐξαφάνιση* f. disappearence
ἐξέλιξη* f. evolution,
development
ἐξετάζω to examine
ἐξέταση* f. examination
ἐξήγηση* f. explanation
ἐξηγῶ to explain

ἐξήντα sixty
ἕξι six
ἔξοδα n. pl. expenses
ἔξοδος f. exit
ἐξοικειώνομαι to become
familiar
ἐξομολόγηση* f. confession
ἐξουσία f. authority, power
ἐξοχή country
ἐξοχικός, -ή, -ό rural, country
ἐξυπνάδα f. cleverness
ἔξυπνος, -η, -ο clever, intelligent,
smart
ἔξω out
ἐξωτερικό, στό abroad
ἐξωτερικός, -ή, -ό external
ἐορτάζω to celebrate
ἐορτασμός m. celebration
ἐορτή f. holiday, feast, festival
ἐπάγγελμα n. profession
ἐπαγγελματικός, -ή, -ό
professional
ἐπαναλαμβάνω to repeat
ἐπανάληψη* f. repetition
ἐπάνω up
ἔπειτα then, afterwards
ἐπηρεασμένος, -η, -ο influenced
ἐπιβιβάζομαι to embark
ἐπιγραφή f. inscription, sign
ἐπιδιορθώνω to repair, to mend
ἐπιδιόρθωση* f. repair
ἐπιδόρπιο n. dessert
ἐπίδραση* f. wish, desire
ἐπιζῶ to survive
ἐπιθυμία f. wish, desire
ἐπιθυμῶ to wish, to desire
ἐπικίνδυνος, -η, -ο dangerous
ἐπιμένω to insist, to persist

επιμονή f. persistence,
perseverence

έπιπλο n. piece of furniture

επιπλωμένος, -η, -ο furnished

επιπλώνω to furnish

επίπλωση* f. furniture

επίσημος, -η, -ο official

επίσης too, also

επισκέπτης, -τρια m., f. visitor

επισκέπτομαι to visit

επίσκεψη* f. visit, call

Επίσκοπος m. Bishop

επιστήμη f. science

επιστημονικός, -ή, -ό scientific

επιστήμων m. scientist

επιστρέφω to return, to come
back

επιστροφή f. return

επιταγή f. check, money order

επιτρέπω to allow, to permit,
to let

επιτροπή f committee

επιτυγχάνω to succeed

επιτυχία f. success

επιφύλαξη* f. reservation

επιχείρημα n. argument

επιχείρηση* f. business,
enterprise

επιχειρηματίας m. businessman

επιχειρώ to attempt

επιχρυσώνω to gild

επόμενος, -η, -ο next

επομένως therefore

εποχή f. season, epoch

επτά seven

εργάζομαι to work

εργαλείο n. tool

εργασία f. work, job

εργαστήριο n. laboratory,
workshop

εργάτης, -τρια m.f. worker

έργο n. work

έργο, θεατρικό n. play

εργοστάσιο n. factory

ερείπιο n. ruin

έρχομαι to come

ερώτηση* f. question

ερωτώ to ask

εσείς you. εσύ you sg., thou

εστιατόριο n. restaurant

εσώρρουχα n. pl. underwear

εσωτερικός, -ή, -ό interior,
internal, inner

εταιρία, εταιρεία f. company,
association, society

ετοιμάζομαι to prepare

έτοιμος, -η, -ο ready

έτσι so, thus

Ευαγγέλιο n. Gospel

ευγένεια f. politeness, courtesy

ευγενής, -ής, -ές polite, noble

ευγενικός, -ή, -ό polite, courteous

ευγνωμοσύνη f. gratitude

ευγνώμων m. f. grateful

ευεξήγητος, -η, -ο easily
explainable

εύθυμος, -η, -ο gay

ευθύνη f. responsibility

ευθύς, -εία, -ύ straight

ευκαιρία f. opportunity

ευκολία f. facility, ease

εύκολος, -η, -ο easy

ευτυχής, -ής, -ές happy

ευτυχία f. happiness

ευτυχώς fortunately

εὐχαριστημένος, -η, -ο pleased,
  satisfied
εὐχαρίστηση* f. pleasure
εὐχάριστος pleasant
εὐχαριστῶ to thank, thank you
εὐχαρίστως with pleasure
εὐωδιάζω to be fragrant
ἐφημερίδα f. newspaper
ἐφ᾽ ὅσον since
ἐχθρικός, -ή, -ό hostile
ἐχθρός m. enemy
ἔχω to have
ἕως till, as far as

Z

ζάλη f. dizziness
ζαλίζομαι to be dizzy
ζαλισμένος, -η, -ο dizzy
ζάχαρη f. sugar
ζαχαροπλαστεῖο n. pastry shop,
  confectionery
ζεσταίνω to warm, to heat
ζέστη f. heat
ζεστός, -ή, -ό warm, hot
ζευγάρι n. pair
ζεῦγος n. couple
ζηλεύω to be jealous of
ζήλια f. jealousy
ζηλιάρης, -α jealous
ζημία f. damage, loss
ζητῶ to ask for, to demand,
  to beg
ζυγαριά f. pair of scales
ζυγίζω to weigh
ζύμη f. dough
ζυμώνω to knead
ζῶ to live
ζωγραφική f. painting
ζωγράφος m. painter

ζωή f. life
ζωηρός, -ή, -ό lively
ζωηρότης f. liveliness
ζώνη f. belt
ζωντανός, -ή, -ό alive
ζῶο n. animal
ζωολογικός κῆπος m. zoo

H

ἤ or
ἠθικός, -ή, -ό moral
ἠλεκτρικός, -ή, -ό electric
ἠλεκτρισμός m. electricity
ἠλίθιος, -α, -ο stupid
ἡλικία f. age
ἡλικιωμένος, -η, -ο aged, old
ἥλιος m. sun
ἡμέρα f. day
ἡμερολόγιο n. calendar
ἡμερομηνία f. date
ἡμερομίσθιο n. day's wages
ἥμερος, -η, -ο tame
ἡμισφαίριο n. hemisphere
Ἡνωμέναι Πολιτεῖαι United
  States
ἤπειρος f. continent
ἠρεμία f. quiet
ἤρεμος, -η, -ο quiet
ἡρωϊκός, -ή, -ό heroic
ἡρωΐδα, ἡρωΐς f. heroine
ἡρωισμός m. heroism
ἥρωας, ἥρως m. hero
ἡσυχάζω to rest
ἡσυχία f. quietness, tranquillity
ἥσυχος, -η, -ο quiet, tranquil
ἥττα f. defeat
ἡφαίστειο n. volcano
ἦχος m. sound

Θ

αλαμηγός f. yacht
άλασσα f. sea
άνατος m. death
άρρος n. courage
αῦμα n. miracle, wonder
αυμάζω to admire
αυμάσιος, -α, -ο wonderful,
  marvelous
αυμασμός m. admiration
αυμαστής, -τρια m. f. admirer,
  fan
εατής m. spectator
εατρικός, -ή, -ό theatrical
έατρο n. theater
είος m. uncle
εία f. aunt
έλγητρο n. charm
έλημα n. will, errand
έληση* f. will
έλω to want
έμα n. subject, topic
εός m. God
εραπεία f. cure, treatment
εραπεύω to cure, to treat
εριεύω to infuriate
ερίζω to reap
ερμόμετρο n. thermometer
έση* f. place, position
εσμός m. institution
ετικός, -ή, -ό positive
έτω to place, to set
εωρία f. theory
εωρῶ to consider
ηλυκός, -ή, -ό feminine, female
ηρίο n. wild animal, beast
ησαυρός m. treasure
λίψη* f. grief

θολός, -ή, -ό muddy, dim
θόρυβος m. noise
θρανίο n. school desk
θράσος n. insolence, audacity
θρεπτικός, -ή, -ό nourishing
θρησκεία f. religion
θρησκευτικός, -ή, -ό religious
θριαμβευτικός, -ή, -ό triumphant
θρίαμβος m. triumph
θύελλα f. storm
θυμίζω to remind
θυμοῦμαι to remember
θυμός m. anger
θυμώνω to be angry
θυρίδα f. ticket window
θυσία f. sacrifice
θυσιάζω to sacrifice

I

'Ιανουάριος m. January
ιατρεῖο n. clinic
ιατρός m. physician, doctor
ιδανικό n. ideal
ιδέα f. idea
ιδεολογία f. ideology
ιδεώδης, -ης, -ες ideal
ιδιαίτερος, -η, -ο private, special
ιδιαιτέρως privately, especially
ιδιοκτησία f. property
ιδιοκτήτης, -τρια owner
ίδιος, -α, -ο same
ιδιοσυγκρασία f. temperament
ιδιότροπος, -η, -ο capricious, odd
ιδιωτικός, -ή, -ό private
ίδρυμα n. institution,
  establishment
ιεραπόστολος m. missionary
ιερέας (-εύς) m. priest
ιέρεια f. priestess

ιερός, -ή, -ό sacred, holy

ικανοποιημένος, -η, -ό satisfied

ικανοποιώ to satisfy

Ιούλιος m. July

Ιούνιος m. June

Ιρλανδία f. Ireland

Ιρλανδός, -ίδα Irish

ίσιος, -α, -ο straight

ίσκιος m. shadow

ίσος, -η, -ο equal

ιστορία f. history

ιστορικός, -ή, -ό historical

ισχυρός, -ή, -ό powerful

ίσως perhaps

ίχνος n. trace, track, footprint

Κ

καθαρίζω to clean

καθαριότης f. cleanliness

καθαρός, -ή, -ό clean

κάθε every, each

καθένας, καθεμία, καθένα everyone

καθεδρικός ναός m. cathedral

καθεστώς n. regime

καθηγητής, -τρια professor

καθήκον n. duty, task

καθημερινός, -ή -ό daily

κάθισμα n. seat

κάθομαι to sit

καθορίζω to define, to determine

καθρέπτης, καθρέφτης m. mirror

καθυστέρηση* f. delay

καθώς as

καί and

καινούργιος, -α, -ο new

καίω to burn

κακός, -ή, -ό bad, mean

καλά well

καλάθι n. basket

καλλιεργώ to cultivate

καλλιτέχνης m. artist

καλλιτεχνικός, -ή, -ό artistic

καλόγηρος m. monk

καλόγρια f. nun

καλοκαίρι summer

καλός, -ή, -ό good, kind

κάλτσα f. sock, stocking

καλύπτω to cover

καλώ to call

καλωσύνη f. kindness

καμαρώνω to be proud of, to take pride in

καμήλα f. camel

καμπάνα f. bell

κάμπος m. plain

Καναδάς m. Canada

καναπές m. sofa

κανείς (κανένας), καμ(μ)ία, κανένα nobody, nothing

κανόνας m. rule

κανονίζω to settle, to regulate

κάνω to make, to do

καπέλ(λ)ο m. hat

καπετάνιος m. captain

καπνίζω to smoke

καπνός m. smoke

κάποιος, -α, -ο someone

κάπου somewhere

κάπως somewhat

καράβι n. boat, sailboat

κάρβουνο n. coal

καρδιά f. heart

καρέκλα f. chair

καρπός m. fruit, wrist

κάρτα f. card

καρύδι n. walnut

καρφί n. nail

καρφώνω to nail
καστανο n. chestnut
καστανός, -ή, -ό brown
καταγγέλω to sue, to denounce
κατάγομαι to be from
καταγωγή f. origin, descent
καταδικάζω to condemn
καταδίκη f. condemnation
καταθέτω to deposit
κατακρίνω to criticize,
  to condemn
καταλαβαίνω to undertsand
καταλαμβάνω to conquer,
  to occupy
κατάλληλος, -η, -ο proper, fit
κατάλογος m. list
κατανόηση* f. understanding
κατάσταση* f. situation
κατάστημα n. store, shop
καταφύγιο n. shelter
κατεβαίνω to go down,
  to descend
κατεύθυνση* f. direction
κατέχω to possess
κατηγορώ to accuse
κατήχηση* f. catechism
κάτι something
κατοχή f. occupation
κάτοικος m. inhabitant, resident
κατόρθωμα n. achievement
κατορθώνω to achieve
κατσίκα f. goat
κάτω down
καφές m. coffee
καφενείο n. coffee house
κάψιμο n. burning
καψούλι n. capsule
κέντημα n. embroidery

κεντρικός, -ή, -ό central
κέντρο n. center
κεραμίδι n. roof tile
κεράσι n. cherry
κεραυνός m. thunderbolt
κερδίζω to win, to earn
κέρδος n. profit, benefit
κερί n. candle, wax
κεφάλαιο n. capital
κεφάλι n. head
κήπος m. garden
κηπουρός m. gardener
κιλό n. kilogram
κινδυνεύω to be in danger
κίνδυνος m. danger
κινηματογράφος m. movies,
  movie theater
κίνηση* f. movement, motion
κινώ to move
κιόλας already
κίτρινος, -η, -ο yellow
κλαδί n. branch
κλαίω to cry, to weep
κλάμμα n. crying, weeping
κλασσικός, -ή, -ό classical
κλέβω to steal
κλειδαριά f. lock
κλειδί n. key
κλειδώνω to lock
κλείνω to close, to shut
κλειστός, -ή, -ό closed, shut
κλέφτης m. thief
κληρικός m. clergyman
κληρονομιά f. inheritance,
  heritage
κληρονόμος m. heir
κλῆρος m. clergy
κλίμα n. climate

κλουβί n. cage
κλωστή f. thread
κόβω to cut
κοιλάδα f. valley
κοιμοῦμαι to sleep
κοινός, -ή, -ό common
κοινόν, τὸ the public
κοινότης f. community
κοινωνία f. society
κοινωνικός, -ή, -ό social
κοιτάζω to look at
κόκκαλο n. bone
κόκκινος, -η, -ο red
κολακεύω to flatter
κόλλα f. glue; sheet of paper; starch
κολλῶ to stick, to attach
κολοκύθι n. pumpkin, squash
κόλπος m. gulf, bay
κολύμπι n. swimming
κολυμπῶ to swim
κόμμα n. party (political); comma
κομμάτι n. piece
κομψός, -ή, -ό elegant
κοντά near
κοντός, -ή, -ό short
κόπος m. pain, fatigue
κορδέλ(λ)α f. ribbon
κορδόνι n. shoelace
κόρη f. daughter; pupil (eye)
κορίτσι n. girl
κορμός m. trunk
κορυφή f. top, summit, peak
κόσμημα n. jewel
κόσμος m. world
κοστίζω to cost
κοστούμι n. suit

κοτόπουλο n. chicken
κουβάρι n. ball (of thread)
κουβέρτα f. blanket
κουδούνι n. bell, doorbell
κουζίνα f. kitchen
κουμπί n. button
κουμπώνω to button
κουνέλι n. rabbit
κουνιάδος, -α m. brother-in-law
    f. sister-in-law
κουνούπι n. mosquito
κουνῶ to shake, to rock, to move
κούπα f. cup
κουπί n. oar
κουράζω to tire
κουρασμένος, -η, -ο tired
κουρδίζω to wind, to tune
κουρέας m. barber, hairdresser
κουτάλι n. spoon
κουτί n. box
κουφός, -ή, -ό deaf
κρασί n. wine
κράτος n. state
κρατῶ to hold, to keep
κρέας n. meat
κρεβάτι n. bed
κρεβατοκάμαρα f. bedroom
κρέμα f. cream
κρεμῶ to hang
κρεμ(μ)ύδι n. onion
κρεοπώλης m. butcher
κριθάρι n. barley
κρίνω to judge
κρίση* f. judgment, crisis
κρίσιμος, -η, -ο critical
κριτήριο n. criterion
κριτικός m. critic
κρύβω to hide

ιύο n. cold	λαός m. people
ιύος, -α, -ο cold	λάσπη f. mud
ιυφός, -ή, -ό secret	λάστιχο n. rubber, tire (car)
ιυφά secretly	λατρεία f. worship
ιύωμα n. cold (sickness)	λατρεύω to worship
ιυώνω to feel cold	λαχανικά n. pl. vegetables
ιτήμα f. property	λέγω to say, to tell
ιτίζω to build	λειτουργία f. function, liturgy
ιτίριο n. building	λεκάνη f. bowl, basin
ιυπῶ to hit, to beat, to strike	λεμόνι n. lemon
ιυβέρνηση* f. government	λέξη* f. word
ιβερνητικός, -ή, -ό governmental	λεξικό n. dictionary
ιυβερνήτης m. governor	λεξιλόγιο n. vocabulary
ιβερνῶ to govern, to rule	λεοντάρι n. lion
ικλος m. circle	λέπι n. scale
ικλοφορία f. circulation	λεπίδα f. blade
ιλῶ to roll	λεπτό n. minute
ιμα, κῦμα n. wave	λεπτός, -ή, -ό fine, thin, slender
ιματίζω to wave	λεπτομέρεια f. detail
ινήγι n. hunting	λεπτότης f. delicacy, thinness, refinement
ινηγός m. hunter	λερώνω to dirty, to soil
ινηγῶ to hunt	λέσχη f. club
ιρία f. lady, Mrs., madam	λευκός, -ή, -ό white
ιριακή f. Sunday	λεωφορεῖο n. bus
ίριος m. gentleman, Mr.	λεωφόρος f. avenue, boulevard
ιρίως mainly, especially	ληστής m. robber, highwayman
ιμικός, -ή, -ό funny, comic	λιανικῶς at retail
ιμωδία f. comedy	λιβάδι n. meadow

Λ

ίδι n. oil	λίγος, -η, -ο little
ίθος n. mistake, error	λιγώτερος, -η, -ο less
ίίμαργος, -η, -ο greedy	λιμάνι n. harbor, port
ιιμός m. throat, neck	λίμνη f. lake
ιμβάνω to receive, to take	λινό n. linen
ιμπάδα f. torch, big candle	λίπασμα n. fertilizer
ιμπρός, -ή -ό bright, brilliant	λιποθυμῶ to faint
ιμπτήρας m. bulb, lamp	λίπος n. fat, grease
ίμπω to shine	λογαριασμός m. account, bill

λογική f. logic, reason
λογικός, -ή, -ό reasonable, sensible, logical
λόγος m. speech, word
λογοτέχνης m. writer
λογοτεχνία f. literature
λοιπόν therefore, then, well
λουλούδι n. flower
λού(ζ)ομαι to bathe
λουτρό n. bath
λόφος m. hill
λυγίζω to bend
λύκος m. wolf
λύ(ν)ω to solve, to untie
λύπη f. sorrow, grief
λυπημένος, -η, -ο sad, grieved
λυποῦμαι to be sorry
λύση* f. solution

M

μά but
μαγαζί n. shop
μαγειρεύω to cook
μαγευτικός, -ή, -ό enchanting
μαγικός, -ή, -ό magic
μαγνήτης m. magnet
μαζεύω to gather, to pick
μαζί together, with
μαθαίνω to learn
μάθημα n. lesson
μαθηματικά n. pl. mathematics
μαθητής, -τρια pupil, student
Μάϊος m. May
μακαρίτης deceased, late
μακρινός, -ή, -ό distant
μάκρος n. length
μακρυά far
μακρύς, -ιά, -ύ long
μαλακός, -ή, -ό soft

μαλακώνω to soften, to get milder
μάλιστα yes, especially, even
μαλλί n. wool
μαλλιά n. pl. hair
μᾶλλον rather
μαμά f. mama
μανία f. mania
μανικέτι n. cuff
μανίκι n. sleeve
μαντεύω to guess
μαντήλι n. handkerchief
μαξιλάρι n. pillow
μαραίνομαι to fade, to wither
μαργαρίτα f. daisy
μάρμαρο n. marble
μαρούλι n. lettuce
Μάρτιος m. March
μας our
μᾶς us
μασῶ to chew
μάταια vainly, in vain
μάτι n. eye
ματιά f. glance, look
ματογιάλια n. pl. eyeglasses
μαῦρος, -η, -ο black
μαχαίρι n. knife
μάχη f. battle
μέ with; με me
μεγαλεῖο n. grandeur
μεγαλοπρέπεια f. magnificence
μεγάλος, -η, -ο great, big, large
μεγαλύτερος, -η, -ο greater, bigger
μεγαλώνω to grow, to grow up
μέγεθος n. size
μεθαύριο n. day after tomorrow

μέθοδος f. method

 μελάνη f. ink

μελέτη f. study

μελετῶ to study

μέλι n. honey

μέλισσα f. bee

μέλλον n. future

μελλοντικός, -ή, -ό future

μέλος n. member

μελωδία f. melody

μένω to stay

μερικοί, -ές some

μέρος n. part, place, side

μέσα inside

μεσαῖος, -α, -ο middle

μεσαιωνικός, -ή, -ό medieval

μεσάνυχτα n. pl. midnight

μέση f. middle, waist

μεσημέρι n. noon

μέσο n. means

μετά after, with

μεταβάλλω to change, to transform

μεταβολή change, transformation

μετακομίζω to move

μέταλλο n. metal

μετανάστης m. emigrate, immigrate

μετανοῶ to repent, to change one's mind

μετάξι n. silk

μεταξύ between, among

μεταξωτός, -ή, -ό silk

μεταφέρω to transport

μεταφράζω to translate

μετάφραση* f. translation

μεταχειρίζομαι to use, to treat

μετοχή f. share, participle

μέτοχος m. stockholder, participant

μέτρημα n. measuring

μετρητοῖς, τοῖς cash

μέτριος, -α, -ο medium, moderate, average

μετριοφροσύνη f. modesty

μέτρο n. meter, measure

μετρῶ to measure, to count

μή don't

μηδέν n. zero

μῆλο n. apple

μῆκος n. length

μήνας m. month

μήπως lest, perhaps, if

μητέρα f. mother

μητρόπολη* f. metropolis, cathedral

μηχανή f. engine, machine

μηχάνημα n. machine

μηχανικός m. engineer, mechanic

μῖγμα n. mixture

μικρόβιο n. germ, microbe

μικρός, -ή, -ό small, little

μικρότερος, -η, -ο smaller, younger

μικροσκόπιο n. microscope

μικτός, -ή, -ό mixed

μίλι n. mile

μιλῶ to speak, to talk

μιμοῦμαι to imitate, to mimic

μισός, -ή, -ό half

μῖσος n. hatred

μισῶ to hate

μνῆμα n. grave, monument

μνημεῖο n. monument

μόδα f. fashion

μοιάζω to resemble, to look like

μοιράζομαι to share

μοιράζω to distribute, to divide
μόλις just, as soon as, scarcely, hardly
μολύβι n. pencil
μοναδικός, -ή, -ό unique
μοναχός, -ή, -ό alone
μόνο only
μόνος, -η, -ο alone, single
μορφή f. form, face, figure
μορφώνω to educate, to form
μόρφωση* f. education
μοσχάρι n. calf, veal
μου my, μοῦ me
μουσεῖο n. museum
μουσική f. music
μουσικός m. musician
μουστάκι n. mustache
μπαίνω to enter, to go in
μπαλκόνι n. balcony
μπάνιο n. bath, swimming
μπαοῦλο n. trunk
μπιφτέκι n. steak
μπουκάλι n. bottle
μπλούζα f. blouse
μπορῶ can, may, to be able
μπράτσο n. arm
μπροστά before, in front of
μυαλό n. brain
μυθιστόρημα n. novel
μύθος, μῦθος m. legend, fable
μύγα, μυῖγα f. fly
μύλος m. mill
μυρίζω to smell
μυρμήγκι n. ant
μυρωδιά f. smell
μῦς m. muscle; mouse
μυστήριο n. mystery; sacrament
μυστηριώδης, -ης, -ες mysterious

μυστικός, -ή, -ό secret
μυτερός, -ή, -ό pointed, sharp
μωρό n. baby
μωσαϊκό n. mosaic

N

ναί yes
ναός m. temple, church
ναῦλο n. freight, fare
ναύτης m. sailor
ναυτικό n. navy
ναυτικός m. seaman
νέα n. pl. news
νεκρός, -ή, -ό dead
νεολαία f. youth, young people
νέος m. young man
νέα f. young woman
νέος, -α, -ο new, young
νεότης f. youth
νερό n. water
νεῦρο n. nerve
νεώτερος, -η, -ο younger, modern
νησί n. island
νηστεία f. fast, lent
νηστεύω to fast
νίκη f. victory
νικῶ to win, to defeat, to beat
Νοέμβριος m. November
νόημα n. meaning
νοιώθω to feel
νομίζω to think
νομικός, -ή, -ό legal
νόμισμα n. coin
νόμος m. law
νομός m. prefect
νοσοκομεῖο n. hospital
νοσοκόμος, -α m. f. nurse
νοσταλγία f. nostalgia

νόστιμος, -η, -ο tasty, delicious, pretty

νότος m. south

νοῦς m. mind

ντομάτα f. tomato

ντουλάπι n. cupboard

ντύνομαι to dress

νυστάζω to be sleepy

νύφη f. bride, sister-in-law, daughter-in-law

νύχι n. nail

νύκτα, νύχτα f. night

νωρίς early

Ξ

ξακουστός, -ή, -ό famous

ξανά again

ξανθομαλλούσα f. blond

ξανθός, -ή, -ό blond, fair

ξαφνικά suddenly

ξεκινῶ to start, to set out

ξεκουράζομαι to rest

ξεναγός m. guide

ξενοδοχεῖο n. hotel

ξένος, -η, -ο strange, foreign, alien

ξένος, -η stranger, foreigner

ξεντύνομαι to undress

ξερός, -η, -ο dry

ξεσηκώνω to arouse

ξεχνῶ to forget

ξοδεύω to spend (money)

ξύδι, ξίδι n. vinegar

ξύλο n. wood

ξυλουργός m. carpenter

ξυλώνω to undo

ξυνός, -ή, -ό sour, acid

ξύνω to scratch, to scrape

ξυπνῶ to awake, to get up

ξυράφι n. razor

ξυρίζω to shave

ξωκκλήσι n. country chapel

Ο

ὀγδόντα eighty

ὄγδοος, -η, -ο eighth

ὄγκος n. volume, bulk, mass

ὁδηγία f. instruction, direction

ὁδηγός m. guide, driver, conductor

ὁδηγῶ to guide, to drive

ὀδοντογιατρός m. dentist

ὀδοντόπαστα f. toothpaste

ὁδός f. street

οἰκογένεια f. family

οἰκονομία f. economy, finances, saving

οἰκονομικός, -ή, -ό economic, financial

οἰκονομῶ to save, to economize

οἶκος m. house

οἰνόπνευμα n. alcohol

ὀκτώ eight

Ὀκτώβριος m. October

ὁλόκληρος, -η, -ο entire, whole

ὅλος, -η, -ο all

ὁμάδα f. group

ὁμαλός, -ή, -ό regular, even

ὁμιλητής m. speaker

ὁμιλητικός, -ή, -ό talkative

ὁμιλία f. talk, conversation

ὁμίχλη f. fog

ὁμογενής m. of the same ethnic group

ὅμοιος, -α, -ο same, alike, similar

ὁμοιότης f. resemblance, similarity

ὁμολογία f. confession, admission

ὁμολογῶ to confess, to admit

ὀμπρέλ(λ)α f. umbrella

ὅμως but, yet, however, though

ὀνειρεύομαι to dream

ὄνειρο n. dream

ὄνομα n. name

ὀνομάζομαι to be named, to be called

ὀνομάζω to name

ὀξύ acid

ὀξύς, -εῖα, -ύ sharp

ὅπλο n. weapon, arm

ὁποῖος, -α, -ο who, which, that

ὅπου where

ὁπουδήποτε wherever

ὅπως as, like

ὅραση* f. sight

ὄργανο n. instrument

ὀργανώνω to organize

ὀργάνωση* f. organization

ὀρεκτικός, -ή, -ό appetizing

ὄρεξη* f. appetite

ὄρθιος, -α, -ο standing

ὀρθόδοξος, -η, -ο orthodox

ὀρθός, -ή, -ό right, correct

ὁρίζοντας m. horizon

ὁριζόντιος, -α, -ο horizontal

ὁρίζω to define, to fix

ὅριο n. limit

ὁρκίζομαι to swear, to take an oath

ὅρκος m. oath, vow

ὁρμή f. impetus, impulse

ὁρμητικός, -ή, -ό impetuous

ὁρμῶ to rush, to dash

ὅρος m. condition, term

ὄρος n. mountain

ὀρυχεῖο n. mine

ὀρφανός, -ή, -ό orphan

ὄσπριο n. dry vegetable

ὄστρακο n. shell

ὄσφρηση* f. smelling

ὅταν when

ὅτι that, what

ὁτιδήποτε whatever

οὐδέτερος, -η, -ο neuter

οὐρά f. tail

οὐρανός m. sky

οὐσία f. substance, essence

οὔτε not even

οὔτε ... οὔτε neither ... nor

ὀφείλω to owe, must

ὄχθη f. bank (river)

ὄχι no

ὄψη* f. face, appearance

Π

πάγος m. ice

παγωνιά f. frost

παγώνω to freeze

παγωτό n. ice cream

παθαίνω to suffer

πάθος n. passion

παιγνίδι n. game, toy

παιδεύω to torture

παιδί n. child

παιδικός, -ή, -ό children's, childish

παίζω to play

παίκτης -τρια player

παίρνω to take

παλάμη f. palm (hand)

παλάτι n. palace

πάλη f. fight, wrestling, struggle

παλιός, -ά, -ό old
παλληκάρι n. brave young man
παλτό n. overcoat
πανεπιστήμιο n. university
πανηγύρι n. fair
πανί n. cloth
παντελόνι n. trousers
παντοπωλεῖο n. grocery store
πάντοτε always
παντοῦ everywhere
παντρεύομαι to marry, to get
  married
παπάς, παππᾶς m. priest
πάπια f. duck
παπ(π)ούς, παππποῦς grandfather
παπούτσι n. shoe
παραγγελία f. order
παραγγέλω to order
παράγραφος f. paragraph
παράγω to produce
παραγωγή f. production
παράδειγμα n. example,
  illustration
παράδεισος m. paradise,
  heaven
παραδίδομαι to surrender, to
  give up
παράδοση* f. tradition, lecture
  lesson
παράθυρο n. window
παρακολουθῶ to watch, to
  attend
παρακούω to disobey,
  to hear wrongly
παραλείπω to omit
παράλειψη* f. omission
παραλία f. sea shore
παράλληλος, -η, -ο parallel

παράλυτος, -η, -ο paralytic
παραμονή f. stay
παραμύθι n. story, fable
παράνομος, -η, -ο illegal
παράξενος, -η, -ο strange
παράπονο n. complaint
παραπονοῦμαι to complain
παράσημο n. medal, decoration
Παρασκευή f. Friday
παράσταση* f. show,
  performance
παρατήρηση* f. observation,
  remark
παρατηρῶ to observe
παρέλαση* parade
παρελθόν n. past
παρεξήγηση* f. misunderstanding
πάρκο n. park
παρόμοιος, -α, -ο similar
παρόν n. present
παρουσία f. presence
παρουσιάζομαι to appear
παρουσιάζω to present
Πάσχα n. Easter
πατάτα f. potato
πατέρας m. father
πάτημα n. step
Πατριάρχης m. Patriarch
πατρίδα f. homeland
πατρικός, -ή, -ό fatherly, of the
  father
πατριώτης m. patriot
πατριωτικός, -ή, -ό patriotic
πατριωτισμός m. patriotism
πατῶ to step, to press
πάτωμα n. floor, story
παύω to stop, to end

παύση* f. stop, pause
πάχος n. fat, thickness
παχύς, -ιά, -ύ fat, thick
πεδιάδα f. plain
πεζογράφος m. prose writer
πεζοδρόμιο n. sidewalk
πεζός m. pedestrian
πεθαίνω to die
πεθαμένος, -η, -ο dead
πεθερός, -ά m. father-in-law
   f. mother-in-law
πείθω to convince; to persuade
πεινῶ to be hungry
πείρα, πεῖρα f. experience
πειράζω to annoy, to tease,
   to vex
πείραμα n. experiment
πέλαγος n. sea
πελώριος, -α, -ο enormous, huge
Πέμπτη f. Thursday
πέμπτος, -η, -ο fifth
πένθος n. mourning
πενήντα fifty
πέν(ν)α f. pen
πέντε five
πέπλο n. veil
πέπλος m. veil
περασμένος, -η, -ο past, bygone
περιγραφή f. description
περιγράφω to describe
περιεχόμενο n. the content(s)
περιέχω to contain, to
   include
περιηγητής, -τρια m., f. tourist
περιλαμβάνω to comprise
περιμένω to wait, to wait for
περίοδος f. period, session
περιορίζω to limit, to restrict
περιορισμός restriction

περιουσία f. fortune, property
περιοχή f. district, area
περίπατος m. walk, ride
περ(ι)πατῶ to walk
περιπέτεια f. adventure
περιπλανῶμαι to wander about
περίπου about, nearly
περίπτερο pavilion, news-stand,
   tobacco-stand
περισσότερος, -η, -ο more
πέρισυ last year
περιττός, -ή, -ό superfluous,
   unnecessary
περίφημος, -η, -ο famous
περιωρισμένος, -η, -ο limited
περνῶ to pass, to cross
πέτρα f. stone
πετρέλαιο n. kerosene,
   petroleum
πετσέτα f. napkin, towel
πεῦκο n. pine tree
πέφτω to fall, to drop
πηγάδι n. well
πηγαίνω to go
πήδημα n. jump, leap
πηδῶ to jump
πιά any more
πιάνω to catch, to seize
πιατάκι n. saucer
πιάτο n. plate, dish
πιέζω to press, to squeeze
πίεση* f. pressure
πιθανόν probably
πίθηκος m. monkey, ape
πικρός, -ή, -ό bitter
πίνακας m. blackboard, table,
   index
πίνω to drink
πιπέρι n. pepper

πιστεύω   to believe
πίστη* f. faith
πιστοποιητικό n. certificate
πιστός, -ή, -ό faithful, loyal
πίστωση* f. credit
πίσω   back, behind
πίτα, πήττα f. pie
πλάθω to form, to knead
  (bread)
πλατεία f. square
πλάτος n. width
πλατύς, -ιά, -ύ wide, broad
πλέκω to knit
πλέον more, any more
πλεονέκτημα n. advantage
πλένω wash
πλευρά f. side
πλέω to float, to sail
πληγή f. wound
πληγώνω to wound, to hurt
πλήθος n. multitude, crowd
πληθυσμός m. population
πλήρης, -ης, -ες full, complete
πληροφορία f. information
πληροφορῶ to inform
πληρωμή f. payment
πληρώνω to pay
πλησιάζω to approach,
  to come near
πλοίαρχος m. captain (of a
  ship)
πλοῖο n. ship, boat, vessel
πλοκή f. plot
πλούσιος, -α, -ο rich, wealthy
πλουτίζω to enrich
πλοῦτος m. wealth, riches
πλυντήριο n. laundry
πνεῦμα n. spirit, mind
  intellect, wit

πνευματικός, -ή, -ό intellectual.
  spiritual
πνευματώδης witty
πνεύμονας (πνεύμων) m. lung
πνίγομαι to drown, to choke
πνίγω to strangle, to drown
ποδήλατο n. bicycle
πόδι n. foot, leg, paw
πόθος m. desire, longing
ποίημα n. poem
ποίηση* f. poetry
ποιητής m. poet; maker
ποιητικός, -ή, -ό poetic
ποικιλία f. variety
ποινή f. sentence, punishment
ποιός, -ά, -ό who, which, what
ποιότης f. quality
πόλεμος m. war
πολεμῶ to fight
πόλη* f. city, town
πολιτεία f. state, big city
πολίτης m. citizen
πολιτική f. politics
πολιτικός, -ή, -ό political
πολιτισμός m. civilization,
  culture
πολιτιστικός, -ή, -ό cultural
πολλοί, -ές, -ά many
πόλος m. pole
πολύ very, much, a great deal of
πολυθρόνα f. armchair
πολύς, πολλή, πολύ much
πολυτέλεια f. luxury
πολυτελής, -ής, -ές luxurious
πολύτιμος, -η, -ο precious
πολυύμνητος, -η, -ο famous
  (lit., much sung)
πονηρός, -ή, -ό sly, cunning
πονόδοντος m. toothache

πονοκέφαλος m. headache

πόνος m. pain

ποντίκι (ποντικός) n. (m.) mouse

πονῶ to ache, to feel pain

πόρτα f. door, gate

πορτοκάλι n. orange

ποσό n. amount, sum

πόσος, -η, -ο how much

πόσοι, -ες, -α how many

ποσοστό n. percentage

ποσότης f. quantity

ποτάμι (ποταμός) n. (m.) river

πότε when (interrogative)

ποτήρι n. drinking glass

ποτίζω to water

ποτό n. drink

πού that, who, which

ποῦ where (interrogative)

πούδρα f. powder

πουλί n. bird

πουλῶ to sell

ποῦρο n. cigar

πρᾶγμα n. thing

πράγματι indeed

πραγματικά really, in fact

πραγματικός, -ή, -ό real, actual

πραγματικότης f. reality

πρακτικός, -ή, -ό practical

πράκτορας (πράκτωρ) m. agent

πρακτορεῖο n. agency

πρᾶξη* f. act, action, deed

πράσινος, -η, -ο green

πρέπει must

πρεσβευτής m. ambassador

πρίν before, previously

προάστειο n. suburb

προβάλλω to appear, to show oneself

πρόβατο n. sheep

προβιβάζω to promote

προβλέπω to foresee

πρόβλημα n. problem

πρόγευμα n. breakfast

πρόγονος m. ancestor

πρόγραμμα m. program, time-table

πρόεδρος m. president, chairman

προειδοποίηση* f. warning, notice

προειδοποιῶ to warn

προετοιμάζω to prepare

προετοιμασία f. preparation

προηγούμενος, -η, -ο previous

προηγουμένως previously

προθήκη f. shop-window

προθυμία f. willingness, eagerness, promptness

πρόθυμος, -η, -ο willing, eager prompt

προϊόν n. product

προκαταβολή f. down payment

προκατάληψη* f. prejudice

πρόκληση* f. challenge, provocation

πρόληψη* f. superstition prevention

προμηθεύω to provide, to supply

προνόμιο n. privilege

προξενεῖο n. consulate

πρόξενος m. consul

προοδευτικός, -ή, -ό progressive

προοδεύω to progress

πρόοδος f. progress

προορισμός m. destiny, destination

πρός to, toward, towards

προσαρμόζω to adjust, to adapt

προσβάλλω to offend, to attack

προσβολή f. offense, affront, insult, attack

προσευχή prayer

προσεύχομαι to pray

προσέχω to be careful, to pay attention, to look out

πρόσθεση* f. addition

προσθέτω to add

προσκαλῶ to invite

πρόσκληση* f. invitation

πρόσκοπος m. scout

προσκύνημα n. pilgrimage; shrine

προσκυνητής, -τρια pilgrim

προσοχή f. attention

προσπάθεια f. effort, endeavor

προσπαθῶ to try, to endeavor

προστασία f. protection

προστατεύω to protect

προστάτης m. protector, patron

πρόστιμο n. fine

προσφέρω to offer, to present, to contribute

προσφορά f. offer, contribution

προσωπικός, -ή, -ό personal

πρόσωπο n. person, face

πρόταση* f. proposition, suggestion

προτείνω to propose, to suggest

προτεραιότης f. priority

προτέρημα n. merit, advantage

προτίμηση* f. preference

προτιμότερος, -η, -ο preferable

προτιμῶ to prefer

προτοῦ before

πρόφαση* f. excuse

προφέρω to pronounce

προφήτης m. prophet

προφορά f. pronunciation

προφορικός, -ή, -ό oral

προφυλάγω to protect, to guard

προφύλαξη* f. precaution

πρόχειρος, -η, -ο handy, improvised

προχθές the day before yesterday

προχωρῶ to advance, to go on

πρωΐ n. morning

πρωταγωνιστής, -τρια leading man, woman

πρῶτος, -η, -ο first

πρωτότυπος, -η, -ο original

πτώση* f. fall; case (gramm.)

πυκνός, -ή, -ό thick, dense

πύλη f. gate, door

πύργος m. tower, castle

πυρετός m. fever

πυροβολισμός m. shot, gunshot

πυροτέχνημα n. firework

πωλῶ to sell

πώς that

πῶς how

Ρ

ράβω to sew

ραδιόφωνο n. radio, radio set

ραντεβού n. date

ράφτης m. tailor

ράχη* f. back

ράψιμο n. sewing

ρεῦμα n. current, stream, draught

ρῆμα n. verb
ρητό n. saying
ρίζα f. root
ρίχνω to throw
ρόδα f. wheel
ροδάκινο n. peach
ρουφῶ to guzzle
ροῦχα n. pl. clothes
ρύζι n. rice
ρυθμός m. rhythm, style
ρυτίδα f. wrinkle
Ρωσ(σ)ία f. Russia
Ρῶσ(σ)ος, Ρωσ(σ)ίδα Russian

Σ

Σάββατο n. Saturday
σαγόνι n. chin
σακκί n. bag, sack
σαλάτα f. salad
σάλτσα f. gravy, sauce
σάν like, as
σαπούνι n. soap
σαράντα forty
σας your σᾶς you (accus.)
σάτιρα f. satire
σβήνω to erase, to put out, to
    quench, to extinguish
σέ you (accus.) ; to, at, in, on
σεβασμός m. respect, reverence
σέβομαι to respect, to revere
σειρά f. row, file, line
σελήνη f. moon
σελίδα f. page
Σεπτέμβριος m. September
σηκώνομαι to rise, to get up
σηκώνω to raise, to lift, to carry
σῆμα n. sign, signal, mark, badge
σημάδι n. sign, signal, badge
σημαία f. flag, banner

σημαίνω to mean, to signify;
    to ring (bell)
σημαντικός, -ή, -ό significant,
    considerable
σημασία f. meaning,
    significance, sense
σημεῖο n. sign, spot, point
σημειώνω to mark, to note
σημείωμα n. note,
    memorandum
σημείωση* f. note
σήμερα today
σημερινός, -ή, -ό of today
σιγά slowly, gently, quietly
σιγαρέττο n. cigarette
σίδερο n. iron
σιδερώνω to iron
σιδηρόδρομος m. railroad, train
σιντόνι n. bed sheet
σιρόπι n. sirup
σιτάρι n. wheat
σιχαίνομαι to loathe, to be
    disgusted
σιωπή f. silence
σιωπηλός, -ή, -ό silent
σιωπῶ to be silent
σκάβω to dig
σκάζω to burst, to crack
σκάλα f. staircase, ladder
σκάλες f. pl. stairs
σκαλίζω to hoe, to dig
σκαμνί n. stool
σκελετός m. skeleton, framework
σκεπάζω to cover
σκεπτικός, -ή, -ό thoughtful
σκέπτομαι to think
σκέψη* f. thought
σκηνή f. stage, scene, tent

σκιά f. shade, shadow
σκληρός, -ή, -ό hard, tough, cruel
σκόνη f. dust, powder
σκοπός m. aim, purpose, objective; tune
σκοπού, άπό on purpose
σκορπίζω to scatter, to spread
σκοτάδι n. darkness
σκοτεινός, -ή, -ό dark
σκοτώνω to kill
σκουλήκι n. worm
σκύβω to stoop
σκυλί (σκύλος) n. (m.) dog
σοβαρά seriously
σοβαρός, -ή, -ό serious, grave
σοκολάτα f. chocolate
σούπα f. soup
σοφία f, wisdom
σοφός, -ή, -ό wise, learned
σπάγγος m. string
σπάζω to break
σπαθί n. sword
σπάνια rarely, seldom
σπάνιος, -α, -ο rare
σπατάλη f. waste
σπαταλῶ to waste
σπέρνω to sow
σπεύδω to hurry, to hasten
σπηλιά f. cave, cavern
σπίρτο n. match
σπίτι n. home, house
σπόρος m. seed
σπουδάζω to study
σπουδαῖος, -α, -ο important
σπουδαιότης f. importance
σπουδαστής, -τρια student
σπουδή f. study

σπρώχνω to push
σταγόνα f. drop
στάδιο n. stadium, stage, career
σταδιοδρομία f. career
στάζω to drip, to drop
σταθερός, -ή, -ό stable, firm, steady, constant
σταθερότης f. firmness, stability
σταθμός m. station, stop
στάλα f. drop
σταματῶ to stop
στάση* f. stop
σταῦλος m. stable
σταυρός m. cross
σταφίδα f. raisin, currant
σταφύλι n. grape
στάχτη f. ash
στάχυ n. ear of wheat
στέγη f. roof, shelter
στεγνός, -ή, -ό dry
στεγνώνω to dry
στέκομαι to stand
στέλλω to send
στέμμα n. crown
στεναγμός m. sigh
στενάζω to sigh
στενογραφία f. shorthand
στενοκέφαλος, -η, -ο narrow-minded
στενός, -ή, -ό narrow, tight
στενοχώρια f. distress, trouble, inconvenience
στενοχωρῶ to embarrass, to oppress
στερεός, -ή, -ό solid, fast
στέρηση* f. privation
στεφάνι n. wreath

στέψη* f. coronation, wedding, ceremony
στῆθος n. chest, breast
στήλη f. column, pillar
στήριγμα n. support
στηρίζω to support, to base
στιγμή f. moment, instant
στίχος m. verse, line
στοιχεῖο n. element, rudiment
στοιχειώδης, -ης, -ες elementary
στοίχημα n. bet
στοιχηματίζω to bet
στολή f. uniform
στολίζω to decorate, to trim
στολισμός m. decoration, ornament
στόλος m. fleet
στόμα n. mouth
στομάχι n. stomach
στοργή f. affection, fondness
στόχος m. target
στραβός, -ή, -ό crooked
στραγγίζω to strain, to drain
στρατιώτης m. soldier
στρατιωτικός, -ή, -ό military
στρατόπεδο n. camp
στρατός m. army
στρείδι n. oyster
στρέμμα n. acre
στρέφομαι to turn, to revolve
στρέφω to turn
στρογγυλός, -ή, -ό round
στροφή f. turn, turning, stanza
στρυφνός, -ή, -ό harsh
στρῶμα n. mattress, layer
στυλογράφος n. fountain pen
στῦλος m. pillar, column, post
στυλώνω to support

σύ you (singular)
συγγενής m. f. relative
συγγνώμη f. pardon, forgiveness
συγγραφέας (συγγραφεύς) m. author, writer
συγκεκριμένος, -η, -ο concrete
συγκέντρωση* f. gathering, concentration
συγκίνηση* f. emotion
συγκινητικός, -ή, -ό moving, touching
συγκοινωνία f. communication
συγκοινωνῶ to communicate
συγκρατῶ to restrain, to keep
συγκρίνω to compare
σύγκριση* f. comparison
συγκριτικός, -ή, -ό comparative
σύγκρουση* f. collision, conflict
συγχαίρω to congratulate
συγχαρητήρια n. pl. congratulations
συγχέω to confuse
σύγχρονος, -η, -ο contemporary, modern
σύγχυση* f. confusion
συγχώρηση* f. pardon, forgiveness
συγχωρῶ to forgive, to excuse
συγχωρεῖτε, μέ excuse me, pardon me
συζήτηση* f. discussion, debate, conversation
συζητῶ to discuss, to debate
σύζυγος m. husband, f. wife
σύκο, σῦκο n. fig
συλλαβή f. syllable
συλλαμβάνω to catch, to arrest, to conceive

συλλογή f. collection
συλλογίζομαι to think,
to meditate
σύλλογος m. association, club
συλλυπητήρια n. pl. condolence,
sympathy
συλλυποῦμαι to condole with,
to express sympathy
συμβαίνω to happen
συμβιβάζομαι to compromise,
to settle
συμβιβάζω to reconcile
συμβιβασμός m. settlement,
compromise
συμβολαιογράφος m. notary,
notary public
συμβόλαιο n. contract
συμβολικός, -ή, -ό symbolic(al)
σύμβολο n. symbol
συμβουλεύω to advise
συμβουλή f. advice
συμμαθητής, -τρια school-mate,
class-mate
συμμαχία f. alliance
σύμμαχος m. ally
συμπάθεια f. sympathy,
compassion, liking
συμπαθητικός, -ή, -ό nice;
sympathetic
συμπατριώτης m. fellow country-
man, compatriot
συμπεραίνω to conclude
συμπέρασμα n. conclusion
συμπεριφορά f. behavior
συμπληρώνω to supplement
συμπλοκή f. conflict, fight
συμπονῶ to sympathize, to feel
compassion

σύμπτωμα n. symptom
σύμπτωση* f. coincidence
συμφέρει it is to one's interest
συμφέρον n. interest
συμφοιτητής, -τρια f. fellow
student
σύμφωνα μέ according to,
in accordance with
συμφωνία f. agreement
σύμφωνος, -η, -ο agreeing,
συμφωνῶ to agree
συμφώνως in accordance with
συναγωνισμός m. competition
συνάδελφος m. colleague
συναίσθημα n. feeling, sensation
συναλλαγή f. exchange,
transaction
συνάλλαγμα n. exchange, bill
συναναστροφή f. company
συνάντηση* f. meeting,
encounter
συναντῶ to meet
συναρπαστικός, -ή, -ό exciting
συναυλία f. concert
σύνδεσμος m. bond, tie,
connection
συνδέω to connect, to join
συνδρομή f. subscription,
assistance
συνδρομητής, -τρια subscriber
συνδυάζω to combine
συνδυασμός m. combination
συνεδρίαση* f. meeting, session
συνέδριο n. convention,
congress
συνείδηση* f. conscience
συνεννόηση* f. understanding

συνεννοοῦμαι to come to an understanding
συνέντευξη* f. interview, appointment
συνέπεια f. consequence
συνεργάζομαι to cooperate, to collaborate
συνεργασία f. cooperation, collaboration
συνεργάτης m. coworker, fellow worker, collaborator
συνέταιρος m. partner, associate
συνέχεια f. continuation
συνεχής, -ής, -ές continuous
συνεχίζω to continue, to go on
συνήθεια f. habit, usage
συνήθης, -ης, -ες usual, habitual
συνηθίζω to have the habit of, to get used to, to accustom
συνηθισμένος, -η, -ο used to
σύνθεση* f. composition, formation
συνθέτης m. composer
σύνθετος, -η, -ο compound, complex
συνθέτω to compose
συνθήκη f. treaty, condition
σύνθημα n. signal
συνιστῶ to recommend
συννεφιασμένος, -η, -ο cloudy
σύννεφο n. cloud
συνοδεύω to accompany
συνοικία f. quarter
συνοικισμός m. settlement
συνομιλία f. conversation
συνομιλῶ to talk
σύνορο n. border, frontier
συνταγή f. recipe, formula, prescription

σύνταγμα n. constitution; regiment
συνταγματικός, -ή, -ό constitutional
συντάκτης m. editor
σύνταξη* f. pension, editing
συντήρηση* f. maintenance, support
συντηρητικός, -ή, -ό conservative
συντηρῶ to maintain
συντομεύω to abbreviate, to shorten
σύντομος, -η ,-ο short, brief
συντόμως in short, briefly
συντροφεύω to keep company
συντροφιά f. company
σύντροφος m. companion
σύρμα n. wire
συρτάρι n. drawer
σύρω to draw
σύσταση* f. recommendation
σύστημα n. system
συστηματικός, -ή, -ό systematic
συστήνω to introduce, to recommend
συχνά often, frequently
συχνός, -ή, -ό frequent
σφάζω to slay
σφαίρα, σφαῖρα f. bullet, sphere, globe, ball
σφάλλω to be wrong
σφάλμα n. mistake, error
σφουγγάρι n. sponge
σφραγίδα f. seal, stamp
σφραγίζω to seal
σφυγμός m. pulse
σφυρί n. hammer
σφύριγμα n. whistle
σφυρίζω to whistle

φυρίχτρα f. whistle

χεδιάζω to plan, to design, to draw

χέδιο n. plan, sketch

χεδόν almost, nearly

χέση* f. relation, connection

χῆμα n. form, shape, figure

χηματίζω to form

χηματισμός m. formation

χίζω to tear

χοινί n. rope, string

χολαστικός, -ή, -ό pedantic

χολείο n. school

χολή f. school, faculty

χολιάζω to comment

χολιαστής m. commentator

χολικός, -ή, -ό of school, scholastic

χόλιο n. comment

ώζω to save

ωληνάρι(ο) n. tube

ωλήνας m. pipe

ῶμα m. body

ωματείο n. organization, association

ωματικός, -ή, -ό bodily

ωρός m. pile, heap

ωστά correctly

ωστός, -ή, -ό correct

ωτήρας m. savior

ωτηρία f. salvation

T

χβέρνα f. tavern shop

χινία f. ribbon, tape, film

χιριάζω to fit, to match

χκούνι n. heel

χκτικός, -ή, -ό regular

τακτοποίηση* f. putting in order, arrangement

τακτοποιῶ to arrange

ταλαιπωρία f. suffering. hardship

ταλαιπωροῦμαι to suffer hardships

ταλαιπωρῶ to harass

ταλέντο n. talent

ταμείο n. treasury

ταμίας m. treasurer, cashier

ταμιευτήριο n. savings bank

τάξη* f. class, order

ταξιδεύω to travel

ταξίδι n. travel, trip

ταξιδιώτης m. traveler

ταπεινός, -ή, -ό humble

ταράζω to disturb

ταραχή f. agitation, disturbance

τάση* f. tendency, trend

ταυτότης f. identity

ταφή f. burial

τάφος m. grave, tomb

ταχυδρομείο n. mail, post office

ταχυδρόμος m. mailman

ταχυδρομῶ to mail, to post

ταχύς, -εῖα, -ύ fast, quick

ταχύτης f. speed, rapidity

τέλειος, -α, -ο perfect

τελειόφοιτος, -η graduate

τελειώνω to finish

τελετή f. ceremony

τελευταῖος, -α, -ο last

τελικός, -ή, -ό final

τέλος n. end

τελωνείο n. custom house

τεμπέλης -α lazy

τεμπελιά f. laziness
τέρας n. monster
τέσσερα four
Τετάρτη f. Wednesday
τέταρτος, -η, -ο fourth
τέτοιος, -α, -ο such
τετράγωνο n. square. block
τετράδιο n. note-book
τετρακόσια four hundred
τέχνασμα n. trick
τέχνη f. art
τεχνητός, -ή, -ό artificial
τεχνικός, -ή, -ό technical
τεχνίτης m. technician
τζάμι n. window-pane. glass
τηγάνι n. frying pan
τηγανίζω to fry
τηλεγράφημα n. telegram
τηλεγραφῶ to telegraph, to wire
τηλεόραση* f. television
τηλεφώνημα n. telephone call
τηλεφωνητής, -τρια operator
τηλέφωνο n. telephone
τηλεφωνῶ to telephone, to call
τί what
τιμή f. price, honor
τίμιος, -α, -ο honest
τιμιότης f. honesty
τιμολόγιο n. price-list
τιμόνι n. steering wheel; rudder
τιμῶ to honor
τιμωρία f. punishment
τιμωρῶ to punish
τινάζω to shake
τίποτα nothing
τίτλος m. title
τμῆμα n. section, department
τοῖχος m. wall

τόκος m. interest
τολμηρός, -ή, -ό bold. daring
τολμῶ to dare
τομέας m. sector
τόμος n. volume
τονίζω to accent, to stress
τόνος m. accent, tone
τόξο n. bow, arch
τοπεῖο n. landscape
τοπικός, -ή, -ό local
τοποθεσία f. location
τόπος m. place, site, spot
τόσος, -η, -ο so, so much
τόσο . . . ὅσο as . . . as, so. . . a
τότε then, at that time
τουλάχιστο at least
Τουρκία f. Turkey
τούτοις, ἐν nevertheless
τουφέκι n. gun, rifle
τραβῶ to pull
τραγικός, -ή, -ό tragic
τραγούδι n. song
τραγουδιστής, -τρια singer
τραγουδῶ to sing
τραγωδία f. tragedy
τραῖνο n. train
τράπεζα f. bank
τραπεζαρία f. dining room
τραπέζι n. table
τραπεζομάνδηλο n. tablecloth
τραῦμα n. wound
τραχύς, -εῖα, -ύ rough
τρέλλα f. madness, insanity
τρελλός, -ή, -ό insane, mad,
  crazy
τρέμω to tremble. to shiver,
  to shake
τρέφω to feed

τρέχω to run
τρία three
τριακόσια three hundred
τριάντα thirty
τριαντάφυλλο n. rose
τρίβω to rub
τριγύρω around
τρίγωνο n. triangle
τρικυμία f. storm
Τρίτη f. Tuesday
τρίτος, -η, -ο third
τρίχα f. hair
τρομάζω to terrify; to be terrified
τρομακτικός, -ή, -ό terrible, frightful
τρομερά terribly
τρομερός, -ή, -ό terrible
τρόμος n. terror
τρόπος m. way, manner
τροφή f. food
τρύπα f. hole
τρυπῶ to make a hole
τρυφερός, -ή, -ό tender
τρώγω to eat
τσάϊ n. tea
τσάντα f. purse, handbag
τσέπη f. pocket
τσιγάρο n. cigarette
τυλίγω to wrap
τύμπανο n. drum
τυπικός, -ή, -ό typical
τυπογραφείο n. printing shop
τυπογράφος m. printer
τύπος m. press, type
τυπώνω to print
τυραννία f. tyranny
τυραννῶ to torture

τυρί n. cheese
τυφλός -ή, -ό blind
τυχερός, -ή, -ό lucky, fortunate
τύχη f. luck, fortune
τυχόν by chance
τύψη* f. remorse
τώρα now, at present

Υ

ὑγεία f. health
ὑγιεινός, -ή, -ό healthy
ὑγρασία f. humidity
ὑγρός, -ή, -ό wet, liquid, humid
ὑλικός, -ή, -ό material
ὑλικό n. material
ὕμνος m. hymn
ὕπαιθρο n. outdoor(s), open air
ὑπακούω to obey
ὑπάλληλος m. employee
ὕπαρξη* f. existence
ὑπάρχω to exist
ὑπερασπίζω to defend
ὑπεράσπιση* f. defense
ὑπερβολή f. exaggeration
ὑπερβολικός, -ή, -ό excessive
ὑπερηφάνεια f. pride
ὑπερήφανος, -η, -ο proud
ὑπεύθυνος, -η, -ο responsible
ὑπηρεσία f. service
ὑπηρέτης, -τρια servant, maid
ὑπηρετῶ to serve
ὕπνος m. sleep
ὑποβρύχιο n. submarine
ὑπόγειο n. cellar, basement
ὑπογραμμίζω to underline
ὑπογραφή f. signature
ὑπογράφω to sign

ὑποδέχομαι   to welcome, to receive
ὑποδοχή   f. reception, welcome
ὑπόθεση*   f. supposition; matter, affair; business
ὑποθέτω   to suppose
ὑποκάμισο   n. shirt
ὑποκρισία   f. hypocrisy
ὑποκριτής, -τρια   hypocrite
ὑπολογισμός   m. estimate
ὑπόλοιπο   n. rest, remainder
ὑπομονή   f. patience
ὑπομονητικός, -ή, -ό   patient
ὑποπτεύομαι   to suspect
ὕποπτος, -η, -ο   suspected
ὑποστηρίζω   to support
ὑποστήριξη*   f. support
ὑπόσχεση*   f. promise
ὑπόσχομαι   to promise
ὑποτροφία   f. scholarship
ὑπουργείο   n. ministry, cabinet
ὑπουργός   m. minister
ὑποφέρω   to suffer
ὑποχρεώνω   to oblige, to compel
ὑποχρέωση*   f. obligation
ὑποχρεωτικός, -ή, -ό   compulsory
ὑποχώρηση*   f. retreat
ὑποχωρῶ   to retire, to give in
ὑποψήφιος, -α, -ο   candidate
ὑποψία   f. suspicion
ὕστερα   after, afterwards
ὑφαίνω   to weave
ὕφασμα   n. cloth, fabric
ὕφος   n. style
ὑψηλός, -ή, -ό   high, tall
ὕψος   n. height
ὕψωμα   n. hill

Φ

φαγητό   n. meal. food

φαίνομαι   to seem, to look
φαινομενικός, -ή, -ό   apparent
φάκελος   m. envelope; file; fold
φακός   m. lens; flashlight
φαλακρός   bald
φανατικός, -ή, -ό   fanatic(al)
φανερός, -ή, -ό   evident, obvious
φανερώνω   to reveal, to disclose
φαντάζομαι   to imagine
φαντασία   f. imagination
φάντασμα   n. ghost
φανταστικός, -ή, -ό   imaginary
φαρμακείο   n. drugstore, pharmacy
φάρμακο   n. medicine, drug
φαρμακοποιός   n. pharmacist
φάρος   m. lighthouse
φασόλι   n. bean
φάτνη   f. manger
Φεβρουάριος   m. February
φεγγάρι   n. moon
φέγγω   to shine, to gleam
φελλός   m. cork
φέρ(ν)ω   to bring, to bear
φέρσιμο   n. behavior, conduct
φέτα   f. slice
φεύγω   to leave, to go away
φήμη   f. fame
φθάνω   to arrive, to reach
φθηνός, -ή, -ό   cheap, inexpensiv
φθινόπωρο   n. autumn, fall
φθόνος   m. envy
φθορά   f. ruin, damage, destruction
φίδι   n. snake
φιλάργυρος, -η, -ο   stingy
φιλελεύθερος, -η, -ο   liberal
φιλί   n. kiss
φιλόδοξος, -η, -ο   ambitious

φιλολογικός, -ή, -ό literary
φιλοξενία f. hospitality
φιλόξενος, -η, -ο hospitable
φιλοξενῶ to entertain,
   to extend hospitality
φίλος m. friend
φίλη f. friend
φιλοσοφία f. philosophy
φιλόσοφος m. philosopher
φιλότιμο n. self-respect, self-pride
φιλότιμος, -η, -ο conscientious
φιλῶ to kiss
φλέβα f. vein
φλόγα f. flame
φλυαρία f. chatter
φλύαρος, -η, -ο chatterer,
   talkative
φλυαρῶ to talk, to chatter
φλυτζάνι n. small cup
φοβερός, -ή, -ό dreadful
φοβίζω to frighten
φοβισμένος, -η, -ο frightened
φόβος m. fear
φοβοῦμαι to fear, to be afraid
φοιτητής, -τρια student
φοιτητικός, -ή, -ό student (adj.)
φοιτῶ to attend
φορά f. time, course
φόρεμα n. dress, garment
φορολογία f. taxation
φόρος m. tax
φορτίο n. load, burden
φορτώνω to load
φορῶ to wear
φούντα f. tassel, pompon
φουντώνω to spread, to grow
φουρνάρης m. baker
φουρνίζω to bake

φοῦρνος m. oven
φούσκα f. bubble, blister
φουσκώνω to swell
φούστα f. skirt
φράζω to block up, to obstruct
φράουλα f. strawberry
φράση* f. phrase, sentence
φράχτης m. fence
φρέσκος, -η, -ο fresh
φρικτός, -ή, -ό horrible
φρόνιμος, -η, -ο quiet, wise,
   prudent
φροντίδα f. care, concern
φροντίζω to take care, to look
   after
φρούριο n. fort
φροῦτο n. fruit
φρύδι n. eyebrow
φταρνίζομαι to sneeze
φτέρνα, πτέρνα f. heel (of the
   foot)
φτώχεια f. poverty
φτωχός, -ή, -ό poor
φυλάγω, φυλάσσω to keep,
   to guard
φύλακας m. guard, keeper
φυλακή f. prison, jail
φυλακίζω to imprison
φυλή f. race; tribe
φύλλο n. leaf, sheet
φύλο n. sex
φύση* f. nature
φυσικά naturally
φυσική f. physics
φυσικός, -ή, -ό natural, physical
φυσῶ to blow
φυτεύω to plant
φυτό n. plant

φυτρώνω to sprout
φωλιά f. nest
φωνάζω to cry, to shout
φωνή f. voice, cry
φῶς n. light
φωταέριο n. gas
φωτιά f. fire
φωτίζω to light, to enlighten
φωτογραφία f. photograph, photo
φωτογραφίζω to photograph
φωτογραφικὴ μηχανή f. camera

Χ

χαίρετε good-bye
χαιρετισμός m. greeting; regards
χαιρετῶ to greet, to salute
χαίρομαι to be glad
χαλάζι n. hail
χαλασμένος, -η, -ο out of order
χαλκός m. copper
χαλ(ν)ῶ to spoil
χαμένος, -η, -ο lost
χαμηλός, -ή, -ό low
χαμηλώνω to lower
χαμόγελο n. smile
χαμογελῶ to smile
χάνομαι to get lost
χάνω to lose
χάος n. chaos
χάπι n. pill
χαρά f. joy
χαρακτήρας m. character
χαρακτηριστικός, -ή, -ό characteristic
χάρη* f. favor
χάρις εἰς thanks to
χαρίζω to present, to make a present

χάρισμα n. gift, talent
χαριτωμένος, -η, -ο charming
χάρτης m. map, charter
χαρτί n. paper
χαρτοπωλεῖο n. stationery
χασμουριέμαι to yawn
χείλι n. lip
χειμώνας m. winter
χελιδόνι n. swallow
χέρι n. hand
χημεία f. chemistry
χημικός m. chemist
χήνα f. goose
χήρα f. widow
χῆρος m. widower
χθές yesterday
χθεσινός, -ή, -ό of yesterday
χίλια one thousand
χιλιόμετρο n. kilometer
χιόνι n. snow
χιονίζω to snow
χλιαρός, -ή, -ό tepid, lukewarm
χλωμός, -ή -ό pale
χοῖρος m. swine, hog, pig
χολή f. bile, gall
χονδρικῶς wholesale
χοντρός, -ή, -ό fat, thick
χορδή f. string, cord
χορευτής, -τρια dancer
χορεύω to dance
χορός m. dance, dancing
χορταίνω to be satisfied
χορτάρι, χόρτο n. grass, herb
χορταρικά n. pl. vegetables
χρειάζομαι to need
χρέος n. debt, obligation
χρ(ε)ωστῶ to owe
χρῆμα n. money

Why We Make This Generous Offer

There are three important reasons why the Institute for Language Study is pleased to make this special Free Record and Sample Lesson offer:

First, never before have there been so many fascinating opportunities open to those who speak foreign languages fluently. Besides the cultural and travel benefits, there are many practical dollars-and-cents advantages—and an ever-increasing number of interesting, well-paying jobs.

The Natural Method

Second, our long experience in the language field has convinced us that the "learn-by-listening" method is the fastest, most convenient and most effective one. It enables you to learn *naturally*—the way you learned English as a child. You acquire a perfect accent and perfect grammar—because that's all you hear.

Just Listen—and Learn

Finally, our professional standing in the field of languages has enabled us to make these generous arrangements with one of the foremost language schools—the inventors of the "learn-by-listening" method. And we are pleased to provide this service for those of our students who want to speak and understand a foreign language "like a native."

There is no obligation and *no salesman will call.* Just mail the card TODAY for your FREE Record.

What Others Say:

Bob Hope says... "I am studying the course in French ... I think it's a great way to study a language."

Enjoyed by Children "It is surprising how much our two children have absorbed by listening." —Mrs. C.M.J.

"A Good Investment" "Just returned from Mexico ... Course good investment!" —Phillips B. Iden

---

Institute for Language Study
71 Plymouth Street, Montclair, N.J. 07042

INSTITUTE FOR LANGUAGE STUDY Dept. HVP #9876
71 Plymouth Street, Montclair, N. J. 07042

Gentlemen:
  Please have the originators of the famous "learn-by-listening" method send me, FREE, the Sample Record and Lesson in the one language checked below—also information which describes fully the complete course and method.

(Please check FREE Language Record and Lesson you wish)

☐ Spanish   ☐ French   ☐ German   ☐ Italian   ☐ Brazilian-Portuguese
☐ Russian   ☐ Japanese   ☐ Modern Greek   ☐ English (for Spanish-or
☐ Arabic   Portuguese-speaking people)

Name _____

Address _____

City _____ State _____

Zip Code _____ Phone _____

BK **HVP**/54321

χρηματιστήριο n. stock exchange

χρήση* f. use

χρησιμεύω to be of use, to be used for

χρησιμοποιῶ to use

χρήσιμος, -η, -ο useful

χριστιανικός -ή, -ό Christian

χριστιανισμός m. Christianity

χριστιανός -ή Christian

Χριστός m. Christ

Χριστούγεννα n. pl. Christmas

χρονολογία f. date

χρόνος m. time, year

χρυσάνθεμο n. chrysanthemum

χρυσάφι n. gold

χρυσός m. gold

χρυσός, -ή, -ό gold, golden

χρῶμα n. color

χτένι n. comb

χτενίζω to comb

χτυπῶ to beat, to hit, to strike

χυδαῖος, -α, -ο vulgar, rude

χυμός m. juice

χῶμα n. earth, soil

χωνεύω to digest

χώρα f. country, land

χωράφι n. field

χωριάτης, -τισσα peasant

χωρίζω to separate, to divide

χωρικός, -ή peasant, villager

χωριό n. village

χωρίς without

χωρισμός m. separation

χωριστός, -ή, -ό separate

Ψ

ψαλίδι n. scissors

ψάλλω to sing, to chant

ψαλμός m. psalm, chant

ψάλτης m. chanter

ψαρεύω to fish

ψάρι n. fish

ψάχνω to look for, to search

ψέμμα n. lie

ψεύτης, -τρα liar

ψεύτικος, -η, ο false

ψηλός, -ή, -ό high, tall

ψήνω to roast, to bake

ψητός, -ή, -ό roast, roasted

ψηφίζω to vote

ψῆφος f. vote

ψιθυρίζω to whisper

ψυγεῖο n. refrigerator

ψύξη* f. refrigeration

ψυχαγωγία f. recreation

ψυχή f. soul

ψυχολογία f. psychology

ψύχρα f. chill

ψυχραιμία f. coolness, composure

ψύχραιμος, -η, -ο cold-blooded

Ω

ὠκεανός m. ocean

ὦμος m. shoulder

ὠμός, -ή, -ό raw

ὥρα f. hour, time

ὡραῖος, -α, -ο beautiful, handsome

ὡραιότης f. beauty

ὠριμάζω to mature, to ripen

ὥριμος, -η, -ο ripe, mature

ὡς until, as far as

ὥστε so that

ὠφέλεια f. profit, benefit

ὠφέλιμος, -η -ο useful

ὠφελῶ to benefit, to be of use

ὠχρός, -ή, -ό pale

ENGLISH-GREEK
DICTIONARY

A

able ἱκανός, -ή, -ό
able, to be μπορῶ
abroad στὸ ἐξωτερικό
absolutely ἀπολύτως
accept, to δέχομαι
accident (τὸ) δυστύχημα
accompany, to συνοδεύω
ache (ὁ) πόνος
across ἀπέναντι
act (ἡ) πράξη*
act, to ἐνεργῶ
action (ἡ) ἐνέργεια, (ἡ) δράση
add, to προσθέτω
addition (ἡ) πρόσθεση*
address (ἡ) διεύθυνση*
admire, to θαυμάζω
advice (ἡ) συμβουλή
advise, to συμβουλεύω

afraid, to be φοβοῦμαι
afternoon (τὸ) ἀπόγευμα
afterwards ἔπειτα
again ξανά
age (ἡ) ἡλικία
agency (τὸ) πρακτορεῖο
agreeable εὐχάριστος, -η, -ο
ahead μπροστά
air (ὁ) ἀέρας
airplane (τὸ) ἀεροπλάνο
airport (τὸ) ἀεροδρόμιο
alcohol (τὸ) οἰνόπνευμα
alive ζωντανός, -ή, -ό
all ὅλος, -η, -ο
allow, to ἐπιτρέπω
almost σχεδόν
alone μόνος, -η, -ο
already ἤδη, κιόλας
also ἐπίσης

In the English-Greek dictionary the following points should be noted: In the case of nouns, gender is indicated by the definite article placed in parentheses before the noun it refers to; (ὁ) stands for masculine, (ἡ) for feminine, (τὸ) for neuter. Adjectives and participles are given in all three genders: χρήσιμος m., χρήσιμη f., χρήσιμο n. (useful), χρήσιμος, -η, -ο. In the case of verbs, the infinitive form is given in English as *be able, to* or *play, to*. The corresponding Greek translation is given in the first person singular of the present indicative which is the basic verbal form in Greek, as μπορῶ or παίζω. Numerals, pronouns, prepositions, and conjunctions are not included in the English-Greek part of this two-way dictionary because their forms, meaning, and function can be better explained in a Reference Grammar. Therefore, look for them in the respective chapters of the Reference Grammar

• The feminine nouns marked with an asterisk have, in addition to the form given, another form in Puristic in -ις (gen. -εως), as πρόσθεσις (addition), προσθέσεως.

always πάντοτε, πάντα

America (ή) Ἀμερική

American (ό) Ἀμερικανός
(ή) Ἀμερικανίδα

amount (τό) ποσό

amusing διασκεδαστικός, -ή, -ό

ancient ἀρχαῖος, -α, -ο

angry θυμωμένος, -η, -ο

angry, to be θυμώνω

animal (τό) ζῶο

answer (ή) ἀπάντηση*

anywhere ὁπουδήποτε

apartment (τό) διαμέρισμα

appear, to ἐμφανίζομαι

appearance (ή) ἐμφάνιση*

appetite (ή) ὄρεξη*

apple (τό) μῆλο

appointment (ή) συνάντηση*,
(τό) ραντεβού

appreciate, to ἐκτιμῶ

approach, to πλησιάζω

approve, to ἐγκρίνω

approximately περίπου

April (ό) Ἀπρίλιος

arm (τό) μπράτσο

armchair (ή) πολυθρόνα

army (ό) στρατός

arrive, to φθάνω

art (ή) τέχνη

article (τό) ἄρθρο,
(τό) ἀντικείμενο

artificial τεχνητός, -ή, -ό

artist (ό) καλλιτέχνης,
(ή) καλλιτέχνιδα or καλλιτέχ-
νις**

ask, to (ἐ)ρωτῶ, ζητῶ

assure, to βεβαιώνω

at once ἀμέσως

attend, to παρακολουθῶ

attractive ἑλκυστικός,-ή. -ο

August (ό) Αὔγουστος

aunt (ή) θεία

authentic αὐθεντικός, -ή, -ό

author (ό) συγγραφέας

authorities οἱ ἀρχές or αἱ ἀρχαί

automatic αὐτόματος, -η, -ο

automobile (τό) αὐτοκίνητο

autumn (τό) φθινόπωρο

avenue (ή) λεωφόρος

avoid, to ἀποφεύγω

awaken, to ξυπνῶ

B

bad κακός, -ή, -ό

baggage (οἱ) ἀποσκευές

bank (ή) τράπεζα, (ή) ὄχθη

basket (τό) καλάθι

bath (τό) μπάνιο, (τό) λουτρό

bathe, to λού(ζ)ομαι

bathroom (τό) λουτρό, (τό)
μπάνιο

battle (ή) μάχη

beach (ή) ἀκρογιαλιά

beautiful ὡραῖος, -α, -ο

beauty (ή) ὀμορφιά, (ή) ὡ-
ραιότης, (ή) καλλονή, (τό)
κάλλος

become γίνομαι

bed (τό) κρεβάτι

bedroom (ή) κρεβατοκάμαρα

beef (τό) βωδινό (κρέας)

begin, to ἀρχίζω

Belgium (τό) Βέλγιο

---

* * Regarding doublets given in this dictionary, the first is either the Demotic or the most frequently used spelling variant in contemporary books.

believe, to πιστεύω

bell (ή) καμπάνα,
(τὸ) κουδούνι

belt (ή) ζώνη

bet, to στοιχηματίζω

better καλύτερος or καλλίτερος, -η, -ο

bicycle (τὸ) ποδήλατο

big μεγάλος, -η, -ο

bill (ὁ) λογαριασμός,
(τὸ) χαρτονόμισμα

bird (τὸ) πουλί

birth (ή) γέννηση*

birthday (τὰ) γενέθλια

bite, to δαγκάνω or δαγκώνω

bitter πικρός, -ή, -ό

black μαῦρος, -η, -ο

blade (ή) λεπίδα

blanket (ή) κουβέρτα

blond ξανθός, -ή, -ό

blood (τὸ) αἷμα

blouse (ή) μπλούζα

blow φυσῶ

blue γαλάζιος, -α, -ο, μπλέ

boat (τὸ) πλοῖο, (τὸ) καράβι,
(ή) βάρκα

body (τὸ) σῶμα

boil, to βράζω

bottle (τὸ) μπουκάλι

box (τὸ) κουτί

boy (τὸ) ἀγόρι

branch (τὸ) κλαδί

bread (τὸ) ψωμί

break, to σπάζω

breakfast (τὸ) πρόγευμα

breath (ή) ἀναπνοή, (ή) ἀνάσα

breathe, to ἀναπνέω

bride (ή) νύφη

bridge (ή) γέφυρα

brief σύντομος, -η, -ο,
βραχύς, -εῖα, -ύ

bright or brilliant
λαμπρός, -ή, -ό

bring, to φέρ(ν)ω

broad πλατύς, -εῖα, -ύ

brother (ὁ) ἀδελφός

brown καφέ, καστανός, -ή, -ό

brush (ή) βούρτσα

brush, to βουρτσίζω

build, to κτίζω

building (τὸ) κτίριο

burn, to καίω

bus (τὸ) λεωφορεῖο

business (ή) ἐπιχείρηση*

busy ἀπασχολημένος, -η, -ο

butcher (ὁ) κρεοπώλης,
(ὁ) χασάπης

butter (τὸ) βούτυρο

button (τὸ) κουμπί

buy, to ἀγοράζω

C

cabin (ή) καμπίνα

calendar (τὸ) ἡμερολόγιο

call, to καλῶ, φωνάζω

camera (ή) φωτογραφική
μηχανή

Canada (ὁ) Καναδάς

captain (ὁ) πλοίαρχος,

car (τὸ) αὐτοκίνητο

car (railroad) (τὸ) βαγόνι

card (ή) κάρτα

career (ή) σταδιοδρομία

carry, to μεταφέρω

cash τοῖς μετρητοῖς

cash, to ἐξαργυρώνω

cashier (ὁ) ταμίας

cat (ὁ) γάτος, (ή) γάτα

catch, to πιάνω, ἁρπάζω

cathedral (ὁ) καθεδρικὸς ναός, (ἡ) μητρόπολη*
cause (ἡ) αἰτία
celebrate, to ἑορτάζω
cemetery (τὸ) νεκροταφεῖο
center (τὸ) κέντρο
central κεντρικός, -ή, -ό
century (ὁ) αἰών(ας)
certain βέβαιος, -α, -ο
certainly βεβαίως, ἀσφαλῶς
chair (ἡ) καρέκλα
change (ἡ) ἀλλαγή, (τὰ) ψιλά
change, to ἀλλάζω
character (ὁ) χαρακτήρ(ας)
cheap φθηνός, -ή, -ό
check (ἡ) ἐπιταγή
check, to ἐλέγχω
cheese (τὸ) τυρί
chestnut (τὸ) κάστανο
chicken (ἡ) κότα
chief (ὁ) ἀρχηγός
child (τὸ) παιδί
chin (τὸ) σαγόνι
chocolate (ἡ) σοκολάτα
choose, to διαλέγω, ἐκλέγω
Christmas (τὰ) Χριστούγεννα
church (ἡ) ἐκκλησία
cigar (τὸ) ποῦρο
cigarette (τὸ) τσιγάρο, (τὸ) σιγαρέττο
city (ἡ) πόλη*
civilization (ὁ) πολιτισμός
class (ἡ) τάξη*
clean καθαρός, -ή, -ό
clean, to καθαρίζω
climate (τὸ) κλίμα or κλίμα
close, to κλείνω

closet (τὸ) ντουλάπι
cloth (τὸ) πανί
clothes (τὰ) ροῦχα
cloud (τὸ) σύννεφο
coal (τὸ) κάρβουνο
coat (τὸ) (ἐ)πανωφόρι, (τὸ) παλτό
coffee (ὁ) καφές
cold κρύος, -α, -ο
collar (ὁ) γιακάς
collection (ἡ) συλλογή
color (τὸ) χρῶμα
comb (τὸ) χτένι, (ἡ) τσατσάρα
comb, to χτενίζω
come, to ἔρχομαι
come in, to μπαίνω
comfortable ἄνετος, -η,- ο
commerce (τὸ) ἐμπόριο
commercial ἐμπορικός, -ή, -ό,
company (ἡ) συντροφιά, (ἡ) ἑταιρεία or ἑταιρία
compare, to συγκρίνω
comparison (ἡ) σύγκριση*
complain, to παραπονοῦμαι
complete πλήρης, -ης, -ες
completely πλήρως
concert (ἡ) συναυλία
confession (ἡ) ἐξομολόγηση*
continue, to συνεχίζω
cook, to μαγειρεύω
cool δροσερός, -ή, -ό
copy (τὸ) ἀντίγραφο
corner (ἡ) γωνία
correct σωστός, -ή. -ό, ὀρθός, -ή, -ὸ
correspondence (ἡ) ἀλληλογραφία
cost, to στοιχίζω, κοστίζω
cotton (τὸ) βαμβάκι

cough, to βήχω

count, to μετρῶ

country (ἡ) χώρα, (ἡ) ἐξοχή

couple (τὸ) ζεῦγος

courage (τὸ) θάρρος

course, of βεβαίως

cousin (ὁ) ἐξάδελφος,
  (ἡ) ἐξαδέλφη

cover, to σκεπάζω

cow (ἡ) ἀγελάδα

cream (ἡ) κρέμα

credit (ἡ) πίστωση*

crisis (ἡ) κρίση*

cry, to κλαίω

cuff (τὸ) μανικέτι

cup (ἡ) κούπα, (τὸ) φλιτζάνι
  or φλυτζάνι

curtain (ἡ) κουρτίνα,
  (τὸ) παραπέτασμα

custom (τὸ) ἔθιμο

customs (τὸ) τελωνεῖο

cut, to κόβω

cutlet (ἡ) κοτολέτα

D

daily καθημερινός, -ή, -ό

damage (ἡ) ζημία

damp ὑγρός, -ή, -ό,
  βρεγμένος, -η, -ο

dance (ὁ) χορός

dance, to χορεύω

danger (ὁ) κίνδυνος

dangerous ἐπικίνδυνος, -η, -ο

dare, to τολμῶ

dark σκοτεινός, -ή, -ό,
  σκοῦρος, -η, -ο

darkness (τὸ) σκοτάδι

darling ἀγαπημένος, -η, -ο

date (ἡ) ἡμερομηνία,

(ἡ) χρονολογία,

(τὸ) ραντεβού

daughter (ἡ) κόρη,
  (ἡ) θυγατέρα

dawn (ἡ) αὐγή

day (ἡ) ἡμέρα or μέρα

dead νεκρός, -ή, -ό,
  πεθαμένος, -η, -ο

deaf κουφός, -ή, -ό

dear ἀγαπητός, -ή, -ό,
  ἀκριβός, -ή, -ό

death (ὁ) θάνατος

debt (τὸ) χρέος

deceive ἀπατῶ, ἐξαπατῶ, γελῶ

December (ὁ) Δεκέμβριος

decide, to ἀποφασίζω

decision (ἡ) ἀπόφαση*

declare, to δηλώνω

deed (ἡ) πράξη*

deep βαθύς, -εῖα, -ύ

defend, to ὑπερασπίζω

degree (ὁ) βαθμός,
  (τὸ) πτυχίο

delay (ἡ) καθυστέρηση*

delay, to καθυστερῶ

delicious νόστιμος, -η, -ο

deliver, to διανέμω, παραδίδω

demand, to ἀπαιτῶ

dentist (ὁ) ὀδοντογιατρός

deny, to ἀρνοῦμαι

depart, to ἀναχωρῶ

departure (ἡ) ἀναχώρηση*

depend, to ἐξαρτῶμαι

deposit, to καταθέτω

descend, to κατεβαίνω

describe, to περιγράφω

description (ἡ) περιγραφή

deserve, to ἀξίζω

desire, to ἐπιθυμῶ, ποθῶ

desk (τό) γραφεῖο

dessert (τό) ἐπιδόρπιο

detail (ἡ) λεπτομέρεια

develop, to ἀναπτύσσω, ἀναπτύσσομαι

diamond (τό) διαμάντι, (ὁ) ἀδάμας

dictionary (τό) λεξικό

die, to πεθαίνω

difference (ἡ) διαφορά

different διαφορετικός, -ή, -ό

difficult δύσκολος, -η, -ο

difficulty (ἡ) δυσκολία

dinner (τό) γεῦμα

dining-room (ἡ) τραπεζαρία

diploma (τό) δίπλωμα

direction (ἡ) διεύθυνση*, (ἡ) κατεύθυνση*

directly ἀπ' εὐθείας, ἄμεσα

dirty ἀκάθαρτος, -η, -ο, βρώμικος, -η, -ο

disappear, to ἐξαφανίζομαι

discover, to ἀνακαλύπτω

discuss, to συζητῶ, μελετῶ

disgust (ἡ) ἀηδία

dish (τό) πιάτο

distance (ἡ) ἀπόσταση*

distant μακρινός, -ή, -ό

distinguish, to διακρίνω, ξεχωρίζω

disturb, to ἀνησυχῶ, ἐνοχλῶ

divide, to διαιρῶ

dizziness (ἡ) ζάλη

do, to κάνω

doctor (ὁ) γιατρός or ἰατρός

dog (τό) σκυλί, (ὁ) σκύλος

dollar (τό) δολλάριο

donkey (τό) γαϊδούρι, (ὁ) ὄνος

door (ἡ) πόρτα

double διπλός, -ή, -ό

doubt (ἡ) ἀμφιβολία

doubt, to ἀμφιβάλλω

down κάτω

dozen (ἡ) δωδεκάδα, (ἡ) ντουζίνα

draft (τό) ρεῦμα

drama (τό) δράμα

dream (τό) ὄνειρο

dress (τό) φόρεμα

dress, to ντύνομαι

dressmaker (ὁ) ράφτης, (ἡ) ράφτρια, (ἡ) μοδίστ(ρ)α

drink (τό) ποτό

drink, to πίνω

drive, to ὁδηγῶ

driver (ὁ) ὁδηγός

drugstore (τό) φαρμακεῖο

dry στεγνός, -ή. -ό, ξηρός or ξερός, -ή. -ό

duck (ἡ) πάπια

dye, to βάφω

E

each κάθε

eager πρόθυμος, -η, -ο

ear (τό) αὐτί

early (ἐ)νωρίς

earn, to κερδίζω

earth (ἡ) γῆ

Easter (τό) Πάσχα

easy εὔκολος, -η, -ο

eat, to τρώγω

egg (τό) αὐγό

elbow (ὁ) ἀγκών(ας)

electric ἠλεκτρικός, -ή, -ό

electricity (ὁ) ἠλεκτρισμός
elegant κομψός, -ή, -ό
elevator (τὸ) ἀσανσέρ,
   (ὁ) ἀνελκυστήρ(ας)
embrace, to ἀγκαλιάζω
employe (ὁ) (ἡ) ὑπάλληλος
empty ἄδειος, -α, -ο
enchanting μαγευτικός, -ή, -ό
end (τὸ) τέλος
enemy (ὁ) ἐχθρός
engineer (ὁ) μηχανικός
England (ἡ) Ἀγγλία
English (ὁ) Ἄγγλος,
   (ἡ) Ἀγγλίδα· (τὰ) ἀγγλικά
enjoy, to ἀπολαμβάνω,
   χαίρομαι
enough ἀρκετά, ἀρκετός, -ή, -ό
enter, to μπαίνω, εἰσέρχομαι
enthusiasm (ὁ) ἐνθουσιασμός
enthusiastic ἐνθουσιώδης,
   -ης, -ες
entire ὁλόκληρος, -η, -ο
entrance (ἡ) εἴσοδος
envelope (ὁ) φάκελος
equal ἴσος, -η, -ο
error (τὸ) λάθος
escape, to ἀποδρῶ
especially ἰδίως
evening (τὸ) βράδυ
event (τὸ) γεγονός
everywhere παντοῦ
exactly ἀκριβῶς
exaggerate, to ὑπερβάλλω
examine, to ἐξετάζω
examination (ἡ) ἐξέταση*
example (τὸ) παράδειγμα
excellent ἄριστος, -η, -ο
exchange (ἡ) συναλλαγή

exciting συναρπαστικός, -ή, -ό
excuse, to δικαιολογῶ,
   συγχωρῶ
excuse me μὲ συγχωρεῖτε,
   συγγνώμη
exist, to ὑπάρχω
exit (ἡ) ἔξοδος
expensive ἀκριβός, -ή, -ό
experience (ἡ) πείρα or πεῖρα
explain, to ἐξηγῶ
explanation (ἡ) ἐξήγηση*
export, to ἐξάγω
express, to ἐκφράζω
expression (ἡ) ἔκφραση*
extinguish, to σβήνω or σβύνω
eye (τὸ) μάτι
eyeglasses (τὰ) ματογιάλια
eyesight (ἡ) ὅραση*

F

fabric (τὸ) ὕφασμα
face (τὸ) πρόσωπο
factory (τὸ) ἐργοστάσιο
faint, to λιποθυμῶ
faith (ἡ) πίστη*
fall, to πέφτω, πίπτω
false ψεύτικος, -η, -ο
family (ἡ) οἰκογένεια
famous περίφημος, -η, -ο
far μακρυά
farmer (ὁ) γεωργός,
   (ὁ)· ἀγρότης
fashion (ἡ) μόδα
fast γρήγορα, γοργά
fat παχύς, -ιά, -ύ, λιπαρός, -ή, -ό
father (ὁ) πατέρας
favor (ἡ) χάρη*, (ἡ) εὔνοια
favorable εὐνοϊκός, -ή, -ό
favorite εὐνοούμενος, -η, -ο

fear (ὁ) φόβος
February (ὁ) Φεβρουάριος
feel, to αἰσθάνομαι
festival (ἡ) ἑορτή or γιορτή
fever (ὁ) πυρετός
field (τὸ) χωράφι, (ὁ) ἀγρός
fill, to γεμίζω
film (ἡ) ταινία, (τὸ) φίλμ
find, to βρίσκω or εὑρίσκω
find out, to ἀνακαλύπτω,
  πληροφοροῦμαι
finger (τὸ) δάκτυλο
finish, to τελειώνω
fire (ἡ) φωτιά
fish (τὸ) ψάρι
flame (ἡ) φλόγα
floor (τὸ) πάτωμα
flower (τὸ) λουλούδι,
  (τὸ) ἄνθος
fly (ἡ) μύγα or μυῖγα
fly, to πετῶ
fog (ἡ) ὁμίχλη, (ἡ) καταχνιά
follow, to ἀκολουθῶ
food (τὸ) φαγητό, (ἡ) τροφή
foot (τὸ) πόδι
force (ἡ) δύναμη*
force, to βιάζω*
foreign ξένος, -η, -ο
foreigner (ὁ) ξένος
forget, to ξεχνῶ
forgive, to συγχωρῶ
form (τὸ) σχῆμα, (ἡ) μορφή
fortunately εὐτυχῶς
forward μπροστά, ἐμπρός
France (ἡ) Γαλλία
free ἐλεύθερος, -η, -ο
freedom (ἡ) ἐλευθερία
freeze, to παγώνω

French (ὁ) Γάλλος,
  (ἡ) Γαλλίδα· (τά) γαλλικά
frequently συχνά
fresh φρέσκος, -η, -ο,
  νωπός, -ή, -ό
Friday (ἡ) Παρασκευή
friend (ὁ) φίλος, (ἡ) φίλη
friendship (ἡ) φιλία
frightened φοβισμένος, -η, -ο
frost (ἡ) παγωνιά
fruit (τὸ) φροῦτο
fry, to τηγανίζω
funny ἀστεῖος, -α, -ο
fur (ἡ) γούνα
furnished ἐπιπλωμένος, -η, -ο
furniture (ἡ) ἐπίπλωση*

G

game (τὸ) παιγνίδι
garage (τὸ) γκαράζ
garden (ὁ) κῆπος
gas (τὸ) φωταέριο
gasoline (ἡ) βενζίνη
gather μαζεύω
gay εὔθυμος, -η, -ο
general γενικός, -ή, -ό
general (ὁ) στρατηγός
generally γενικά or γενικῶς
Germany (ἡ) Γερμανία
German (ὁ) Γερμανός,
  (ἡ) Γερμανίδα· (τά) γερμα-
  νικά
get up, to σηκώνομαι
gift (τὸ) δῶρο
give, to δίνω
glad χαρούμενος, -η, -ο,
  εὐχαριστημένος, -η, -ο
glass (τὸ) ποτήρι,
  (τὸ) τζάμι, (τὸ) γιαλί

glory (ἡ) δόξα

glove (τὸ) γάντι

go, to ·ηγαίνω

go up, to ἀνεβαίνω

goat (ἡ) κατσίκα, (ἡ) γίδα

gold (ὁ) χρυσός, (τὸ) χρυσάφι

good καλός, -ή, -ό

good-bye χαίρετε, ἀντίο

government (ἡ) κυβέρνηση*

granddaughter (ἡ) ἐγγονή

grandfather (ὁ) παππούς
  or παπποῦς

grandmother (ἡ) γιαγιά

grandson (ὁ) ἐγγονός

grape (τὸ) σταφύλι

grapefruit (ἡ) φράπα

grateful εὐγνώμων, -ων, -ον

grass (τὸ) χορτάρι,
  (τὸ) χόρτο, (τὸ) γρασίδι

grave (ὁ) τάφος, (τὸ) μνῆμα

gravy (ἡ) σάλτσα

gray γκρί, γκρίζος, -α, -ο

great μεγάλος, -η, -ο

Greece (ἡ) Ἑλλάδα or Ἑλλάς

Greek (ὁ) Ἕλλην(ας),
  (ἡ) Ἑλληνίδα (τὰ) ἑλληνικά

green πράσινος, -η, -ο

greet, to χαιρετῶ

greeting (ὁ) χαιρετισμός

grocery (τὸ) παντοπωλεῖο,
  (τὸ) μπακάλικο

grow, to μεγαλώνω, αὐξάνω

guess, to μαντεύω

guest προσκεκλημένος, -η

guide, to ὁδηγῶ

H

hair (τὰ) μαλλιά

hairdresser (ὁ) κουρέας,

(ἡ) κομμώτρια

half μισός, -ή. -ό

ham (τὸ) ζαμπόν,
  (τὸ) χοιρομέρι

hammer (τὸ) σφυρί

hand (τὸ) χέρι
  (ὁ) δείκτης

handkerchief (τὸ) μαντήλι
  or μαντίλι

hang, to κρεμῶ

happiness (ἡ) εὐτυχία

happy εὐτυχής, -ής, -ές,
  εὐτυχισμένος, -η, -ο

hard σκληρός, -ή, -ό,
  δύσκολος, -η, -ο

hat (τὸ) καπέλο or καπέλλο

hate, to μισῶ

have, to ἔχω

head (τὸ) κεφάλι

headache (ὁ) πονοκέφαλος

health (ἡ) ὑγεία

healthy ὑγιής, -ής, -ές

hear, to ἀκούω

heart (ἡ) καρδιά

heat (ἡ) ζέστη

heat, to ζεσταίνω

heavy βαρύς, -ιά, -ύ

heel (τὸ) τακούνι,
  (ἡ) φτέρνα

height (τὸ) ὕψος

help (ἡ) βοήθεια

help, to βοηθῶ

here ἐδῶ

hesitate, to διστάζω

hide, to κρύβω

high (ὑ)ψηλός, -ή, -ό

high school (τὸ) γυμνάσιο

I

hill (ὁ) λόφος,
(τὸ) ὕψωμα

historical ἱστορικός, -ή, -ό

history (ἡ) ἱστορία

hit, to κτυπῶ

hold, to κρατῶ

holiday (ἡ) γιορτή or ἑορτή

holy ἅγιος, -α, -ο

home (τὸ) σπίτι

honest τίμιος, -α, -ο

honesty (ἡ) τιμιότης

honey (τὸ) μέλι

honor (ἡ) τιμή

honor, to τιμῶ

hope (ἡ) ἐλπίδα

hope, to ἐλπίζω

horn (car) (τὸ) κλάξον

horse (τὸ) ἄλογο

hospital (τὸ) νοσοκομεῖο

hospitality (ἡ) φιλοξενία

hot ζεστός, -ή, -ό

hotel (τὸ) ξενοδοχεῖο

hour (ἡ) ὥρα

house (τὸ) σπίτι, (ἡ) οἰκία

how πῶς

how much πόσο

human ἀνθρώπινος, -η, -ο

humanity (ἡ) ἀνθρωπότης

humidity (ἡ) ὑγρασία

hunger (ἡ) πείνα or πεῖνα

hungry, to be πεινῶ

hunt, to κυνηγῶ

hunting (τὸ) κυνήγι

hurry, to βιάζομαι

hurt, to πληγώνω, προσβάλλω

husband (ὁ) σύζυγος,
(ὁ) ἄντρας

ice (ὁ) πάγος

ice cream (τὸ) παγωτό

idea (ἡ) ἰδέα

ill, to be εἶμαι ἄρρωστος,
ἀσθενῶ

imagine, to φαντάζομαι

immediately ἀμέσως

import, to εἰσάγω

important σπουδαῖος, -α, -ο

impression (ἡ) ἐντύπωση*

impossible ἀδύνατο(ν)

improve, to βελτιώνω

include, to περιλαμβάνω

income (τὸ) εἰσόδημα

indeed πράγματι

industry (ἡ) βιομηχανία

inform, to πληροφορῶ

information πληροφορία,
(οἱ) πληροφορίες

ink (ἡ) μελάνη

insect (τὸ) ἔντομο

insecticide (τὸ) ἐντομοκτόνο

insist, to ἐπιμένω

insurance (ἡ) ἀσφάλεια

intelligent ἔξυπνος, -η, -ο,
εὐφυής, -ής, -ές

interest (τὸ) ἐνδιαφέρον

interesting ἐνδιαφέρων,
-ουσα, -ον

interrupt, to διακόπτω

introduce, to συστήνω, συνιστῶ

introduction (ἡ) εἰσαγωγή,
(ἡ) σύσταση*

invitation (ἡ) πρόσκληση*

invite, to προσκαλῶ

iron (τὸ) σίδερο

irony (ἡ) εἰρωνία

island (τὸ) νησί, (ἡ) νῆσος
Italian (ὁ) Ἰταλός,
   (ἡ) Ἰταλίδα˙ (τὰ) ἰταλικά
Italy (ἡ) Ἰταλία

J

jacket (ἡ) ζακέτα
jam (τὸ) γλυκό
January (ὁ) Ἰανουάριος
jealous (ὁ) ζηλιάρης
Jew (ὁ) Ἑβραῖος,
   (ἡ) Ἑβραία
join, to ἑνώνω
joke (τὸ) ἀστεῖο
joke, to ἀστειεύομαι
joy (ἡ) χαρά
July (ὁ) Ἰούλιος
jump, to πηδῶ
June (ὁ) Ἰούνιος
justice (ἡ) δικαιοσύνη

K

keep, to κρατῶ, φυλάγω
key (τὸ) κλειδί
kilogram (τὸ) κιλό,
   (τὸ) χιλιόγραμμο
kilometer (τὸ) χιλιόμετρο
kind καλός, -ή, -ό
kind (τὸ) εἶδος
kindness (ἡ) καλωσύνη
king (ὁ) βασιλιάς
   or βασιλεύς
kiss, to φιλῶ
kitchen (ἡ) κουζίνα
knee (τὸ) γόνατο
knife (τὸ) μαχαίρι
knock, to κτυπῶ
know, to γνωρίζω, ξέρω
knowledge (ἡ) γνώση*,
   (οἱ) γνώσεις

L

labor (ἡ) ἐργασία
lace, shoe (τὸ) κορδόνι
lady (ἡ) κυρία
lake (ἡ) λίμνη
lamb (τὸ) ἀρνί
lamp (ἡ) λάμπα
lamp bulb (ὁ) λαμπτήρ(ας)
land, to προσγειώνομαι
language (ἡ) γλώσσα
   or γλῶσσα
large μεγάλος, -η, -ο
last τελευταῖος, -α, -ο
last, to διαρκῶ
late ἀργά
later ἀργότερα
laugh, to γελῶ
laughter (τὸ) γέλιο
laundry (τὸ) πλυντήριο
law (ὁ) νόμος
lazy (ὁ) τεμπέλης,
   (ἡ) τεμπέλα
leaf (τὸ) φύλλο
learn, to μαθαίνω
least, at τουλάχιστο
leather (τὸ) δέρμα
leave, to ἀφήνω, φεύγω ἀπό
lecture (ἡ) διάλεξη*
left ἀριστερός, -ή, -ό,
   ἀριστερά
leg (ἡ) κνήμη, (τὸ) μπούτι
lemon (τὸ) λεμόνι
lend, to δανείζω
less λιγώτερο
lesson (τὸ) μάθημα
let, to ἀφήνω, ἐπιτρέπω
letter (τὸ) γράμμα
lettuce (τὸ) μαρούλι

ibrary (ἡ) βιβλιοθήκη
ie (τὸ) ψέμα or ψέμμα
ie, to ψεύδομαι, λέγω ψέματα
ife (ἡ) ζωή
ift, to σηκώνω
ight (τὸ) φῶς
ight ἐλαφρός, -ή, -ό
ight, to ἀνάβω (τὸ φῶς)
ighter (ὁ) ἀναπτήρας,
ightning (ἡ) ἀστραπή
ike, to μοῦ ἀρέσει
    or μ' ἀρέσει, ἀγαπῶ
ine (ἡ) γραμμή
inen (τὸ) λινό,
    (τὰ) ἀσπρόρουχα
ion (τὸ) λιοντάρι, (ὁ) λέων
ip (τὸ) χείλι, (τὸ) χεῖλος
ist (ὁ) κατάλογος
isten, to ἀκούω
iterature (ἡ) λογοτεχνία
ittle μικρός, -ή, -ό, λίγο
ive, to ζῶ, κατοικῶ, μένω
oad, to φορτώνω
obster (ὁ) ἀστακός
ocated, to be βρίσκομαι
    or εὑρίσκομαι
ock (ἡ) κλειδωνιά
ogical λογικός, -ή, -ό
ong μακρύς, -ιά, -ύ
ook at, to κοιτάζω or κυττάζω
ook for, to ψάχνω, γυρεύω
ook like, to μοιάζω
ose, to χάνω
ost χαμένος, -η, -ο
oud δυνατός, -ή, -ό
ove (ἡ) ἀγάπη
ove, to ἀγαπῶ
ow χαμηλός, -ή, -ό

luck (ἡ) τύχη
lucky τυχερός, -ή, -ό
lunch (τὸ) γεῦμα
lung (τὸ) πλεμόνι, (ὁ) πνεύ-
    μονας or πνεύμων
luxury (ἡ) πολυτέλεια

M

machine (ἡ) μηχανή,
    (τὸ) μηχάνημα
magic μαγικός, -ή, -ό
maid (ἡ) ὑπηρέτρια
mail (τὸ) ταχυδρομεῖο
main κύριος, -α, -ο
make, to κάνω
man (ὁ) ἄνθρωπος,
    (ὁ) ἄνδρας
manage διευθύνω, κατορθώνω
manager (ὁ) διευθυντής
manner (ὁ) τρόπος
many πολλοί, -ές, -ά
map (ὁ) χάρτης
marble (τὸ) μάρμαρο
March (ὁ) Μάρτιος
mark (τὸ) σημεῖο,
    (τὸ) σημάδι
market (ἡ) ἀγορά
marriage (ὁ) γάμος
marry, to παντρεύομαι
marvelous θαυμάσιος, -α, -ο
match (τὸ) σπίρτο
match, to ταιριάζω
mathematics (τὰ) μαθηματικά
material (τὸ) ὑλικό
mattress (τὸ) στρῶμα
May (ὁ) Μάϊος
may μπορῶ
mayor (ὁ) δήμαρχος

mean, to σημαίνω, ἐννοῶ

meaning (ἡ) σημασία,
  (ἡ) ἔννοια

means (τὸ) μέσο

measure (τὸ) μέτρο

meat (τὸ) κρέας

medicine (τὸ) φάρμακο,
  (ἡ) ἰατρική

meet, to συναντῶ

meeting (ἡ) συνάντηση*,
  (ἡ) συνεδρίαση*

melody (ἡ) μελωδία

mend, to μπαλώνω,
  ἐπιδιορθώνω

menu (τὸ) μενού,
  (ὁ) κατάλογος φαγητῶν

merchandise (τὸ) ἐμπόρευμα

merchant (ὁ) ἔμπορος

metal (τὸ) μέταλλο

meter (τὸ) μέτρο

midnight (τὰ) μεσάνυχτα

milk (τὸ) γάλα

mind (τὸ) μυαλό,
  (τὸ) πνεῦμα

mine (τὸ) ὀρυχεῖο

minute (τὸ) λεπτό

mirror (ὁ) καθρέπτης

Miss (ἡ) Δεσποινίς

miss, to χάνω, μοῦ λείπει

mistaken, to be κάνω λάθος

mister (ὁ) κύριος; (voc.) κύριε

misunderstand, to παρεξηγῶ

misunderstanding
  (ἡ) παρεξήγηση*

mix, to ἀνακατεύω

moderate μέτριος, -α, -ο

modern σύγχρονος, -η, -ο,
  μοντέρνος, -α, -ο

moment (ἡ) στιγμή

Monday (ἡ) Δευτέρα

money (τὸ) χρῆμα,
  (τὰ) χρήματα

month (ὁ) μήνας

monthly μηνιαῖος, -α, -ο

monument (τὸ) μνημεῖο

moon (τὸ) φεγγάρι,
  (ἡ) σελήνη

more περισσότερο

morning (τὸ) πρωΐ

mosquito (τὸ) κουνούπι

most πιὸ πολύ

mother (ἡ) μητέρα

motion picture (ἡ) ταινία,
  (τὸ) φίλμ

motor (ἡ) μηχανή

motorcycle (ἡ) μοτοσυκλέτα

mountain (τὸ) βουνό

mouth (τὸ) στόμα

move, to μετακινῶ, κινοῦμαι

movement (ἡ) κίνηση*

movie theater
  (ὁ) κινηματογράφος

much πολύ

mud (ἡ) λάσπη

museum (τὸ) μουσεῖο

music (ἡ) μουσική

musician (ὁ) μουσικός

must πρέπει

mustache (τὸ) μουστάκι

mysterious μυστηριώδης,
  -ης, -ες

N

nail (τὸ) νύχι, (τὸ) καρφί

name (τὸ) ὄνομα

napkin (ἡ) πετσέτα

narrow στενός, -ή, -ό

nation (τὸ) ἔθνος
national ἐθνικός, -ή, -ό
nationality (ἡ) ἐθνικότης,
(ἡ) ὑπηκοότης
natural φυσικός, -ή, -ό
naturally φυσικά
nature (ἡ) φύση*
navy (τὸ) ναυτικό
near κοντά, πλησίον
nearly σχεδόν
necessary ἀναγκαῖος, -α, -ο
neck (ὁ) λαιμός
necktie (ἡ) γραβάτα
need (ἡ) ἀνάγκη
need, to χρειάζομαι
needle (ἡ) βελόνα,
(τὸ) βελόνι
neighbor (ὁ) γείτονας,
(ἡ) γειτόνισσα
neighborhood (ἡ) γειτονιά
nephew (ὁ) ἀνεψιός
or ἀνιψιός
never ποτέ
new νέος, -α, -ο,
καινούργιος, -α, -ο
newlyweds (οἱ) νεόνυμφοι
news (τὰ) νέα
newspaper (ἡ) ἐφημερίδα
next ἑπόμενος, -η, -ο
night (ἡ) νύκτα
no ὄχι
noise (ὁ) θόρυβος
noon (τὸ) μεσημέρι
north (ὁ) βορρᾶς or βοριάς
not δέν, μή
notebook (τὸ) σημειωματάριο,
(τὸ) τετράδιο
nothing τίποτε or τίποτα

notice (ἡ) εἰδοποίηση*
(ἡ) σημείωση*
November (ὁ) Νοέμβριος
now τώρα
number (ὁ) ἀριθμός
nurse (ἡ) νοσοκόμα
nut (τὸ) καρύδι

O

object (τὸ) ἀντικείμενο
obligation (ἡ) ὑποχρέωση*
occupation (τὸ) ἐπάγγελμα,
(ἡ) ἀπασχόληση*, (ἡ) κα-
τοχή
occupy, to κατέχω
ocean (ὁ) ὠκεανός
October (ὁ) Ὀκτώβριος
offer, to προσφέρω
office (τὸ) γραφεῖο
officer (ὁ) ἀξιωματικός
official ἐπίσημος, -η, -ο
often συχνά
oil (τὸ) λάδι
ointment (ἡ) ἀλοιφή
O.K. ἐν τάξει
old παλιός or παληός
or παλαιός, -α, -ο
olive (ἡ) ἐλιά or ἐληά
once μιὰ φορά, ἅπαξ
onion (τὸ) κρεμύδι
only μόνο(ν)
open ἀνοικτός, -ή, -ό
open, to ἀνοίγω
opinion (ἡ) γνώμη
opportunity (ἡ) εὐκαιρία
oppose, to εἶμαι ἐναντίον,
ἀντιτίθεμαι
orange (τὸ) πορτοκάλι

order (ἡ) διαταγή,
 (ἡ) παραγγελία
order, to διατάζω, παραγγέλλω
organization (ἡ) ὀργάνωση*
other ἄλλος, -η, -ο
otherwise ἀλλιῶς
out or outside ἔξω
out of order χαλασμένος, -η, -ο
overcoat (τὸ) παλτό,
 (ἐ)πανωφόρι
owe, to ὀφείλω
owner (ὁ) ἰδιοκτήτης
ox (τὸ) βόδι
oyster (τὸ) στρείδι

P

package (τὸ) δέμα
page (ἡ) σελίδα
pain (ὁ) πόνος
paint (ἡ) βαφή, (τὸ) χρῶμα
paint, to βάφω, ζωγραφίζω
painter (ὁ) ζωγράφος
pair (τὸ) ζευγάρι
palace (τὸ) παλάτι
pale χλωμός, -ή, -ό
palm (ἡ) παλάμη
pan (τὸ) τηγάνι
paper (τὸ) χαρτί
parents (οἱ) γονεῖς
park (τὸ) πάρκο
part (τὸ) μέρος
pass, to περνῶ
passport (τὸ) διαβατήριο
past (τὸ) παρελθόν
pastry (τὸ) γλύκισμα
patriarch (ὁ) Πατριάρχης
patriotism (ὁ) πατριωτισμός
pattern (τὸ) σχέδιο
pay, to πληρώνω

payment (ἡ) πληρωμή
peace (ἡ) εἰρήνη
peach (τὸ) ροδάκινο
pear (τὸ) ἀχλάδι, (ἡ) ἀχλάδα
peasant (ὁ) χωρικός
pen (ἡ) πένα
pen, fountain στυλο(γράφος)
pencil (τὸ) μολύβι or μολίβι
people (ὁ) κόσμος, (ὁ) λαός
pepper (τὸ) πιπέρι
per cent τοῖς ἑκατό
perfect τέλειος, -α, -ο
performance (ἡ) παράσταση*
perfume (τὸ) ἄρωμα,
 (ἡ) μυρωδιά
perhaps ἴσως
period (ἡ) περίοδος
perish, to χάνομαι
permit, to ἐπιτρέπω
person (τὸ) πρόσωπο
personal προσωπικός, -ή, -ό
perspire, to ἱδρώνω
perspiration (ὁ) ἱδρωτας
persuade, to πείθω
petroleum (τὸ) πετρέλαιο
photograph (ἡ) φωτογραφία
photograph, to φωτογραφίζω
picture (ἡ) εἰκόνα
pie (ἡ) πίτα or πήττα
piece (τὸ) κομμάτι
pier (ἡ) ἀποβάθρα
pile (ὁ) σωρός
pill (τὸ) χάπι
pillow (τὸ) μαξιλάρι
 (ἡ) καρφίτσα
pipe (ὁ) σωλήν(ας),
 (ἡ) πίπα

pitcher (τό) κανάτι,
   (ή) κανάτα
place (ό) τόπος, (τό) μέρος
plan (τό)˙ σχέδιο
plane, by ἀεροπορικῶς
plant (τό) φυτό
plant, to φυτεύω
play (τό) παιγνίδι,
   (τό) (θεατρικό) ἔργο
play, to παίζω
pleasant εὐχάριστος, -η, -ο
please παρακαλῶ
please, to εὐχαριστῶ
pleasure (ή) εὐχαρίστηση*
pocket (ή) τσέπη
poem (τό) ποίημα
poet (ό) ποιητής
poetry (ή) ποίηση*
point (τό) σημεῖο
point out, to δείχνω
Poland (ή) Πολωνία
police (ή) ἀστυνομία
policeman (ό) ἀστυφύλακας,
   χωροφύλακας
police officer (ό) ἀστυνόμος
police station
   (τό) ἀστυνομικό τμῆμα
polite εὐγενής
political πολιτικός, -ή, -ό
politics (ή) πολιτική
poor πτωχός, -ή, -ό
popular δημοφιλής, -ής, -ές
pork (τό) χοιρινό
port (τό) λιμάνι,
   (ό) λιμένας or λιμήν
porter (ό) ἀχθοφόρος, χαμάλης
position (ή) θέση*
possible δυνατό(ν)

postman (ό) ταχυδρόμος
post office (τό) ταχυδρομεῖο
postpone, to ἀναβάλλω
potato (ή) πατάτα
pound (ή) λίτρα
poverty (ή) φτώχια,
   (ή) ἔνδεια
powder (ή) πούδρα
power (ή) δύναμη*, (ή) ἰσχύς
powerful ἰσχυρός, -ή, -ό
practical πρακτικός, -ή, -ό
practice (ή) ἄσκηση*
praise, to ἐπαινῶ
pray, to προσεύχομαι
prayer (ή) προσευχή
precious πολύτιμος, -η, -ο
precisely ἀκριβῶς
prefer, to προτιμῶ
prejudice (ή) προκατάληψη*
prepare, to προετοιμάζω
prescription (ή) συνταγή
present (τό) παρόν
present, to παρουσιάζω
press (ό) τύπος
press, to πιέζω
pretend, to ὑποκρίνομαι
pretty ὄμορφος, -η, -ο
prevent, to ἐμποδίζω
previous προηγούμενος, -η, -ο
previously προηγουμένως
price (ή) τιμή
prince (ό) πρίγκηπας
princess (ή) πριγκήπισσα
print, to τυπώνω
printed matter (τό) ἔντυπο
private ἰδιωτικός, -ή, -ό
prize (τό) βραβεῖο
probably πιθανῶς

proceed, to προχωρῶ
produce, to παράγω
product (τὸ) προϊόν
profit (τὸ) κέρδος
program (τὸ) πρόγραμμα
promise, to ὑπόσχομαι
pronounce, to προφέρω
pronunciation (ἡ) προφορά
propose, to προτείνω
protest (ἡ) διαμαρτυρία
protest, to διαμαρτύρομαι
prove, to ἀποδεικνύω
pull, to τραβῶ
pure ἁγνός, -ή, -ό
purpose (ὁ) σκοπός
purpose, on ἐπίτηδες,
    ἀπό σκοποῦ
push, to σπρώχνω
put, to βάζω, θέτω
put on, to βάζω, φορῶ

Q

quality (ἡ) ποιότης
quantity (ἡ) ποσότης
quarter (τὸ) τέταρτο
queen (ἡ) βασίλισσα
question (ἡ) ἐρώτηση*
quick ταχύς, -εῖα, -ύ
    or γρήγορος, -η, -ο
quickly γρήγορα
quit, to παραιτοῦμαι

R

rabbit (τὸ) κουνέλι
race (ἡ) φυλή
radio (τὸ) ραδιό(φωνο)
railroad (ὁ) σιδηρόδρομος
rain (ἡ) βροχή
rain, to βρέχει
raincoat (τὸ) ἀδιάβροχο

raise, to σηκώνω
rare σπάνιος, -α, -ο
rather μᾶλλον
raw ὠμός, -ή, -ό
razor (τὸ) ξυράφι
razor blade (ἡ) λεπίδα
    ξυραφιοῦ, (τὸ) ξυραφάκι
reach, to φθάνω
react, to ἀντιδρῶ
read, to διαβάζω
ready ἕτοιμος, -η, -ο
real πραγματικός, -ή, -ό
really πραγματικά,
    ἀλήθεια, πράγματι
reason (ἡ) αἰτία
reasonable λογικός, -ή, -ό
receipt (ἡ) ἀπόδειξη*
receive, to λαμβάνω, δέχομαι
recently προσφάτως,
    τελευταίως
reception (ἡ) δεξίωση*
recognize, to ἀναγνωρίζω
recommend, to συστήνω,
    συνιστῶ
recover, to γίνομαι καλά,
    ἀνακτῶ
red κόκκινος, -η, -ο,
    ἐρυθρός, -ά, -ό
refreshment (τὸ) ἀναψυκτικό
refrigerator (ἡ) παγωνιέρα
    (τὸ) ψυγεῖο
refuse, to ἀρνοῦμαι
register, to ἐγγράφω
registered letter
    (ἡ) συστημένη ἐπιστολή
regret, to λυποῦμαι
relation (ἡ) σχέση*
relative (ὁ) (ἡ) συγγενής

religion (ἡ) θρησκεία
religious θρησκευτικός, -ή, -ό
remain, to (παρα)μένω
remainder (τὸ) ὑπόλοιπο
remember, to θυμοῦμαι
   or θυμᾶμαι
remind, to θυμίζω
rent (τὸ) ἐνοίκιο
rent, to ἐνοικιάζω
repair, to ἐπιδιορθώνω
repeat, to ἐπαναλαμβάνω
replace, to ἀντικαθιστῶ
represent, to ἀντιπροσωπεύω
representative
   (ὁ) ἀντιπρόσωπος
republic (ἡ) δημοκρατία
resemblance (ἡ) ὁμοιότης
resemble, to ὁμοιάζω
reservation (ἡ) ρεζερβασιόν,
   (ἡ) ἐπιφύλαξη*
respect (ὁ) σεβασμός
respect, to σέβομαι
responsible ὑπεύθυνος, -η, -ο
rest (τὸ) ὑπόλοιπο,
   (ἡ) ἀνάπαυση*
rest, to ἀναπαύομαι,
   ξεκουράζομαι
restaurant (τὸ) ἑστιατόριο
restriction (ὁ) περιορισμός
return, to ἐπιστρέφω
ribbon (ἡ) κορδέλα
   or κορδέλλα
rice (τὸ) ρύζι
rich πλούσιος, -α, -ο
right σωστός, -ή, -ό,
   δεξιός, -ά, -ό
right, to the δεξιά
right away ἀμέσως

ring (τὸ) δαχτυλίδι
ring, to χτυπῶ (τὸ κουδούνι)
rise, to σηκώνομαι
river (ὁ) ποταμός,
   (τὸ) ποτάμι
road (ὁ) δρόμος
roast (τὸ) ψητό
rock (ὁ) βράχος
roll, to τυλίγω, κυλῶ
roof (ἡ) στέγη
room (τὸ) δωμάτιο
rose (τὸ) τριαντάφυλλο,
   (τὸ) ρόδο
rough τραχύς, -εῖα, -ύ
round στρογγυλός, -ή, -ό
ruin (τὸ) ἐρείπιο
rule, to κυβερνῶ
Rumania (ἡ) Ρουμανία
run, to τρέχω
Russia (ἡ) Ρωσ(σ)ία
Russian (ὁ) Ρῶσ(σ)ος,
   (ἡ) Ρωσ(σ)ίδα

S

sad λυπημένος, -η, -ο,
   λυπητερός, -ή, -ό
sadness (ἡ) λύπη
safe ἀσφαλής, -ής, -ές
safety (ἡ) ἀσφάλεια
sail, to πλέω
salad (ἡ) σαλάτα
salt (τὸ) ἁλάτι
salty ἁλμυρός, -ή, -ό
same ἴδιος, -α, -ο
sand (ὁ) ἄμμος
satisfy, to ἱκανοποιῶ
Saturday (τὸ) Σάββατο
saucer (τὸ) πιατάκι
save, to σώζω

say, to λέγω

scene (ἡ) σκηνή

school (τὸ) σχολεῖο

science (ἡ) ἐπιστήμη

scientist (ὁ) (ἡ) ἐπιστήμων

scissors (τὸ) ψαλίδι

sea (ἡ) θάλασσα

seal (ἡ) σφραγίδα

seashore (ἡ) ἀκρογιαλιά

season (ἡ) ἐποχή

seat (τὸ) κάθισμα

second (τὸ) δευτερόλεπτο

see, to βλέπω

seek, to γυρεύω, ψάχνω

seem, to φαίνομαι

sell, to πουλῶ οr πωλῶ

send, to στέλλω

sentence (ἡ) πρόταση*,
    (ἡ) ποινή

September (ὁ) Σεπτέμβριος

serious σοβαρός, -ή, -ό

seriously σοβαρά

servant (ὁ) ὑπηρέτης

serve, to ὑπηρετῶ

sew, to ράβω

shade (ἡ) σκιά

shadow (ὁ) ἴσκιος

shake, to κουνῶ, τρέμω,
    τινάζω

share (τὸ) μερίδιο

share, to μοιράζομαι

sharp ὀξύς, -εῖα, -ύ,
    μυτερός, -ή, -ό

shave, to ξυρίζω, ξυρίζομαι

sheep (τὸ) πρόβατο

sheet (τὸ) σιντόνι

sheet of paper φύλλο χαρτιοῦ

shell (τὸ) ὄστρακο

shine, to λάμπω

ship (τὸ) πλοῖο

shirt (τὸ) ὑποκάμισο
    οr πουκάμισο

shoe (τὸ) παπούτσι

shop (τὸ) μαγαζί

short κοντός, -ή, -ό

shoulder (ὁ) ὦμος

shout, to φωνάζω

show (τὸ) θέαμα

show, to δείχνω

shower (τὸ) ντούς

shut, to κλείνω

sick ἄρρωστος, -η, -ο

sick, to get ἀρρωσταίνω

side (ἡ) πλευρά

sidewalk (τὸ) πεζοδρόμιο

sign (τὸ) σημεῖο,
    (ἡ) ἐπιγραφή

sign, to ὑπογράφω

signature (ἡ) ὑπογραφή

silence (ἡ) σιωπή

silent σιωπηλός, -ή, -ό

silk (τὸ) μετάξι

silver (τὸ) ἀσήμι,
    (ὁ) ἄργυρος

silverware (τὰ) ἀσημικά

similar παρόμοιος, -α, -ο

simple ἁπλός, -ή, -ό

simplicity (ἡ) ἁπλότης

sincere εἰλικρινής, -ής, -ές

sincerity (ἡ) εἰλικρίνεια

sing, to τραγουδῶ

single μόνος, -η, -ο

sister (ἡ) ἀδελφή

sister-in-law (ἡ) νύφη,
    (ἡ) κουνιάδα

sit (down), to κάθομαι

size (τὸ) μέγεθος, νούμερο
skin (τὸ) δέρμα
skirt (ἡ) φούστα
sky (ὁ) οὐρανός
skyscraper (ὁ) οὐρανοξύστης
sleep, to κοιμοῦμαι
sleeve (τὸ) μανίκι
slice (ἡ) φέτα
slip (τὸ) κομπινεζόν,
    (τὸ) μεσοφόρι
slip, to γλιστρῶ
slow ἀργός, -ή, -ό
slowly σιγά
small μικρός, -ή, -ό
smell, to μυρίζω
smile, to χαμογελῶ
smoke (ὁ) καπνός
smoke, to καπνίζω
sneeze, to φταρνίζομαι
snow (τὸ) χιόνι
snow, to χιονίζει
so ἔτσι, τοιουτοτρόπως
soak μουσκεύω
soap (τὸ) σαπούνι
sock (ἡ) κάλτσα
sofa (ὁ) καναπές
soft μαλακός, -ή, -ό,
    ἀπαλός, -ή, -ό
soldier (ὁ) στρατιώτης
sole (ἡ) σόλα
sometimes κάποτε,
    μερικὲς φορές
something κάτι
somewhere κάπου
son (ὁ) γιός or γυιός
song (τὸ) τραγούδι
soon σὲ λίγο, σύντομα
sorrow (ἡ) λύπη

sorry, to be λυποῦμαι
soul (ἡ) ψυχή
sound (ὁ) ἦχος
soup (ἡ) σούπα
south (ὁ) νότος
souvenir (τὸ) ἐνθύμιο
Spain (ἡ) Ἱσπανία
Spanish (ὁ) Ἱσπανός,
    (ἡ) Ἱσπανίδα
speak, to (ὁ) μιλῶ
special εἰδικός, -ή, -ό
specify, to καθορίζω
speed (ἡ) ταχύτης
spend, to (ἐ)ξοδεύω
    περνῶ
spoil, to χαλνῶ
sponge (τὸ) σφουγγάρι
spoon (τὸ) κουτάλι
sports (ὁ) ἀθλητισμός
spread, to ἀπλώνω
spring (ἡ) ἄνοιξη*
spring (τὸ) ἐλατήριο
square (τὸ) τετράγωνο
square (ἡ) πλατεία
    or πλατεῖα
stage (ἡ) σκηνή
stairs (οἱ) σκάλες
stairway (ἡ) σκάλα
stamp (τὸ) γραμματόσημο
stand, to στέκομαι
star (τὸ) ἀστέρι, (τὸ) ἄστρο
start, to ἀρχίζω, ξεκινῶ
state (ἡ) πολιτεία,
    (τὸ) κράτος, (ἡ) κατάσταση*
statement (ἡ) δήλωση*
station (ὁ) σταθμός
stay, to μένω
steak (τὸ) μπιφτέκ(ι)

steal, to κλέβω

steam heat (τὸ) καλοριφέρ

steering wheel (τὸ) τιμόνι

still ἀκόμη, ὅμως

stocking (ἡ) κάλτσα

stomach (τὸ) στομάχι

stone (ἡ) πέτρα

stop, to σταματῶ

stop (ἡ) στάση*

store (τὸ) κατάστημα

store, to ἀποθηκεύω

storm (ἡ) θύελλα

story (ἡ) ἱστορία

story (floor) (τὸ) πάτωμα

straight ἴσιος, -α, -ο

strange παράξενος, -η, -ο

strawberry (ἡ) φράουλα

street (ὁ) δρόμος, (ἡ) ὁδός

strike, to κτυπῶ

string (ὁ) σπάγγος,
(ἡ) χορδή

strong δυνατός, -ή, -ό

student (ὁ) μαθητής,
(ἡ) μαθήτρια, (ὁ) φοιτητής,
(ἡ) φοιτήτρια

study (ἡ) μελέτη

study, to μελετῶ

stupid ἠλίθιος, -α, -ο, βλάκας

subject (τὸ) θέμα,
(τὸ) ὑποκείμενο

suburb (τὸ) προάστειο

subway (ὁ) ὑπόγειος
(σιδηρόδρομος)

succeed πετυχαίνω
or ἐπιτυγχάνω

success (ἡ) ἐπιτυχία

such τέτοιος, -α, -ο

sudden ξαφνικός, -ή, -ό

suddenly ξαφνικά, ἔξαφνα

suffer, to ὑποφέρω

sugar (ἡ) ζάχαρη

suit (τὸ) κοστούμι

suitcase (ἡ) βαλίτσα

sum (τὸ) ποσό

summer (τὸ) καλοκαίρι

sun (ὁ) ἥλιος

Sunday (ἡ) Κυριακή

sunrise (ἡ) ἀνατολή
(τοῦ ἡλίου)

sunset (ἡ) δύση* (τοῦ ἡλίου)

superior ἀνώτερος, -η, -ο

supper (τὸ) δεῖπνο, (τὸ) σουπέ

supply, to προμηθεύω

support, to ὑποστηρίζω

suppose, to ὑποθέτω

sure βέβαιος, -α, -ο

surprise (ἡ) ἔκπληξη*

surprise, to ἐκπλήττω

surround, to τριγυρίζω

suspect, to ὑποπτεύομαι

sweep, to σκουπίζω

sweet γλυκός, -ιά, -ό

swim, to κολυμπῶ

swimming (τὸ) κολύμπι

Swiss (ὁ) Ἑλβετός,
(ἡ) Ἑλβετίδα

Switzerland (ἡ) Ἑλβετία

sympathy (ἡ) συμπάθεια,
(ἡ) συμπόνια

symptom (τὸ) σύμπτωμα

system (τὸ) σύστημα

T

table (τὸ) τραπέζι

tablecloth
(τὸ) τραπεζομάνδηλο

tailor (ὁ) ράφτης

take, to παίρνω

take off, to βγάζω

tall (ὑ)ψηλός, -ή, -ό

taste (ἡ) γεύση*, (τό) γοῦστο

taste, to γεύομαι

tax (ὁ) φόρος

taxi (τό) ταξί

tea (τό) τσάι

teach, to διδάσκω

teacher (ὁ) δάσκαλος,
    (ἡ) δασκάλα

tear (τό) δάκρυ

tear, to σχίζω

telegram (τό) τηλεγράφημα

telegraph, to τηλεγραφῶ

telephone (τό) τηλέφωνο

telephone, to τηλεφωνῶ

telephone call (τό) τηλεφώνημα

telephone operator
    (ἡ) τηλεφωνήτρια

television (ἡ) τηλεόραση*

tell, to λέγω

temperature (ἡ) θερμοκρασία

tender τρυφερός,-ή, -ό

terrible τρομερός, -ή, -ό

thank, to εὐχαριστῶ

theater (τό) θέατρο

then τότε, ἔπειτα

there ἐκεῖ

there is, are ὑπάρχει,
    ὑπάρχουν, ἔχει

thermometer (τό) θερμόμετρο

thin ἀδύνατος, -η, -ο,
    λεπτός, -ή, -ό

thing (τό) πρᾶγμα
    or πράγμα

think, to σκέπτομαι

thirst (ἡ) δίψα

thirsty, to be διψῶ

thought (ἡ) σκέψη*

thread (ἡ) κλωστή

threaten, to ἀπειλῶ

throat (ὁ) λαιμός

throw, to ρίχνω

thunder (ἡ) βροντή

Thursday (ἡ) Πέμπτη

ticket (τό) εἰσιτήριο

ticket window (ἡ) θυρίδα

tight στενός, -ή, -ό

time (ὁ) χρόνος, (ὁ) καιρός

time table (τό) δρομολόγιο

tip (τό) πουρμπουάρ,
    (τό) φιλοδώρημα

tire λάστιχο αὐτοκινήτου

tired κουρασμένος, -η, -ο

tobacco (ὁ) καπνός

today σήμερα

together μαζί

toilet (τό) μέρος,
    (ἡ) τουαλέτα

tomato (ἡ) ντομάτα

tomb (ὁ) τάφος

tomorrow αὔριο(ν)

tongue (ἡ) γλώσσα
    or γλῶσσα

tonight ἀπόψε

too ἐπίσης

too much παρὰ πολύ

tooth (τό) δόντι

toothbush (ἡ) ὀδοντόβουρτσα

toothpaste (ἡ) ὀδοντόπαστα

top (ἡ) κορυφή

touch, to ἀγγίζω or ἐγγίζω

tough σκληρός, -ή, -ό

tourist (ὁ) περιηγητής,
    (ἡ) περιηγήτρια

towel (ή) πετσέτα
tower (ό) πύργος
town (ή) πόλη*
toy (τό) παιγνίδι
trade (τό) ἐμπόριο
tragedy (ή) τραγωδία
train (τό) τραῖνο
translate, to μεταφράζω
travel, to ταξιδεύω
traveler (ό) ταξιδιώτης
tray (ό) δίσκος
tree (τό) δέντρο
trial (ή) δίκη
trip (τό) ταξίδι
trouble (ή) φασαρία,
(ή) ἐνόχληση*, (ή) δυσκολία
trousers (τό) παντελόνι
truck (τό) φορτηγό
(αὐτοκίνητο)
true ἀληθής, -ής, -ές
trunk (τό) μπαοῦλο,
(ό) κορμός
truth (ή) ἀλήθεια
try, to δοκιμάζω,
προσπαθῶ, δικάζω
Tuesday (ή) Τρίτη
Turkey (ή) Τουρκία
turn, to γυρίζω,
στρέφω, στρέφομαι
turn on the light, to
ἀνάβω τό φῶς
turn off the light, to
σβήνω τό φῶς
twice δύο φορές
twin δίδυμος, -η, -ο
typewrite, to δακτυλογραφῶ
typewriter (ή) δακτυλογραφική
μηχανή

U

ugly ἄσχημος, -η, -ο
umbrella (ή) ὀμπρέλα
or ὀμπρέλλα
uncle (ό) θεῖος
understand, to καταλαβαίνω
underwear (τά) ἐσώρρουχα
undoubtedly ἀναμφιβόλως
undress, to ξεντύνομαι
unfortunately δυστυχῶς
unhealthy ἀνθυγιεινός, -ή, -ό
uniform (ή) στολή
union (ή) ἕνωση*
united ἑνωμένος, -η, -ο
United States (αἱ) Ἡνωμέναι
Πολιτεῖαι
university (τό) πανεπιστήμιο
unpleasant δυσάρεστος, -η, -ο
up ἐπάνω
upset, to ἀναστατώνω
upstairs στό ἐπάνω πάτωμα
urgent ἐπείγων, -ουσα, -ον
use (ή) χρήση*
use, to χρησιμοποιῶ
useful χρήσιμος, -η, -ο
useless ἄχρηστος, -η, -ο
usually συνήθως

V

vacation (οἱ) διακοπές
vain, in ματαίως, μάταια
valley (ή) κοιλάδα
value (ή) ἀξία
variety (ή) ποικιλία
veal (τό) μοσχάρι
vegetables (τά) χορταρικά
velvet (τό) βελοῦδο
very πολύ
vest (τό) γελέκο or γιλέκο

victory (ή) νίκη

view (ή) άποψη*, (ή) θέα

vinegar (τό) ξύδι or ξίδι

visit (ή) έπίσκεψη*

visit, to έπισκέπτομαι

visitor (ό) έπισκέπτης,
(ή) έπισκέπτρια

voice (ή) φωνή

W

waist (ή) μέση

wait, to περιμένω

waiter (τό) γκαρσόν(ι)

waiting room (ή) αἴθουσα
άναμονῆς

wake up, to ξυπνῶ

walk (ό) περίπατος

walk, to περιπατῶ

wall (ό) τοῖχος

want, to θέλω

war (ό) πόλεμος

wardrobe (ή) ντουλάπα

warm ζεστός, -ή, -ό

warm, to ζεσταίνω

warn, to προειδοποιῶ

wash, to πλένω or πλύνω

wash oneself, to πλένομαι
or πλύνομαι

wash basin (ή) λεκάνη

waste, to σπαταλῶ

watch (τό) ρολό(γ)ι

watch, to παρακολουθῶ,
φυλάγω, προσέχω

watchmaker (ό) ὡρολογοποιός,
(ό) ρολογάς

watch out προσέξτε

water (τό) νερό

wave (τό) κύμα or κῦμα

way (ό) δρόμος, (ό) τρόπος

wealth (τά) πλούτη

weather (ό) καιρός

Wednesday (ή) Τετάρτη

week (ή) έβδομάδα

weigh, to ζυγίζω

weight (τό) βάρος

welcome καλῶς ὡρίσατε

well καλά

west (ή) δύση*

wet ὑγρός, -ή, -ό,
βρεμμένος, -η, -ο

wheat (τό) σιτάρι

wheel (ή) ρόδα, (ό) τροχός

when ὅταν, πότε

where ὅπου, ποῦ

white ἄσπρος, -η, -ο,
λευκός, -ή, -ό

wholesale χονδρικῶς

why γιατί

wide πλατύς, -ιά, -ύ
φαρδύς, -ιά, -ύ

wife (ή) σύζυγος,
(ή) γυναίκα

will (ή) θέληση*,
(ή) διαθήκη

win, to κερδίζω, νικῶ

wind (ό) ἄνεμος

wind, to κουρδίζω

window (τό) παράθυρο

wine (τό) κρασί, (ό) οἶνος

wing (ή) πτέρυγα,
(ή) φτερούγα

winter (ό) χειμώνας

wish (ή) έπιθυμία,
(ή) εὐχή

wish, to έπιθυμῶ, εὔχομαι

witty πνευματώδης, -ης, -ες

wolf (ό) λύκος

woman (ἡ) γυναίκα
wonderful θαυμάσιος, -α, -ο
wood (τὸ) ξύλο
wool (τὸ) μαλλί
word (ἡ) λέξη*
work (ἡ) ἐργασία,
   (ἡ) δουλειά
work, to ἐργάζομαι,
   δουλεύω
work (of art) ἔργο (τέχνης)
world (ὁ) κόσμος
worry (ἡ) φροντίδα,
   (ἡ) στενοχώρια, (ἡ) ἔγνοια
worse χειρότερος,-η, -ο
worth (ἡ) ἀξία
worthy ἄξιος, -α, -ο
wrap, to τυλίγω
wrinkle (ἡ) ρυτίδα
wrinkle, to τσαλακώνω

wrist (ὁ) καρπός
wrist watch ρολόγι τοῦ χεριοῦ
write, to γράφω
writer (ὁ) συγγραφέας
wrong, to be δὲν ἔχω δίκαιο,
   ἔχω ἄδικο, κάνω λάθος

Y

year (ὁ) χρόνος,
   (ἡ) χρονιά, (τὸ) ἔτος
yellow κίτρινος, -η, -ο
yes ναί, μάλιστα
yesterday χθές
yet ἀκόμη, καὶ ὅμως
young νέος, -α, -ο
youth (ἡ) νεότης, (ἡ) νεολαία

Z

zero μηδέν
zone (ἡ) ζώνη

One of the best ways to continue your study of Greek is by listening to Greek radio programs and by reading Greek newspapers like «Ἀτλαντίς» and «Ἐθνικὸς Κῆρυξ» and Greek magazines like the monthly "Atlantis", the Athenian «Εἰκόνες», «Ταχυδρόμος», «Θησαυρός», «Ρομάντζο», «Θεατής», the literary «Νέα Ἑστία», «Κρίκος», «Ἀκτίνες», and the organ of the Greek Archdiocese «Ὀρθόδοξος Παρατηρητής». In order to read newspapers and magazines you would probably need a larger dictionary than this. Anyone of the following may be recommended:

English-Modern Greek and Modern Greek-English Dictionary published by Atlantis. Thumb indexed. Pocket size, 389 pp. $3.00.

English - Greek and Greek - English Dictionary of the *National Herald* (Ἐθνικὸς Κῆρυξ), compiled by Carroll N. Brown. Thumb indexed, 935 pp., $6.00.

Divry's English - Greek and Greek - English Dictionary. 469 pp. Cloth with indexes, $4.00. Leather, with indexes and maps, $5.00

English - Greek and Greek-English Dictionary by I. Kykkotis. Regular Edition, 644 pp., $3.95. Available through the R. D. Cortina Co., Inc., 136 West 52nd Street, New York 19, N. Y.